WHAT
WE'VE
LOST

WHAT WE'VE LOST

.

GRAYDON CARTER

LITTLE, BROWN

A *Little, Brown* Book

First published in Great Britain in 2004 by Little, Brown

Copyright © Graydon Carter 2004

The moral right of the author has been asserted.
Some of this material appeared, in different form, in *Vanity Fair*.

A CIP catalogue record for this book
is available from the British Library.

ISBN 0 316 72867 5

Typeset in Fairfield by M Rules
Printed and bound in Great Britain
by Clays Ltd, St Ives plc

Little, Brown
An imprint of
Time Warner Book Group UK
Brettenham House
Lancaster Place
London WC2E 7EN

www.twbg.co.uk

For Ash, Max, Spike, and Bronwen

CONTENTS

ACKNOWLEDGMENTS

So many people to thank.

For a start, my children, who never once complained that I was spending every evening and weekend working on this book.

My employers at Condé Nast – Charles Townsend, James Truman, and especially S. I. Newhouse Jr. – for establishing and maintaining a culture that encourages freedom, risk, and creativity. The same goes for Jonathan Newhouse and Nicholas Coleridge in London.

My remarkable editor, Jonathan Galassi, and all the great people at Farrar, Straus and Giroux. This book was Jonathan's idea, as was the title. The people he has gathered around him at FSG have made working on this book one of the most pleasant professional experiences I have had outside of *Vanity Fair*.

My agent, Andrew Wylie. He's a friend, too, but he's also a hell of an agent.

My friends, so many of whom provided encouragement and guidance. I'd name them all, but I don't want them to be embarrassed if this gets crummy reviews.

My colleagues at *Vanity Fair*, including, but not limited to, John Banta, Chris Garrett, Beth Kseniak, Fran Lebowitz, Meg Nolan, and Henry Porter. Also, Aimee Bell, Dana Brown, Patrick Christell, David Friend, Bruce Handy, David Harris, Punch Hutton, Wayne Lawson, David Margolick, Chris Mueller, Matt Tyrnauer, and Julie Weiss.

My superb research team, made up of Sue Carswell, Eric

Drilling, Matt Kapp, Ben Kalin, Rob Mackey, Tim McConville, Austin Merrill, John Ortved, and Anne Phalon.

My chief researcher, who shepherded this book through all its various stages – the incomparable Heather Fink.

And above all, Anna Scott, my researcher, editor, and guide, without whose wisdom, patience, and encouragement this book never would have been written.

WHAT
WE'VE
LOST

'Trying to eliminate Saddam . . . would have incurred incalculable human and political costs. Apprehending him was probably impossible . . . We would have been forced to occupy Baghdad and, in effect, rule Iraq . . . There was no viable "exit strategy" we could see, violating another of our principles. Furthermore, we had been self-consciously trying to set a pattern for handling aggression in the post-Cold War world. Going in and occupying Iraq, thus unilaterally exceeding the United Nations' mandate, would have destroyed the precedent of international response to aggression that we hoped to establish. Had we gone the invasion route, the United States could conceivably still be an occupying power in a bitterly hostile land.'

– PRESIDENT GEORGE H. W. BUSH AND HIS
NATIONAL SECURITY ADVISER, BRENT SCOWCROFT,

in their memoir *A World Transformed*

TO BEGIN WITH . . .

IN making his final decision to launch an invasion of Iraq, President George W. Bush did not seek the advice of his father, a veteran of World War II and a former president who had gone to battle with the same foe a decade earlier. Nor did he seek the overall final recommendation of his secretary of defense, or of his secretary of state, the only man in his cabinet who had been decorated for military service in wartime with the medals befitting a national hero. Instead, as Bob Woodward wrote in his book *Plan of Attack,* he consulted his God – a God that the president presumes takes sides in disputes between peoples.

That reckless, unnecessary, and unforgiving decision – to wage a war of choice with a country that was neither an enemy nor a real threat – is at the very root of all we've lost during George W. Bush's presidency. We've lost our good reputation and our standing as a great and just superpower. We've lost the sympathy of the world following September 11 and turned it into an alloy of fear and hatred. We've lost lives and allies. We've lost liberties and freedoms. We've lost billions of dollars that could have gone toward a true assault on terrorism. It could fairly be said that in the age of George W. Bush, we have lost our way.

The deceptions that took the United States into Iraq were the work of an administration without care for logic or truth. The aftermath, a war seemingly without end and one that is costing the country tens of billions of dollars and the lives of about thirteen young American soldiers every week, is the work of an administration without judgment or foresight. The United States is a warrior nation with a heart of peace and a history of generally doing the right thing. The cry-wolf invasion of Iraq has not only shaken that opinion of the United States, it will make it difficult for future American leaders to rally nations against an enemy that actually is a credible global threat.

The sideshow in the Middle East proved in the end to be a convenient diversion for the Bush White House: It distracted Americans' attention from the administration's domestic agenda, its ideological war at home. Iraq also served as a shield for the administration, in the sense that the White House defined any opposition to or criticism of what it was up to in those early days as the work of the unpatriotic or the traitorous. With the country looking the other way, Bush and Cheney began dismantling decades' worth of advances in civil liberties, health care, education, the economy, the judiciary, and the environment. It is difficult to point to a single element of American society that comes under federal jurisdiction which is not worse off than it was an administration ago.

The Bush White House inherited a military greater than any ever assembled and spread it so thin that it ultimately had to order thousands of troops to stay in war zones months longer than the terms of their service contracts. At a time of war, the administration tried to cut back on benefits for veterans and soldiers still in the field of battle.

The Bush White House inherited a robust economy brimming with jobs and budget surpluses. It may well end its four years with a net loss of jobs during Bush's first term, a feat unsurpassed since the Hoover administration. In its desire to create tax cuts for the wealthiest Americans, it created a horizon of budget deficits, crippling debt, and trade imbalances.

The Bush White House inherited an education system that, while not perfect, was in many ways the envy of the world. Its unreasonable and underfunded No Child Left Behind program hobbled state systems by placing rigid demands on school districts but pledging little money to meet those demands.

The Bush White House inherited an environment that had been all but saved by the Clean Air and Clean Water acts of the 1970s. The administration, many of whose members were plucked from the oil and gas industries, turned its back on more than thirty years of advances in environmental legislation and global treaties to reward its campaign backers from the petro-chemical industry.

The Bush White House inherited a health-care system that favored the rich, then made it worse, turning it into a complex apparatus that will produce unprecedented profits for another set of major campaign backers – the health and pharmaceutical industries – all at the expense of regular patients, the elderly, and the poor.

The Bush White House inherited a government of model transparency and purposefully bent it to the will of the most secretive administration in recent American history.

The Bush White House inherited a judicial system that was America's centrist, if not conservative, legal safeguard and turned it into an ideological, right-wing juggernaut.

The Bush White House took the world's warm feelings toward America – remember the days following September 11, when all citizens of the world proclaimed themselves to be New Yorkers? – and turned them into confusion and then rage.

The Bush White House took a nation that was both the cradle and the missionary of democratic freedoms and civil liberties and reduced rights under both for America's own citizens.

At the heart of all of this loss were two unforgivable deceptions embedded in George W. Bush's 2000 presidential campaign: that he was a 'uniter and not a divider,' and that he was a 'compassionate conservative.' This 'uniter' became 'the great polarizer,' a president who has divided Americans more than at any time since the Civil War. 'Compassionate conservative' was a meaningless bit of public relations designed by Karen Hughes to appease the middle ground of the Republican Party and the conservative flank of the Democratic Party. Once in office, the Bush administration pursued not a compassionate course, but rather a harsh, far-right-wing effort to roll back decades of liberal legislation. In a May 2004 interview in *The New York Times*, the billionaire George Soros said, 'The government of the most powerful country on earth has fallen into the hands of extremists.' It seems as if post–September 11 America has been in a slumber – brought on by an anesthetic of fear and patriotism – and is only now beginning to wake up.

I am an American by choice rather than by birth. I'm a white, fifty-five-year-old Episcopalian. Born in Canada, I've lived in America for half my life. I've raised four children here, have done reasonably well professionally, and am by most measures a happy man. I've followed politics all my life, but politics has never *been* my life, if you know what I mean. To be honest, I really never had much truck with politicians of any stripe. But I love this country, its land, its soul, and above all its people.

So what does it say about us that we let a man of such blind conviction and willful ignorance lead us? George W. Bush may be the most incurious American president ever. He reads little and is far and away the least traveled president of the last half century. Indeed, most of his trips outside this country have been aboard Air Force One. When he was on the David Frost show in late 2003 before his official state visit to London, Frost brought up previous trips Bush had made there. 'Laura and I went to see *Cats*,' was the president's chief recollection. Former treasury secretary Paul O'Neill describes meetings with the president as short, limited, and without discussion or inquiry. Five, ten minutes, tops, then Bush is up and out of the room.

In polls, America is now regularly listed as one of the most dangerous nations on earth, sometimes ahead of even North Korea. The world, simply put, doesn't like Bush — or Americans — anymore. And Americans, a great people with high ideals, like to be liked. Well, Americans like to be *feared* and liked, but liked is an important part of the equation. Electing George W. Bush was seen in many quarters of the world as a mistake, a voters' aberration. His re-election would send those same quarters a message of intent and hostility on the part of the United States that may take decades fully to recover from.

One can only hope that this war, this period, this administration, is not the beginning of a new age. That it is not the true story of our times, a terrible dream from which we will wake up one day only to realize what we've lost.

1

■

THE PRESIDENT'S WARS

THE WAR ON TERROR

'I'm not going to play like I've been a person who's spent hours involved with foreign policy. I am who I am.'
— GEORGE W. BUSH, April 2000

'I don't think our troops ought to be used for what's called nation building.'
— GEORGE W. BUSH, April 1999

'People say, how can I help on this war against terror? How can I fight evil? You can do so by mentoring a child; by going into a shut-in's house and say I love you.'
— GEORGE W. BUSH, September 2002

WHILE Americans and much of the rest of the world mourned the dead from September 11, the administration reacted reasonably and proportionately. It launched a full-out manhunt for the leaders of Al Qaeda that stretched to the far corners of the earth. But in the smoldering ruins of the World

Trade Center, members of the Bush White House also found arguments they could use to sell the American public on an invasion of Iraq – part of a grand plan to 'rid the world,' the president said, 'of the evil-doers.'

In early 2004, a spate of books came out that showed what many suspected all along: In the days after the attacks, when the administration's resources should have been completely focused on the search for the terrorists and protecting Americans at home, the White House was almost irrationally keyed up on Iraq. A December 2003 report by Dr. Jeffrey Record for the Army War College summed up the situation thus: 'The result has been an unnecessary preventive war of choice against a deterred Iraq that has created a new front in the Middle East for Islamic terrorism and diverted attention and resources away from securing the American homeland against further assault by an undeterrable al-Qaeda. The war against Iraq was not integral to the [global war on terror], but rather a detour from it.'

You would think that if we were to lash out at anybody it would have been against the Saudis, given that fifteen of the nineteen terrorists responsible for the September 11 attacks were from Saudi Arabia. The Saudis are friends, though. Not necessarily friends of ours – but friends of the Bushes. Indeed, in the president's three post–September 11 State of the Union addresses, he didn't once even mention Saudi Arabia's role as an incubator of terrorists.

Not only were the Saudis ignored in the days immediately following September 11, they were actively aided by the Bush administration. Within minutes of the terrorist attacks, the Federal Aviation Administration grounded all planes in the United States – an order that stood for the next two days. Former vice president Al Gore couldn't get back from Austria. Even former president Bill Clinton had to cancel his travel plans. As Craig Unger, author of *House of Bush, House of Saud: The Secret Relationship Between the World's Two Most Powerful Dynasties*, initially pointed out in a report in *Vanity Fair*, 'For the first time in a century, American skies were nearly as empty as they had been when the Wright brothers first flew at Kitty Hawk.'

On September 13, in a meeting scheduled before the attacks, President Bush sat down with Prince Bandar, the well-connected Saudi ambassador to the United States (very well connected: he had been a racquetball partner of Secretary of State Colin Powell's years earlier, and in July 2003 he gave President Bush a painting worth $1 million). According to Unger, Bandar had been busy working the phones for two days, trying to get influential Saudis out of the United States. And though the nation's airspace was severely restricted, he was shockingly successful. Coincidentally, the day he met with the president, according to Unger, three Saudi men, all apparently in their twenties, were escorted to a private hangar in Tampa, where they boarded an eight-passenger Learjet and took off for Blue Grass Airport in Lexington, Kentucky. There they were greeted by an American who helped them with their baggage as they made their way onto a waiting Boeing 747 with Arabic writing on it, which then departed.

Over the next few days, planes around the country shuttled wellborn Saudis and members of the bin Laden family to East Coast airports for flights home. Incredibly, departure points along the way included Boston's Logan and Newark airports, two of the airports where the hijackers had boarded their planes on September 11 – and ones that would likely have instituted the greatest degree of lockdown in the days following the attacks.

On September 18, at least five members of the bin Laden family flew back to Saudi Arabia in a specially reconfigured Boeing 727. The next day, according to Unger, even as the president was crafting a speech to announce that 'our war on terror . . . will not end until every terrorist group of global reach has been found, stopped, and defeated,' a private plane that had originated in Los Angeles and made stops in Orlando and Washington, DC, arrived at Logan – where, Unger says, at least eleven bin Laden family members came on board – soon to exit the country under the cover of darkness. In all, some 140 Saudis, including more than a dozen bin Laden family members, made it out of the United States by the third week in September. Not only had they not been fully vetted by the FBI, but the FAA and the White House denied that the September 13 flight even took place. So close was Bandar to the Bush administration that, according to Bob Woodward's book *Plan of Attack*, the vice president told the Saudi ambassador of the White House's decision to invade Iraq even before he told Secretary of State Colin Powell. Woodward quotes Cheney as saying, 'Prince Bandar, once we start, Saddam is toast.'

The invasion of Iraq – so costly in terms of lives, dollars, and our international reputation – diverted attention and resources that could have gone toward securing the nation. The Bush administration tried to convince Americans it was doing everything in its power to ensure the country's safety on land and in the air. The truth of the matter is somewhat different. In almost every single instance, tax cuts took priority over security. 'President Bush vetoed several specific (and relatively cost-effective) measures proposed by Congress that would have addressed critical national vulnerabilities,' a 2002 report from the Brookings Institution said. 'As a result, the country remains more vulnerable than it should be today.' At one point Cheney was actually sent over to Congress to lobby for *less* spending on counterterrorism measures, rather than more.

About a month after September 11, a New York *Daily News* investigative team attempted to take utility knives, razor knives, and pepper spray aboard twelve flights taking off from eleven different airports. They succeeded on all but one flight. A year later the paper tried again, boarding fourteen flights taking off from eleven airports while carrying the same banned items. They succeeded every time. Of even greater concern are the nation's general aviation airports like the ones at which the terrorists trained. There are nineteen thousand of these small airfields, according to CBS News, and few of them have much in the way of security, or even fences. Despite all the warnings about the possibility of passenger jets being attacked by shoulder-fired surface-to-air missiles, the perimeters of even big American airports are woefully unsecured. In the summer of 2003, a boat containing three young men washed ashore at New York's John F. Kennedy International Airport. The men freely walked up and down the runways until they stumbled upon a police station.

And although passenger luggage is now more thoroughly screened at the gate, the vast majority of the nearly three million tons of cargo shipped in the holds of regular commercial airliners is not checked for weapons or explosives. *Time* reported that 'security experts shiver when they talk about the nation's cargo-handling procedures. Thousands of low-paid workers have carte blanche to roam airports, ramps and runways without undergoing personal inspections or having their belongings checked.'

Underscoring these vulnerabilities was the bizarre case in September 2003 of a man who shipped himself as air cargo from New York to Dallas undetected. 'Today it was just a guy trying to fly cheaply from New York to Dallas to visit his parents,' Representative Edward Markey told CNN, 'but in the future, a member of al Qaeda could have himself packed into an air cargo container.' A report issued by the Century Foundation in early 2004 stated that the Transportation Security Administration 'estimates there is a 35 to 65 percent chance that terrorists are planning to place a bomb in the cargo of a U.S. passenger plane. Yet, only about 5 percent of air cargo is screened, even if it is transported on passenger planes.'

Ninety-five percent of all foreign goods are shipped to America by sea – some eight million containers a year. Of those, only one in fifty is subjected to anything more than a cursory inspection, wrote Jonathan Chait in *The New Republic* in March 2003. Stephen Flynn, a former coast guard commander who oversaw a

2004 report on homeland security prepared by the Council on Foreign Relations, told Chait, 'We have virtually no security there.' To test security at the ports, ABC News bundled just under fifteen pounds of depleted uranium in a lead-lined steel pipe and shipped it in a container from Jakarta, Indonesia – a notorious Al Qaeda rallying ground and a departure point that should have raised all sorts of flags. The container went out, bound for Los Angeles, a week before the August 2003 bombing of the Jakarta Marriott that killed twelve people. It arrived in LA intact and undetected. Rather than being embarrassed by the incident, the Department of Homeland Security and the FBI investigated the ABC staff responsible for the shipment, claiming they may have broken smuggling laws. Criminal charges were threatened.

The coast guard says it would cost $5.5 billion to fully secure U.S. ports over the next ten years. And although the White House has said that seaport security is a priority in keeping the nation safe from terrorist attacks, the Bush administration's budget for 2005 calls for just $46 million for port security grants. But that's better than 2003 and 2004, when port security didn't get a penny.

In late 2002, the administration succeeding in getting the United Nations' International Maritime Organization to pass a new law of the sea. The pact requires ships around the world to be installed with communications equipment, security personnel, computers, and surveillance cameras. The treaty also sets strict security standards for the ports of call of ships coming into U.S. waters. It was a worthy idea, but like so many Bush initiatives, because of the administration's tax cuts, there was no funding to back it up. Not only can foreign ports in developing countries not afford to comply with the new standards, many American ports can't either. For U.S. ports, the cost of compliance was estimated at $7 billion – 152 times Bush's allocation for port security grants for 2005. And this is despite the terrorists' track record of attacks by boat – on the USS *Cole*, the French supertanker *Limburg*, Basra's oil terminals. Osama bin Laden may have ties to as many as three hundred vessels, reported the New York *Daily News* in September 2003, 'ranging from a shadowy fleet of small fishing trawlers to freighters, experts say.'

One thing Bush did do to make our ports safer: He issued a proclamation in early 2004 directing the Department of Homeland Security to seize any vessel, anywhere in U.S. waters, if it is believed that the boat might sail into Cuban waters. Amazingly, the proclamation went on to say that 'unauthorized entries' into Cuban waters facilitate 'the Cuban government's support of terrorism.' 'Aside from the order being a possible violation of the Bill of Rights,' wrote Paul Magnusson in *Businessweek*, 'the U.S. Coast Guard has had to draw up regulations and enlist cash-strapped local police departments and harbor patrols in the effort.' (The order even managed to anger recreational boaters. 'That's right, Popeye,' said the editor of one boating magazine. 'If you're unlucky enough to be reading this magazine in the cockpit of your most cherished possession – be it in San Diego, Seattle, Saginaw, or South Florida – and you wonder aloud how you'd always wanted to chase Hemingway's wake, by the letter of this new edict you have now forfeited the right to keep your boat.')

The administration allocated $115 million for rail security in the last two budgets – a paltry sum, especially in light of the Madrid train bombings in March 2004 that killed nearly two hundred people and the fact that, according to *Time*, five times as many people take trains than take planes on a given day. Lowly buses, which have virtually no security equipment or supervision, are a worry. Often you don't even need a key to start a bus – you just push a button. In late 2003, a man walked into the Port Authority Bus Terminal in New York and got behind the wheel of a fifty-six-seater. He drove it out of the station and all the way to Terminal 4 at JFK airport, where police arrested him. (His blood alcohol tested above the legal limit.)

Of immediate worry is the safety of the nation's existing nuclear storage facilities and laboratories. Rich Levernier, a specialist with the Department of Energy, spent more than half a decade organizing mock-terrorist squads made up of U.S. military commandos, who would attempt to infiltrate the Los Alamos National Laboratory in New Mexico and nine other nuclear facilities. At risk nationwide are more than sixty metric tons of plutonium and many times that amount of highly enriched uranium. (To make a crude nuclear weapon requires just eleven pounds of plutonium or forty-five pounds of uranium.)

Levernier told Mark Hertsgaard in a report in *Vanity Fair* that 'some of the facilities would fail year after year. In more than 50% of our tests of the Los Alamos facility, we got in, captured the plutonium, got out again, and in some cases didn't fire a shot, because we didn't encounter any guards.' This despite the fact that the facilities had been told months in advance both the day and approximate time the attacks would take place. The faux attackers were handicapped in other ways that real terrorists wouldn't be: Grenades, body armor, and armed helicopters couldn't be used, and safety guidelines had to be adhered to, which meant the mock terrorists couldn't drive over the speed limit.

During one pretend attack, after Levernier's squad managed to get into Los Alamos and make off with weapons-grade nuclear material, the facility complained, almost comically, that the attack shouldn't count because the 'terrorists' carried the material off in a vehicle not on the approved list of weapons for war games – a Home Depot cart.

When Energy Secretary Spencer Abraham asked for $379.7 million in 2002 for added security measures at the country's nuclear facilities, the administration approved only $26.4 million, according to a story by Jonathan Chait in *The New Republic*. 'The list of improvements Bush declined to fund included more secure barriers and fences, computer improvements to defend against hackers, equipment to detect explosives in packages and vehicles entering department sites, and a reduction in the overall number of sites that store bomb-grade plutonium and uranium,' Chait wrote.

There are similar problems with the nation's nuclear power plants. New York State's Indian Point facility, which is only an hour's drive north of Times Square, is a case in point. For decades, environmental and other groups have fought to have the plant closed. In 2003, in an effort to quiet fears, the Nuclear Regulatory Commission proudly announced that Indian Point had thwarted a mock-terrorist attack. That drill was as slanted in the facility's favor as the ones Levernier had staged at Los Alamos. Guards were reportedly told in advance when the attack would occur, and there were only three 'terrorists.' They were required to attack during daylight hours.

A 2003 report called 'Controlling Nuclear Warheads and Materials: A Report Card and Action Plan' prepared by Harvard University found that Al Qaeda has been trying to get hold of nuclear weapons since the early 1990s. The report said that Chechen terrorists, who have close ties to Al Qaeda, made four reconnaissance missions to Russia between 2001 and 2002, checking out nuclear storage facilities and train yards where the material is moved. The report was commissioned by the Nuclear Threat Initiative, whose members include former senator Sam Nunn and Senator Richard Lugar. In 1991, they had created the Cooperative Threat Reduction Program, which sought to destroy the unprotected stockpiles of warheads and bomb-grade material in the former Soviet Union. The Bush administration has been reluctant to give it much in the way of funding. Duncan Hunter, a California Republican who is chairman of the House Armed Services Committee, somewhat enigmatically called the plan 'open-ended, unfocused and . . . self-defeating.' According to James Traub in *The New York Times*, in early 2004, the White House at first tried to eliminate the program but finally agreed to keep it funded at $451 million per year – about 5 percent of what the Pentagon spends on missile defense.

Responding to a request by Senate Minority Leader Tom Daschle, a group that included Clinton's former secretary of state

Madeleine Albright and former national security adviser Sandy Berger prepared a study in July 2003 called 'An American Security Policy.' The report listed six major areas of concern. Number one they called 'The Loose Nukes Crisis in North Korea.' Number two was weapons of mass destruction in Russia and other countries. Iraq came in at number four. Graham Allison of the Kennedy School of Government at Harvard told *The Times*'s James Traub in early 2004 that 'Iraq was a Level 2 issue. The Level 1 issue is that a terrorist could detonate a nuclear bomb in New York City instead of flying two planes into the World Trade Center.' Traub quoted Allison as saying that the eventuality of this occurring was 'more likely than not.'

'America at Risk,' a report released in 2004 by Democratic members of the House Select Committee on Homeland Security, stated that since the anthrax scare of 2001–02, not a single drug or vaccine for the pathogens rated as most dangerous by the Centers for Disease Control had been developed. The Pentagon's own review of the situation found weaknesses in 'almost every aspect of U.S. biopreparedness and response.' The Pentagon attempted to suppress its report, but parts of it were read to a reporter for *The New York Times*. One passage stated, 'The fall 2001 anthrax attacks may turn out to be the easiest of bioterrorist strikes to confront.' *60 Minutes* reported that 'just a few miles across the Hudson River from New York City, tucked underneath a heavily trafficked overpass, sits a nondescript chemical plant that manufactures disinfectant. According to government records, nearly 1,000 tons of deadly chlorine gas is stored here – the first agent ever used in chemical warfare during World War I . . . [and] twelve million people . . . within a fourteen-mile radius of the plant could be affected if the cloud of chlorine gas was released.'

You would think that 'first responders' – firefighters and emergency crews, like the ones who spent months at the World Trade Center and the Pentagon – would be a priority for a president who called the nation's security his 'highest priority.' They aren't. In his

2005 budget, Bush proposed reducing the $750 million allocated to the Assistance to Firefighters Grant Program to $500 million. When House Democratic Whip Steny H. Hoyer of Maryland wrote the president urging him to reconsider his decision, he was ignored.

The overall budget for first responders is $27 billion, to be spent between 2004 and 2008. When a task force from the Council on Foreign Relations surveyed emergency responder groups nationwide as to what programs and equipment they deemed necessary for a 'minimum' response to another terrorist attack, the amount they came up with was $98.4 billion – almost four times what the Bush administration was giving them. In early 2004, the U.S. Conference of Mayors released findings from a survey that said that of the 215 cities queried, 76 percent had yet to receive a penny from Washington for first response units. Senator Hillary Rodham Clinton did a survey of her own in early 2003. Of the New York towns and cities she polled, 70 percent had not received any first response funding.

When it came to dividing up the first $3 billion in funds allocated by the administration to homeland security, the amounts per capita in no way reflected the level of probable danger to the individuals in the states receiving the money. An Associated Press study in 2003 showed that New York State got $17 per person. The highest per capita payout for a state was nearly $36 for residents of Wyoming – the vice president's home state. American Samoa, the U.S. territory in the Pacific Ocean twenty-three hundred miles from Hawaii, received $94.40 for every resident.

In New York City, police officials say they need $900 million for preparedness alone. They received just $84 million. Of fifty major American cities, wrote Richard Schwartz in the *Daily News*, New York had the forty-ninth lowest per capita allotment – $5.87. The city that had the highest payout was New Haven, Connecticut, home to Yale University, alma mater of the president, his father, and his grandfather – it received $77.92 per person. Governor Jeb

Bush's state, Florida, also did well, with Miami getting $52.82 per person; Orlando, $47.14; and Tampa, $30.57. *USA Today* reported in July 2003 that a harbor on Martha's Vineyard and the ferry company that runs boats between mainland Massachusetts and the Vineyard, where many legislators summer, received $900,000 for increased security. The paper said that when Todd Alexander, one of the harbormasters, told *The Vineyard Gazette*, 'Quite honestly, I don't know what we're going to do, but you don't turn down grant money,' the poor fellow was told not to speak to the press again.

In 2002, just as the whole Homeland Security apparatus was being set up, the Immigration and Naturalization Service – which, according to Chait in *The New Republic*, has a total of fourteen agents to track down twelve hundred illegal immigrants in the United States known to have come from Al Qaeda–breeding countries – asked for $52 million to hire more staff. The request was denied in the interests of the tax cuts. Along the five thousand-mile U.S.-Canadian border and the two thousand-mile U.S.-Mexican border pass some four hundred million people each year. The borders are notoriously porous, and although there is rising concern that terrorists could easily slip into the United States across the Canadian border, there is, on average, only one guard every ten miles.

According to a March 2004 article in *The New York Times*, the Internal Revenue Service requested funds to hire eighty additional criminal investigators, to add to the '160 it has already assigned to penetrate the shadowy networks that terrorist groups use to finance plots like the Sept. 11 attacks and the recent train bombings in Madrid. But the Bush administration did not include funds for them in the president's proposed budget for the 2005 fiscal year.' Although the White House is fond of making pronouncements stating that it has frozen $136.7 million in terrorists' funds, Rachel Ehrenfeld, the author of *Funding Evil*, a book about terrorists' money operations, said that amount is 'a drop in the bucket.'

In late 2003, the General Accounting Office reported that the

IRS didn't have a plan for sharing information about terrorist financing with other government agencies. The GAO also said that both the Justice Department and the Department of the Treasury were a year behind in coming up with programs to investigate terrorist money-laundering operations and the money they get from selling black market gold and precious gems.

The Council on Foreign Relations summed up the overall state of the nation's safety in 2003, following an investigation headed by former senator Warren Rudman. 'Although in some respects the American public is now better prepared to address aspects of the terrorist threat than it was two years ago,' the report states, 'the United States remains dangerously ill-prepared to handle a catastrophic attack on American soil.'

THE WAR IN AFGHANISTAN

'An attack on one is an attack on all.'

– NATO SECRETARY-GENERAL GEORGE ROBERTSON

September 2001

With this statement, the North Atlantic Treaty Organization's nineteen members invoked Article 5 of the group's charter to justify the eventual attack on Afghanistan in retaliation for the ones on September 11. It was the first time NATO had dipped into the part of the treaty that says that an attack on a member nation is an attack on the whole organization and therefore justifies a military response. In the White House Treaty Room shortly after the Afghan bombing began, Bush pronounced his resolve to the nation. 'The battle is now joined on many fronts,' he said. 'We will not waver. We will not tire. We will not falter. And we will not fail. Peace and freedom will prevail.'

Politicians, and especially presidents, have short and selective attention spans. The administration was never fully committed to rooting out Al Qaeda in Afghanistan. Its hearts and minds were always on the oil-rich nation eight hundred miles to the west. As former security czar Richard Clarke told Seymour Hersh of *The New Yorker*, 'One, they did not want to get involved in Afghanistan like Russia did. Two, they were saving forces for the war in Iraq. And, three, Rumsfeld wanted to have a laboratory to prove his theory about the ability of small numbers of ground troops, coupled with airpower, to win decisive battles.' Clarke added that 'the U.S. has succeeded in stabilizing only two or three cities. The President of Afghanistan is just the mayor of Kabul.'

The Iraq invasion essentially left Afghanistan in the dust. Funding and human resources were shifted to the new theater of battle. In *Plan of Attack*, Bob Woodward reports that in July 2002, the administration diverted $700 million from the Afghanistan conflict to General Tommy Franks so that he could begin preparing for war in Iraq. The diversion was not only kept from Congress, it was also in violation of the Constitution. By the end of 2003, the United States had budgeted more for just bringing oil into Iraq ($690 million) than for rebuilding Afghanistan ($672 million). Almost 50 percent of the commando units and intelligence specialists who had been combing the hills and mountains of Afghanistan and Pakistan looking for Osama bin Laden and other members of Al Qaeda were reportedly diverted to Iraq when the war started there. *USA Today* stated in March 2004 that 'Bob Andrews, former head of a Pentagon office that oversaw special operations, says that removing Saddam Hussein was a good idea but "a distraction." The war in Iraq, Andrews notes, entailed the largest deployment of special operations forces – about 10,000 – since the Vietnam War. That's about 25% of all U.S. commandos.'

The aftermath is as dispiriting as it is potentially explosive. A World Bank conference in 2002 estimated that Afghanistan would need $15 billion over the next ten years to get back on its feet. The

United States spent $500 million over two years to create and train an Afghan army. As of March 2004, according to *Time*, only fifty-seven hundred soldiers – in a nation of twenty-eight million – had been hired and trained. The soldiers rarely leave the confines of Kabul, and desertion rates are running at 22 percent, according to NATO. By comparison, the armed followers of former Afghan president Burhanuddin Rabbani number close to fifty thousand in Kabul alone. The United Nations, says *Time*, 'has managed to register just 9% of the country's 10.5 million eligible voters. Taliban rebels have threatened to kill U.N.-sponsored election teams and burn down schools and mosques where Afghans are signing up to vote.'

The Center on International Cooperation estimated that by early 2004, only about $120 million of the $2.9 billion disbursed by donors toward reconstruction had resulted in any projects being completed. A 2004 report by the UN's Development Program stated that aid 'has been much lower than expected or promised . . . In comparison to other conflict or post-conflict situations, Afghanistan appears to have been neglected.' The report went on to say that despite similarly sized populations, Iraq is receiving ten times the development aid that Afghanistan is receiving. Even citizens of Bosnia and Herzegovina get 3.7 times more per capita in foreign aid than Afghans.

In mid-2003, the Council on Foreign Relations and the Asia Society issued a joint report that said, 'Unless the situation improves, Afghanistan risks sliding back into the anarchy and warlordism that prevailed in the 1990s and helped give rise to the Taliban. Such a reversion would have disastrous consequences for Afghanistan and would be a profound setback for the US war on terrorism.'

The Taliban is regrouping under its leader, Mullah Mohammad Omar, who is still in hiding and now has a hold on roughly a third of the country. The nation's warlords are again carving up other regions. Ismail Khan, the governor of western Afghanistan, and others have brought back the Taliban's infamous department of 'Vice and Virtue,' which sends young hoodlums into the streets to enforce segregation. Khan had previously made a radio announcement that women who walk with men other than their husbands should be beaten. On a visit to Afghanistan in April 2002, Donald Rumsfeld described Khan as 'an appealing person, thoughtful, measured and self-confident.'

In the eastern provinces, Hazrat Ali's forces are still being supported by the U.S. military because they had pitched in during the battle in Tora Bora against Al Qaeda. Human Rights Watch calls Ali one of the country's worst violators of human rights. His followers have been accused of raping women, sodomizing young boys, and stealing and kidnapping.

Human Rights Watch has also been critical of Amniate Milli, the intelligence division of the interim Afghan government, which is backed by the United States. The *Australian Financial Review* reported, 'Its members regularly torture prisoners [and] often innocent citizens whom officials shake down for money. Prisoners are shackled, beaten, hung upside down, given electric shocks or hung from their fingertips and covered with a thick blanket teeming with lice. The editor of a Kabul magazine that published an offending cartoon was told by an Amniat official, "Look, we have 30 bullets in our clip. I can shoot 30 of these bullets into your chest right now and there is no-one who can stop us."'

The situation in the country is especially harmful to women, whose rights – or, rather, lack thereof – have essentially returned to the state they were under the Taliban. Colin Powell had stated definitively in November 2001 that the restoration of women's rights would 'not be negotiable.' Other members of the administration didn't share his conviction. In early 2002, the White House told the Senate it wanted to ratify the Convention on the Elimination of All Forms of Discrimination Against Women. Signed by Jimmy Carter in 1980 but never ratified by the Senate, the UN pact, the administration said, was 'generally desirable and should be approved.' The White House soon changed course. Powell began talking about its 'vagueness' and 'complexity' and thought the Justice Department should have a look at it. But Attorney General John Ashcroft had been a vocal critic of the treaty back when he was a member of the Senate and offered no endorsement of it this time. The White House walked away from the pact. 'Standing with the United States in failing to ratify the convention,' wrote the *Houston Chronicle*, 'are nations known for their oppressive treatment of women, such as Afghanistan under the Taliban, Iran, Sudan, Somalia, Syria, the United Arab Emirates and Qatar.' Under Democratic leadership in July 2002, the Senate Foreign Relations Committee took matters into its own hands and voted to put the measure to the full Senate for a vote. But nothing happened before that session of Congress adjourned. The Republicans won the Senate in 2002, and so the treaty sits, stalled and unratified. In early 2004, *The New York Times* reported that in Herat alone, more than forty women had chosen self-immolation over life during the previous six months.

Afghanistan is once again the leading producer of opium in the world, supplying 75 percent of the global market. Crop acreage is 36 times greater than it was during the Taliban regime, the White House said in November 2003. The harvest now brings in $2.3 billion a year. More than 1.7 million Afghans – 6 percent of the population – are currently involved in opium production. In late 2003, the United Nations estimated that the average Afghan family brought in $184 a year; the average family involved in opium growing brought in $3,900 a year.

Where does the money go? Much of it winds up in the hands of the warlord militias, the Taliban, and other terrorist organizations like Al Qaeda and Hezb-i-Islami. 'Any operation that Al Qaeda or the Taliban could conceive of could be funded right now,' a diplomat told a reporter for the *Chicago Tribune*. 'In terms of their needs, it's an unlimited source of financing.' In early 2004, a UN report warned that Afghanistan was becoming an opium-based economy and a 'terrorist breeding ground.'

> 'Peace will be achieved by helping Afghanistan develop its own stable government.'
>
> – GEORGE W. BUSH, April 2002

THE WAR IN IRAQ

> 'I analyzed a thorough body of intelligence – good, solid, sound intelligence – that led me to come to the conclusion that it was necessary to remove Saddam Hussein from power.'
>
> – GEORGE W. BUSH, July 2003

> 'I'm also not very analytical. You know I don't spend a lot of time thinking about myself, why I do things.'
>
> – GEORGE W. BUSH, June 2003

'People don't want war . . . but [they] can always be brought to the bidding of the leaders. That is easy. All you have to do is tell them they are being attacked and denounce the pacifists for lack of patriotism and exposing the country to danger.' That may sound like a quote from the Karl Rove playbook or a snippet from an internal memo from Rumsfeld's office. But it actually was said by Hitler's Luftwaffe chief and designated successor, Hermann Goering, to a psychologist in 1946, at the time of the Nuremberg war-crimes trials.

For Americans, September 11 was most certainly the defining single-day tragedy of our age. But, to put it in perspective, it was, however devastating, the only attack by a foreign element on U.S. soil in more than half a century – outside of the 1993 World Trade Center bombing. European, African, and Middle Eastern countries have grown wearily accustomed to death tolls by terrorism that are registered almost weekly; month in, month out; year in, year out.

Make no mistake about it. September 11 was about terrorism – a new type of enemy for the United States. But it's an enemy without borders, capitals, or diplomatic structure. And yet in what may come to be seen as one of the most critical blunders in military history, the White House and the Pentagon irrationally picked Iraq as the target on which they would stake their careers – and the lives and reputation of the American people. Iraq was always the G-spot for the Bush administration. September 11 gave them a pretext they could manipulate to sell the nation on an invasion. As *The Daily Show*'s Jon Stewart says, the United States is really bad at fear. And that climate of fear and patriotism in the wake of the attacks only made the administration's public relations job easier.

As Paul O'Neill, former treasury secretary under Bush, and journalist Ron Suskind point out in their book *The Price of Loyalty*, ten days into the administration, Iraq was officially on the Bush agenda. The attacks of September 11 gave the White House an excuse to carry out a radical restructuring of the Middle East. Rumsfeld seemed more keyed up on hitting targets – and fast – than on finding who and where the enemy was. On September 12, 2001, Richard Clarke says in his book *Against All Enemies*, 'Secretary Rumsfeld complained that there were no decent targets for bombing in Afghanistan and that we should consider bombing Iraq, which, he said, had better targets. At first I thought Rumsfeld was joking. But he was serious and the President did not reject out of hand the idea of attacking Iraq.'

Egged on by the trio of neoconservatives who had the president's ear – Deputy Secretary of Defense Paul Wolfowitz, defense adviser Richard Perle, and Undersecretary of Defense for Policy Douglas Feith – the administration assembled a PR calculus for invading the country that it thought Americans would swallow:

- Iraq equals terrorism.
- Iraq equals biological weapons.

- Iraq equals weapons of mass destruction – in the president's words, 'the smoking gun . . . a mushroom cloud.'

Except that:

- Saddam Hussein's regime was a secular one and Al Qaeda is a fundamentalist terror group dedicated in part to the overthrow of secular leaderships. There is no evidence whatsoever that Saddam ever funneled money to the terrorist organization. And, as the Europeans know but this administration has yet to figure out, the invasion of Iraq was not a blow against terrorism but rather a growth hormone for more of it.
- Inspectors, including Scott Ritter, Hans Blix, and most recently David Kay, all say that the international community's efforts – begun in the early 1990s after the Gulf War – to rid Saddam of stockpiles of biological and other weapons systems had been successful.
- There was no 'smoking gun' in the way of weapons of mass destruction, merely 'weapons of mass destruction–related program activities,' whatever that means.

The miscalculations in going to war were endless. Vice President Dick Cheney predicted that American troops would be welcomed as liberators. Just over a month after the invasion of Iraq began, Rumsfeld compared the operation to the liberation of Paris after World War II. Except there was a big difference between Paris in 1944 and Baghdad in 2003: France was occupied by Germany, a foreign power. Iraq was in the grip of a native Iraqi. Not a very nice one, mind you, but an Iraqi nevertheless – which, if you live in the country being occupied, is a big difference. Foreigners dominating your country versus one of your own dominating your country? People of pride choose the latter any day. And the Iraqis are nothing if not proud people.

In its rush to war, the Bush administration bullied traditional allies who failed to see the logic of an invasion of Iraq. And it derided the United Nations for trying to maintain world order and the delicate dance of diplomacy necessary to avoid wars. Shortly after the invasion began, Perle callously dismissed the organization as 'the looming chatterbox on the Hudson.' (Perle's geography is a little off. The UN headquarters overlooks New York's East River.)

You've got to give it to the Bush administration, though – it's focused. When it wants to go to war, it goes to war come hell or high water, and never mind what anyone else thinks. In no particular order, in its rush to invade Iraq, the Bush White House did the following:

- It co-opted the CIA and other intelligence agencies. Mel Goodman, a twenty-four-year veteran of the agency, told *Vanity Fair* that CIA and Defense Intelligence Agency analysts were being called into their superiors' offices and told that their careers would be on the line if they didn't produce findings backing up the administration's desires on Iraq.
- It then cherry-picked intelligence favorable to its philosophy and its goals.
- It deceived Congress (a felony, by the way).
- It deceived the American people (not a felony, but it should be). The deceit worked. In August 2002, an ABC News/*Washington Post* poll found that 79 percent of Americans felt that Iraq posed a threat to the United States. An October 2002 Gallup poll showed 56 percent of Americans in favor of going into Iraq. And a December 2002 *Los Angeles Times* poll showed that 90 percent of Americans thought Saddam was developing WMDs. (Incredibly, a September 2003 *Washington Post* poll found that 69 percent of Americans believed Saddam was

personally involved in the September 11 attacks.)

- It deceived the United Nations. Not only that, it asked Britain to bug six Security Council members during the 2002–03 debate over enforcing Resolution 1441. Tony Blair's government may even have bugged the offices of UN Secretary-General Kofi Annan.

- It strong-armed some traditional allies into going along with us and trashed the ones that wouldn't.

- It had its attack machine tar Americans opposed to war as being chickens or, worse, traitors.

Furthermore, when it wanted to go to war, the Bush administration pushed the UN weapons inspectors to the wall, pressuring them to find the WMDs and find them fast. The White House said that time was running out ('the smoking gun . . . the mushroom cloud'). Then, when it wanted to justify the war once 'major combat operations' were over and Iraq had been leveled, the administration told the world not to rush the inspection process, that the inspectors needed more time to find the root reason given for the invasion – weapons of mass destruction. A University of Maryland poll conducted in May 2003 found that 34 percent of Americans believed the United States had found weapons of mass destruction in Iraq, and 22 percent thought Iraq had used chemical or biological weapons during the war.

When all the administration's manufactured justifications for going to war crumbled on a bloody bone pile of deception and dissolution, the White House threw its weight behind another rationale for the war: Saddam had to be toppled for the good of the Iraqi people and stability in the Middle East.

Who are the winners in all of this? The vice president's old firm, Halliburton, is certainly one. Through May 2004, it won $4.7 billion in postwar contracts in Iraq and Afghanistan, according to the Center for Public Integrity, even though it was accused in Congress of overcharging the Pentagon for gas and meals.

Bechtel is another winner. It received contracts totaling $2.8 billion over the same period, despite criticism from the army of the shoddy work it did building schools and other facilities. Few of these contracts were sent out for competitive bidding.

Who are the losers? Where do we begin? Saddam, his sons Uday and Qusay, and his murderous, despotic regime, obviously. Morale at the CIA is at an all-time low. A battered George Tenet resigned in June 2004 after weathering two of the biggest intelligence failures in the agency's history. Morale isn't much better at the FBI. The members of the National Guard who have stayed way past their terms of duty have paid a heavy price, as have their families. We've lost our reputation for being the world's responsible superpower – a standing that took two centuries to establish. And for what? The Iraqis hate us. We've alienated many of our traditional allies. America has been pushed into a conflict in Iraq without purpose and now without conclusion. 'Bush's Vietnam,' Senator Edward Kennedy calls it. The war was also an Al Qaeda recruitment officer's dream. And the Middle East is as unstable as it was before September 11, perhaps more so.

The death toll of Iraqi civilians as a result of the military intervention by spring 2004, has been estimated by iraqbodycount.net at upward of ten thousand. Add to that figure the untold thousands who have been wounded, and it's the highest number of civilian noncombatant casualties involving U.S. troops since Vietnam. The *Los Angeles Times* reported in late 2003 that 'the U.S. military does not keep statistics on the civilian deaths it has caused, saying it is "impossible for us to maintain an accurate account."'

In early November 2003, after a particularly bloody month for U.S. troops, the military adopted a get-tough strategy – encompassing a range of tactics – toward the growing insurgency. 'In selective cases, American soldiers are demolishing buildings thought to be used by Iraqi attackers,' *The New York Times* reported a month later. 'They have begun imprisoning the relatives of suspected guerrillas, in hopes of pressing the insurgents to turn themselves in.' They'd also wrapped entire towns in barbed-wire fences, allowing citizens in and out through a single checkpoint, and imposed curfews after dark. 'This is absolutely humiliating,' a schoolteacher told the *Times*. 'We are like birds in a cage.' Aside from angering the very people the military was trying to win over, 'tactics like these are unethical under any moral code,' reported *The Christian Science Monitor*, 'and illegal under the Fourth Geneva Convention.'

The military's get-tough strategy was also being applied at Iraq's prisons, where thousands of suspected insurgents were being interrogated. Among those detained were innocent Iraqi civilians. Not by accident but by design, according to Hayder Sabbar Abd, one of the detainees forced to pose naked with a bag over his head in the now infamous Abu Ghraib photographs. Abd told the *Times*, 'We were not insurgents. We were just ordinary people. And American intelligence knew this.' The release of the Abu Ghraib photographs broke what little trust remained between Iraqis and their occupiers. As of May 2004, the military continued to battle the insurgency, and America's reputation around the world was at its lowest point in decades.

The cost of the war in terms of dollars? By May 2004, the first anniversary of the official end of combat operations, the U.S. share of the invasion was about $100 billion and climbing at the rate of about $8 billion per month.

On May 1, 2003, Bush, in a borrowed navy pilot's suit, was dropped onto the deck of the USS *Abraham Lincoln*, then sailing in dangerous waters thirty miles offshore from San Diego. The banner behind him reading 'Mission Accomplished' was a clever idea for a photo op backdrop, but it was a foolish, swaggering gesture that has come back to haunt the administration and will for years to come. A year to the day since that landing aboard the *Lincoln*, 833 American and coalition forces had lost their lives in the war and its bloody aftermath.

This is what war really looks like:

The British Toll

Cpl. Stephen John Allbutt, 35 • Sapper Luke Allsopp, 24 • Cpl. Russell Aston, 30 • Maj. Stephen Alexis Ballard, 33 • Fusilier Russell Beeston, 26 • Colour Sgt. John Cecil, 36 • Trooper David Jeffrey Clarke, 19 • Lance Cpl. Andrew Jason Craw, 21 • Staff Sgt. Simon Cullingworth, 36 • Lance Bombardier Llywelyn Karl Evans, 24 • Lt. Philip D. Green, 31 • Capt. Philip Stuart Guy, 29 • Sgt. Alexander Hamilton-Jewell, 41 • Leonard Harvey, 55 • Marine Sholto Hedenskog, 26 • Sgt. Les Hehir, 34 • Lance Cpl. of Horse Matty Hull, 25 • Cpl. Richard Thomas David Ivell, 29 • Capt. David Martyn Jones, 29 • Pvt. Andrew Joseph Kelly, 18 • Lance Cpl. Thomas Richard Keys, 20 • Lt. Antony King, 35 • Lt. Marc A. Lawrence, 26 • Capt. James Linton, 43 • Cpl. Paul Graham Long, 24 • Marine Christopher R. Maddison, 24 • Flight Lt. Kevin Barry Main, 36 • Lance Cpl. Ian Keith Malone, 28 • Lance Cpl. James McCue, 27 • Cpl. Simon Miller, 21 • Staff Sgt. Chris Muir, 32 • Piper Christopher Muzyuru, 21 • Sgt. John Nightingale, 32 • Sgt. Norman Patterson, 28 • Cpl. Ian Plank, 31 • Cpl. Dewi Pritchard, 35 • Gunner Duncan Geoffrey Pritchard, 22 • Sgt. Steven Mark Roberts, 33 • Operator Mechanic (Comm.) Second Class Ian Seymour, 29 • Lance Cpl. Karl Shearer, 24 • Cpl. David John Shepherd, 34 • Pvt. Jason Smith, 32 • Maj. James Stenner, 30 • Lance Cpl. Barry Stephen, 31 • Warrant Officer Second Class Mark Stratford, 39 • Pvt. Ryan Lloyd Thomas, 18 • Sapper Robert Thompson, 22 • Maj. Matthew Titchener, 32 • Fusilier Kelan John Turrington, 18 • Lt. Alexander Tweedie, 25 • Company Sgt. Maj. Colin Wall, 34 • Maj. Jason George Ward, 34 • Lt. Philip West, 32 • Flight Lt. David Rhys Williams, 37 • Lt. James Williams, 28 • Lt. Andrew S. Wilson, 36 • Rifleman Vincent Calvin Windsor, 23

The Italian Toll

Chief Warrant Officer Massimiliano Bruno, 40 • Cpl. Alessandro Carrisi, 23 • Chief Warrant Officer Giovanni Cavallaro, 47 • Sgt. Maj. Giuseppe Coletta, 38 • Cpl. Emanuele Ferraro, 28 • Lt. Massimiliano Ficuciello, 35 • Pvt. Andrea Filippa, 31 • Chief Warrant Officer Enzo Fregosi, 56 • Chief Warrant Officer Daniele Ghione, 31 • Sgt. Maj. Ivan Ghitti, 30 • Pfc. Domenico Intravaia, 46 • Pvt. Horacio Majorana, 29 • Chief Warrant Officer Filippo Merlino, 46 • Warrant Officer Silvio Olla, 32 • Cpl. Pietro Petrucci, 22 • Chief Warrant Officer Alfio Ragazzi, 39 • Chief Warrant Officer Alfonso Trincone, 44

The Spanish Toll

Master Sgt. Alfonso Vega Calvo, 41 • Sgt. Maj. José Lucas Egea, 42 • Sgt. Luis Puga Gandar, 29 • Cmdr. Gonzalo Perez García, 42 • Sgt. José Antonio Bernal Gómez, 34 • Maj. Alberto Martínez González, 43 • Navy Capt. Manuel Martín Oar, 57 • Maj. José Merino Olivera, 49 • Maj. Carlos Barro Ollero, 36 • Maj. José Carlos Rodríguez Pérez, 41 • Sgt. First Class Luis Ignacio Zanon Tarazona, 36

The Bulgarian Toll

Sgt. Dimitar Dimitrov, 25 • Sgt. First Class Ivan Hristov Indjov Jr., 36 • Capt. Georgi Hristov Kachorin, 29 • Pvt. Svilen Simeonov Kirov, 25 • Sgt. Anton Valentinov Petrov, 26 • Second Lt. Nikolai Angelov Saruev, 26

The Ukrainian Toll

Pvt. Ruslan Androschuk, 24 • Capt. Olexei Bondarenko, 34 • Pvt. Konstantin M. Khaliev, 23 • Sr. Sgt. Yuriy Koydan, 23 • Jr. Sgt. Sergiy Suslov, 20 • Yaroslav Zlochevskiy, 23

The Polish Toll

Maj. Hieronim Kupczyk, 44 • Lance Cpl. Gerard Wasilewski, 20

The Thai Toll

Sgt. Amporn Chulert, 46 • Sgt. Mitr Klaharn, 43

The El Salvadoran Toll

Pvt. Natividad Mendez Ramos, 19

The Danish Toll

Cpl. Preben Pedersen, 34

The Estonian Toll

Jr. Sgt. Andres Nuiamäe, 21

The American Toll

ARMY: Sgt. Michael D. Acklin II, 25 • Spc. Genaro Acosta, 26 • Pfc. Steven Acosta, 19 • Capt. James F. Adamouski, 29 • Pvt. Algernon Adams, 36 • First Lt. Michael R. Adams, 24 • Pfc. Michael S. Adams, 20 • Spc. Jamaal R. Addison, 22 • Capt. Tristan N. Aitken, 31 • Spc. Ronald D. Allen Jr., 22 • Sgt. Glenn R. Allison, 24 • Pfc. John D. Amos II, 22 • Spc. Michael Andrade, 28 • Sgt. Edward J. Anguiano, 24 • Spc. Richard Arriaga, 20 • Spc. Robert R. Arsiaga, 25 • Cpl. Evan Asa Ashcraft, 24 • Capt. Matthew J. August, 28 • Spc. Tyanna S. Avery-Felder, 22 • Sgt. First Class Henry A. Bacon, 45 • Sgt. Andrew Joseph Baddick, 26 • Staff Sgt. Daniel Bader, 28 • Staff Sgt. Nathan J. Bailey, 46 • Spc. Ryan T. Baker, 24 • Sgt. Sherwood R. Baker, 30 • Spc.

Solomon C. Bangayan, 24 • Cpl. Juan C. Cabral Banuelos, 25 • Lt. Col. Dominic R. Baragona, 42 • Spc. Jonathan P. Barnes, 21 • Sgt. Michael Paul Barrera, 26 • Spc. Todd M. Bates, 20 • Spc. James L. Beckstrand, 27 • Sgt. Gregory A. Belanger, 24 • Sgt. Aubrey D. Bell, 33 • Pfc. Wilfred D. Bellard, 20 • Staff Sgt. Joseph P. Bellavia, 28 • Sgt. First Class William M. Bennett, 35 • Spc. Robert T. Benson, 20 • First Lt. David R. Bernstein, 24 • Spc. Joel L. Bertoldie, 20 • Staff Sgt. Stephen A. Bertolino, 40 • Cpl. Mark A. Bibby, 25 • Sgt. Benjamin W. Biskie, 27 • Sgt. Jarrod W. Black, 26 • Chief Warrant Officer 2 Michael T. Blaise, 29 • Capt. Ernesto M. Blanco, 28 • Command Sgt. Maj. James D. Blankenbecler, 40 • Spc. Joseph M. Blickenstaff, 23 • Sgt. Trevor A. Blumberg, 22 • Sgt. First Class Craig A. Boling, 38 • Sgt. First Class Kelly Bolor, 37 • Staff Sgt. Stevon A. Booker, 34 • Chief Warrant Officer Clarence E. Boone, 50 • Pfc. Rachel K. Bosveld, 19 • Spc. Mathew G. Boule, 22 • Spc. Edward W. Brabazon, 20 • Staff Sgt. Kenneth R. Bradley, 39 • Staff Sgt. Stacey C. Brandon, 35 • Spc. Artimus D. Brassfield, 22 • Pfc. Joel K. Brattain, 21 • Pfc. Jeffrey F. Braun, 19 • Staff Sgt. Steven H. Bridges, 33 • Staff Sgt. Cory W. Brooks, 32 • Sgt. Thomas F. Broomhead, 34 • Cpl. Henry L. Brown, 22 • Pfc. John E. Brown, 21 • Spc. Larry K. Brown, 22 • Spc. Lunsford B. Brown II, 27 • Pfc. Nathan P. Brown, 21 • Pfc. Timmy R. Brown Jr., 21 • Second Lt. Todd J. Bryant, 23 • Sgt. Ernest G. Bucklew, 33 • Spc. Roy Russell Buckley, 24 • Spc. Paul J. Bueche, 19 • Lt. Col. Charles H. Buehring, 40 • Sgt. George Edward Buggs, 31 • Staff Sgt. Christopher Bunda, 29 • Staff Sgt. Richard A. Burdick, 24 • Sgt. Travis L. Burkhardt, 26 • Pfc. Charles E. Bush Jr., 43 • Pvt. Matthew D. Bush, 20 • Pfc. Damian S. Bushart, 22 • Sgt. Jacob L. Butler, 24 • Capt. Joshua T. Byers, 29 • Sgt. Charles T. Caldwell, 38 • Spc. Nathaniel A. Caldwell, 27 • Staff Sgt. Joseph Camara, 40 • Sgt. Ryan M. Campbell, 25 • Spc. Marvin A. Camposiles, 25 • Spc. Isaac Campoy, 21 • Spc. Adolfo C. Carballo, 20 • Cpl. Richard P. Carl, 26 • Spc. Ryan G. Carlock,

25 • Staff Sgt. Edward W. Carman, 27 • Spc. Jocelyn L. Carrasquillo, 28 • Pfc. José Casanova, 23 • Spc. Ahmed A. Cason, 24 • Capt. Paul J. Cassidy, 36 • Staff Sgt. Roland L. Castro, 26 • Sgt. Sean K. Cataudella, 28 • Spc. Doron Chan, 20 • Spc. James A. Chance III, 25 • Spc. Jason K. Chappell, 22 • Pfc. Jonathan M.Cheatham, 19 • Sgt. Yihjyh L. Chen, 31 • Spc. Andrew F. Chris, 25 • Staff Sgt. Thomas W. Christensen, 42 • Spc. Brett T. Christian, 27 • Spc. Arron R. Clark, 20 • First Sgt. Christopher D. Coffin, 51 • Cpl. Gary B. Coleman, 24 • Second Lt. Benjamin J. Colgan, 30 • Staff Sgt. Gary L. Collins, 32 • Chief Warrant Officer 2 Lawrence S. Colton, 32 • Spc. Zeferino E. Colunga, 20 • Sgt. Timothy M. Conneway, 22 • Spc. Steven D. Conover, 21 • Command Sgt. Maj. Eric F. Cooke, 43 • Sgt. Dennis A. Corral, 33 • Chief Warrant Officer Alexander S. Coulter, 35 • Sgt. Michael T. Crockett, 27 • Staff Sgt. Ricky L. Crockett, 37 • Pvt. Rey D. Cuervo, 24 • Spc. Daniel Francis J. Cunningham, 33 • Spc. Michael Edward Curtin, 23 • Staff Sgt. Christopher E. Cutchall, 30 • Pfc. Anthony D. D'Agostino, 20 • Capt. Nathan S. Dalley, 27 • Pfc. Norman Darling, 29 • Pvt. Brandon L. Davis, 20 • Staff Sgt. Craig Davis, 37 • Spc. Raphael S. Davis, 24 • Staff Sgt. Wilbert Davis, 40 • Staff Sgt. Jeffrey F. Dayton, 27 • Pfc. Jason L. Deibler, 20 • Sgt. Felix M. Delgreco, 22 • Spc. Darryl T. Dent, 21 • Pfc. Ervin Dervishi, 21 • Pfc. Michael R. Deuel, 21 • Pvt. Michael J. Deutsch, 21 • Spc. Jeremiah J. DiGiovanni, 21 • Spc. Michael A. Diraimondo, 22 • Sgt. Michael E. Dooley, 23 • Chief Warrant Officer Patrick Dorff, 32 • Master Sgt. Robert J. Dowdy, 38 • Staff Sgt. Joe L. Dunigan Jr., 37 • Spc. William Dave Dusenbery, 30 • Second Lt. Seth J. Dvorin, 24 • Staff Sgt. Richard S. Eaton Jr., 37 • Sgt. William C. Eckhart, 25 • Spc. Marshall L. Edgerton, 27 • Pfc. Shawn C. Edwards, 20 • Spc. Peter G. Enos, 24 • Sgt. Adam W. Estep, 23 • Pvt. Ruben Estrella-Soto, 18 • Pvt. David Evans Jr., 18 • Pfc. Jeremy Ricardo Ewing, 22 • Pvt. Jonathan I. Falaniko, 20 • Capt. Brian R. Faunce, 28 • Capt. Arthur L. Felder, 36 • Spc. Rian C. Ferguson,

22 • Master Sgt. Richard L. Ferguson, 45 • Master Sgt. George A. Fernandez, 36 • Staff Sgt. Clint D. Ferrin, 31 • Spc. Jon P. Fettig, 30 • Sgt. Paul F. Fisher, 39 • Pfc. Jacob S. Fletcher, 28 • Spc. Thomas A. Foley III, 23 • Spc. Jason C. Ford, 21 • Chief Warrant Officer 3 Wesley C. Fortenberry, 38 • Sgt. First Class Bradley C. Fox, 34 • Staff Sgt. Bobby C. Franklin, 38 • Pvt. Robert L. Frantz, 19 • Pvt. Benjamin L. Freeman, 19 • Sgt. David T. Friedrich, 26 • Spc. Luke P. Frist, 20 • Spc. Adam D. Froehlich, 21 • Pvt. Kurt R. Frosheiser, 22 • Pfc. Nichole M. Frye, 19 • Sgt. First Class Dan H. Gabrielson, 39 • Sgt. Landis W. Garrison, 23 • Sgt. Justin W. Garvey, 23 • Spc. Israel Garza, 25 • First Sgt. Joe J. Garza, 43 • Spc. Christopher D. Gelineau, 23 • Pvt. Kyle C. Gilbert, 20 • Sgt. Maj. Cornell W. Gilmore I, 45 • Pfc. Jesse A. Givens, 34 • Spc. Michael T. Gleason, 25 • Spc. Christopher A. Golby, 26 • Spc. David J. Goldberg, 20 • Pfc. Gregory R. Goodrich, 37 • Sgt. First Class Richard S. Gottfried, 42 • Spc. Richard A. Goward, 32 • Second Lt. Jeffrey C. Graham, 24 • Spc. Kyle A. Griffin, 20 • Cpl. Sean R. Grilley, 24 • Pvt. Joseph R. Guerrera, 20 • Chief Warrant Officer Hans N. Gukeisen, 31 • Pfc. Analaura Esparza Gutierrez, 21 • Pfc. Richard W. Hafer, 21 • Spc. Charles G. Haight, 23 • Pvt. Jesse M. Halling, 19 • Chief Warrant Officer Erik A. Halvorsen, 40 • Capt. Kimberly N. Hampton, 27 • Sgt. Michael S. Hancock, 29 • Sgt. Warren S. Hansen, 36 • Spc. Kenneth W. Harris Jr., 23 • Pfc. Leroy Harris-Kelly, 20 • Pfc. John D. Hart, 20 • Sgt. Nathaniel Hart Jr., 29 • Sgt. Jonathan N. Hartman, 27 • Staff Sgt. Stephen C. Hattamer, 43 • Pfc. Sheldon R. Hawk Eagle, 21 • Sgt. Timothy L. Hayslett, 26 • Chief Warrant Officer 2 Brian D. Hazelgrove, 29 • Spc. Justin W. Hebert, 20 • Pfc. Damian L. Heidelberg, 21 • Pfc. Raheen Tyson Heighter, 22 • Staff Sgt. Brian R. Hellermann, 35 • Staff Sgt. Terry W. Hemingway, 39 • First Lt. Robert L. Henderson II, 33 • Staff Sgt. Kenneth W. Hendrickson, 41 • Pfc. Clayton W. Henson, 20 • Pfc. Edward J. Herrgott, 20 • Sgt. Jacob R. Herring, 21 • Sgt. First Class Gregory B. Hicks, 35 • Spc.

Christopher K. Hill, 26 • Spc. Stephen D. Hiller, 25 • Sgt. Keicia M. Hines, 27 • Sgt. First Class James T. Hoffman, 41 • Spc. Christopher J. Holland, 26 • Staff Sgt. Lincoln D. Hollinsaid, 27 • Spc. Jeremiah J. Holmes, 27 • Master Sgt. Kelly L. Hornbeck, 36 • Pfc. Bert E. Hoyer, 23 • Spc. Corey A. Hubbell, 20 • Pfc. Christopher E. Hudson, 21 • First Lt. Doyle M. Hufstedler, 25 • Staff Sgt. Jamie L. Huggins, 26 • Spc. Eric R. Hull, 23 • Spc. Simeon Hunte, 23 • First Lt. Joshua C. Hurley, 24 • Pfc. Ray J. Hutchinson, 20 • Pfc. Gregory P. Huxley Jr., 19 • Spc. Craig S. Ivory, 26 • Spc. Marlon P. Jackson, 25 • Chief Warrant Officer Scott Jamar, 32 • Second Lt. Luke S. James, 24 • Spc. William A. Jeffries, 39 • Sgt. Troy David Jenkins, 25 • Spc. Darius T. Jennings, 22 • Pfc. Howard Johnson II, 21 • Spc. John P. Johnson 24 • Spc. Justin W. Johnson, 22 • Spc. Maurice J. Johnson, 21 • Spc. Nathaniel H. Johnson, 22 • Staff Sgt. Paul J. Johnson, 29 • Chief Warrant Officer Philip A. Johnson Jr., 31 • Pfc. Rayshawn S. Johnson, 20 • Pvt. Devon D. Jones, 19 • Staff Sgt. Raymond E. Jones Jr., 31 • Capt. Gussie M. Jones, 41 • Sgt. Curt E. Jordan Jr., 25 • Sgt. Jason D. Jordan, 24 • Cpl. Forest J. Jostes, 22 • Spc. Spencer T. Karol, 20 • Spc. Michael G. Karr Jr., 23 • Second Lt. Jeffrey J. Kaylor, 24 • Spc. Chad L. Keith, 21 • Chief Warrant Officer Kyran E. Kennedy, 43 • Staff Sgt. Morgan D. Kennon, 23 • Spc. Jonathan R. Kephart, 21 • Chief Warrant Officer Erik C. Kesterson, 29 • Spc. James M. Kiehl, 22 • Staff Sgt. Kevin C. Kimmerly, 31 • Spc. Levi B. Kinchen, 21 • Staff Sgt. Lester O. Kinney II, 27 • Pfc. David M. Kirchhoff, 31 • Spc. John K. Klinesmith Jr., 25 • Sgt. Floyd G. Knighten Jr., 55 • Spc. Joshua L. Knowles, 23 • Pfc. Martin W. Kondor, 20 • Chief Warrant Officer 3 Patrick W. Kordsmeier, 49 • Capt. Edward J. Korn, 31 • Sgt. Elmer C. Krause, 40 • Pvt. Dustin L. Kreider, 19 • Capt. John F. Kurth, 31 • Sgt. First Class William W. Labadie Jr., 45 • Spc. James I. Lambert III, 22 • Staff Sgt. Sean G. Landrus, 31 • Spc. Tracy L. Laramore, 30 • Spc. Scott Q. Larson Jr., 22 • Chief Warrant Officer 2 Matthew C. Laskowski, 32 • Staff Sgt. William

T. Latham, 29 • Pfc. Karina S. Lau, 20 • Staff Sgt. Mark A. Lawton, 41 • Spc. Cedric L. Lennon, 32 • Spc. Farao K. Letufuga, 20 • Spc. Roger G. Ling, 20 • Spc. Joseph L. Lister, 22 • Staff Sgt. Nino D. Livaudais, 23 • Sgt. Daniel J. Londono, 22 • Spc. Ryan P. Long, 21 • Spc. Zachariah W. Long, 20 • Pfc. Duane E. Longstreth, 19 • Staff Sgt. David L. Loyd, 44 • Capt. Robert L. Lucero, 34 • Jason C. Ludlam, 22 • Pfc. Vorn J. Mack, 19 • Spc. William J. Maher III, 35 • Staff Sgt. Toby W. Mallet, 26 • Chief Warrant Officer Ian D. Manuel, 23 • Pfc. Pablo Manzano, 19 • Sgt. Atanacio Haro Marin, 27 • Sgt. First Class John W. Marshall, 50 • Sgt. Francisco Martinez, 28 • Chief Warrant Officer Johnny Villareal Mata, 35 • Spc. Clint Richard Matthews, 31 • Pfc. Joseph P. Mayek, 20 • Spc. Dustin K. McGaugh, 20 • Spc. Michael A. McGlothin, 21 • Spc. David M. McKeever, 25 • Pvt. Robert L. McKinley, 23 • Staff Sgt. Don S. McMahan, 31 • Sgt. Heath A. McMillin, 29 • Spc. Irving Medina, 22 • Spc. Kenneth A. Melton, 30 • Staff Sgt. Eddie E. Menyweather, 35 • Spc. Gil Mercado, 25 • Spc. Michael M. Merila, 23 • Sgt. Daniel K. Methvin, 22 • Pfc. Jason M. Meyer, 23 • Sgt. Eliu A. Miersandoval, 27 • Spc. Michael G. Mihalakis, 18 • Pfc. Anthony S. Miller, 19 • Pfc. Bruce Miller Jr., 23 • Staff Sgt. Frederick L. Miller Jr., 27 • Sgt. First Class Marvin L. Miller, 38 • Sgt. Joseph Minucci II, 23 • Spc. George A. Mitchell, 35 • Sgt. Keman L. Mitchell, 24 • Sgt. Michael W. Mitchell, 25 • Spc. Sean R. Mitchell, 24 • Pfc. Jesse D. Mizener, 24 • First Lt. Adam G. Mooney, 28 • Pfc. Stuart W. Moore, 21 • Sgt. Travis A. Moothart, 23 • Spc. José L. Mora, 26 • Master Sgt. Kevin N. Morehead, 33 • Sgt. Gerardo Moreno, 23 • Pfc. Luis A. Moreno, 19 • Spc. Dennis B. Morgan, 22 • Sgt. Keelan L. Moss, 23 • Sgt. Cory R. Mracek, 26 • Spc. Paul T. Nakamura, 21 • Spc. Nathan W. Nakis, 19 • Pvt. Kenneth A. Nalley, 19 • Chief Warrant Officer Christopher G. Nason, 39 • Spc. Rafael L. Navea, 34 • Staff Sgt. Paul M. Neff II, 30 • Pfc. Gavin L. Neighbor, 20 • Spc. Joshua M. Neusche, 20 • Spc. Isaac Michael Nieves, 20 • Sgt. William

J. Normandy, 42 • Spc. Joseph C. Norquist, 26 • First Lt. Leif E. Nott, 24 • Spc. David T. Nutt, 32 • Spc. Donald S. Oaks Jr., 20 • Pfc. Branden F. Oberleitner, 20 • Spc. Richard P. Orengo, 32 • Lt. Col. Kim S. Orlando, 43 • First Lt. Osbaldo Orozco, 26 • Pfc. Cody J. Orr, 21 • Staff Sgt. Billy J. Orton, 41 • Pfc. Kevin C. Ott, 27 • Pvt. Shawn D. Pahnke, 25 • Spc. Gabriel T. Palacios, 22 • Capt. Eric T. Paliwoda, 28 • Staff Sgt. Dale A. Panchot, 26 • Pfc. Daniel R. Parker, 18 • Pfc. James David Parker, 20 • Pfc. Kristian E. Parker, 23 • Sgt. David B. Parson, 30 • Staff Sgt. Esau G. Patterson Jr., 25 • Master Sgt. William L. Payne, 46 • Sgt. Michael F. Pedersen, 26 • Staff Sgt. Abraham D. Penamedina, 32 • Spc. Brian H. Penisten, 28 • Sgt. Ross A. Pennanen, 36 • Staff Sgt. Hector R. Perez, 40 • Sgt. Joel Perez, 25 • Spc. José A. Perez III, 22 • Pfc. Wilfredo Perez Jr., 24 • Staff Sgt. David S. Perry, 36 • Spc. Alyssa R. Peterson, 27 • Staff Sgt. Brett J. Petriken, 30 • Pfc. Jerrick M. Petty, 25 • Sgt. First Class Gladimir Philippe, 37 • Sgt. Ivory L. Phipps, 44 • Capt. Pierre E. Piche, 29 • Pfc. Lori Ann Piestewa, 23 • Spc. James H. Pirtle, 27 • Staff Sgt. Andrew R. Pokorny, 30 • Spc. Justin W. Pollard, 21 • Spc. Larry E. Polley Jr., 20 • Sgt. Darrin K. Potter, 24 • Spc. James E. Powell, 26 • Pvt. Kelley S. Prewitt, 24 • Sgt. Jaror C. Puello-Coronado, 36 • Staff Sgt. Michael B. Quinn, 37 • Staff Sgt. Richard P. Ramey, 27 • Sgt. Christopher Ramirez, 34 • Spc. Eric U. Ramirez, 31 • Pfc. William C. Ramirez, 19 • Pfc. Brandon Ramsey, 21 • Sgt. Edmond L. Randle, 26 • Pfc. Cleston C. Raney, 20 • Spc. Rel A. Ravago IV, 21 • Pfc. Ryan E. Reed, 20 • Staff Sgt. Aaron T. Reese, 31 • Sgt. First Class Randall S. Rehn, 36 • Staff Sgt. George S. Rentschler, 31 • Sgt. Sean C. Reynolds, 25 • Sgt. Ariel Rico, 25 • Pfc. Diego Fernando Rincon, 19 • Capt. Russell B. Rippetoe, 27 • Sgt. First Class José A. Rivera, 34 • Cpl. John T. Rivero, 23 • Spc. Frank K. Rivers Jr., 23 • Sgt. Thomas D. Robbins, 27 • Sgt. Todd J. Robbins, 33 • Spc. Robert D. Roberts, 21 • Staff Sgt. Joseph E. Robsky Jr., 31 • Pfc. Marlin T. Rockhold, 23 • Spc. Philip G. Rogers, 23 • Sgt. First Class Robert E. Rooney, 43 •

Staff Sgt. Victor A. Rosales-Lomeli, 29 • Sgt. Scott C. Rose, 30 • Sgt. Randy S. Rosenberg, 23 • Sgt. Lawrence A. Roukey, 33 • Spc. Brandon J. Rowe, 20 • Sgt. Roger D. Rowe, 54 • Lt. Jonathan D. Rozier, 25 • Sgt. John W. Russell, 26 • Chief Warrant Officer Scott A. Saboe, 33 • Spc. Rasheed Sahib, 22 • First Lt. Edward M. Saltz, 27 • Spc. Gregory P. Sanders, 19 • Spc. Matthew J. Sandri, 24 • Staff Sgt. Barry Sanford Sr., 46 • Staff Sgt. Cameron B. Sarno, 43 • Spc. Justin B. Schmidt, 23 • Pfc. Sean M. Schneider, 22 • Maj. Mathew E. Schram, 36 • Spc. Christian C. Schulz, 20 • Pfc. Kerry D. Scott, 21 • Spc. Stephen M. Scott, 21 • Spc. Marc S. Seiden, 26 • Capt. Christopher Scott Seifert, 27 • Sgt. Juan M. Serrano, 31 • Staff Sgt. Wentz Jerome Henry Shanaberger III, 33 • Spc. Casey Sheehan, 24 • Lt. Col. Anthony L. Sherman, 43 • Capt. James A. Shull, 32 • Pvt. Sean A. Silva, 23 • Sgt. Leonard D. Simmons, 33 • Pfc. Charles M. Sims, 18 • Spc. Uday Singh, 21 • Spc. Aaron J. Sissel, 22 • Pfc. Christopher A. Sisson, 20 • First Lt. Brian D. Slavenas, 30 • Pvt. Brandon Ulysses Sloan, 19 • Pfc. Corey L. Small, 20 • Sgt. Keith L. Smette, 25 • Capt. Benedict J. Smith, 29 • Chief Warrant Officer Bruce A. Smith, 41 • Cpl. Darrell L. Smith, 28 • Chief Warrant Officer Eric A. Smith, 41 • Pfc. Jeremiah D. Smith, 25 • Spc. Orenthial J. Smith, 21 • Sgt. First Class Paul R. Smith, 33 • Capt. Christopher F. Soelzer, 26 • Sgt. Roderic A. Solomon, 32 • Pfc. Armando Soriano, 20 • Cpl. Tomas Sotelo Jr., 20 • Pfc. Kenneth C. Souslin, 21 • Maj. Christopher J. Splinter, 43 • Pvt. Bryan Nicholas Spry, 19 • Sgt. Maj. Michael B. Stack, 48 • Staff Sgt. Robert A. Stever, 36 • Pfc. William R. Strange, 19 • Spc. William R. Sturges Jr., 24 • Spc. Paul J. Sturino, 21 • Spc. Joseph D. Suell, 24 • Spc. John R. Sullivan, 26 • Spc. Narson B. Sullivan, 21 • Pfc. Ernest Harold Sutphin, 21 • Staff Sgt. Michael J. Sutter, 28 • Chief Warrant Officer Sharon T. Swartworth, 43 • Sgt. Thomas J. Sweet II, 23 • Staff Sgt. Christopher W. Swisher, 26 • Sgt. Patrick S. Tainsh, 33 • Spc. Christopher M. Taylor, 25 • Maj. Mark D. Taylor, 41 • Capt. John R. Teal, 31 • Master Sgt.

Thomas R. Thigpen Sr., 52 • Spc. Kyle G. Thomas, 23 • Sgt. Anthony O. Thompson, 26 • Spc. Jarrett B. Thompson, 27 • Spc. Brandon S. Tobler, 19 • Sgt. Lee D. Todacheene, 29 • Sgt. Nicholas A. Tomko, 24 • Spc. Ramon Reyes Torres, 29 • Second Lt. Richard Torres, 25 • Sgt. Michael L. Tosto, 24 • Spc. Richard K. Trevithick, 20 • Staff Sgt. Roger C. Turner Jr., 37 • Pvt. Scott M. Tyrrell, 21 • Spc. Eugene A. Uhl III, 21 • Sgt. Melissa Valles, 26 • Spc. Allen J. Vandayburg, 20 • Chief Warrant Officer Brian K. Van Dusen, 39 • Staff Sgt. Mark D. Vasquez, 35 • Spc. Frances M. Vega, 20 • First Lt. Michael W. Vega, 41 • Staff Sgt. Paul A. Velazquez, 29 • Staff Sgt. Kimberly A. Voelz, 27 • Sgt. Jeffrey C. Walker, 33 • Sgt. Donald Ralph Walters, 33 • Pvt. Jason M. Ward, 25 • Chief Warrant Officer Aaron A. Weaver, 32 • Spc. Douglas J. Weismantle, 28 • Pfc. Michael Russell Creighton Weldon, 20 • Chief Warrant Officer 2 Stephen M. Wells, 29 • Spc. Jeffrey M. Wershow, 22 • Spc. Christopher J. Rivera Wesley, 26 • Spc. Donald L. Wheeler, 22 • Sgt. Mason Douglas Whetstone, 30 • Pfc. Marquis A. Whitaker, 20 • Sgt. Steven W. White, 29 • Pfc. Joey D. Whitener, 19 • Sgt. Eugene Williams, 24 • Spc. Michael L. Williams, 46 • Sgt. Taft V. Williams, 29 • Sgt. First Class Christopher R. Willoughby, 29 • Command Sgt. Maj. Jerry L. Wilson, 45 • Staff Sgt. Joe N. Wilson, 30 • Spc. Trevor A. Win'E, 22 • Spc. Robert A. Wise, 21 • Spc. Michelle M. Witmer, 20 • Spc. James R. Wolf, 21 • Second Lt. Jeremy L. Wolfe, 27 • Sgt. Brian M. Wood, 21 • Capt. George A. Wood, 33 • Spc. Michael R. Woodliff, 22 • Sgt. Elijah Tai Wah Wong, 42 • Spc. James C. Wright, 27 • Pfc. Jason G. Wright, 19 • Pfc. Stephen E. Wyatt, 19 • Sgt. Michael E. Yashinski, 24 • Sgt. Henry Ybarra III, 32 • Sgt. Ryan C. Young, 21 **NAVY:** Lt. Thomas Mullen Adams, 27 • Petty Officer Third Class Doyle W. Bollinger Jr., 21 • Petty Officer Third Class Christopher M. Dickerson, 33 • Petty Officer 2nd Class Jason B. Dwelley, 31 • Petty Officer Second Class Michael J. Gray, 32 • Petty Officer Third Class Michael Vann Johnson Jr., 25 • Lt. Kylan A. Jones-Huffman, 31 • Seaman Joshua McIntosh,

22 • Petty Officer Third Class David J. Moreno, 26 • Boatswain's Mate First Class (SW) Michael J. Pernaselli, 27 • Signalman Second Class (SW) Christopher E. Watts, 28 • Lt. Nathan D. White, 30 **AIR FORCE:** Tech. Sgt. Bruce E. Brown, 32 • Capt. Eric B. Das, 30 • Staff Sgt. Patrick Lee Griffin Jr., 31 • Airman First Class Antoine J. Holt, 20 • Master Sgt. Jude C. Mariano, 39 • Staff Sgt. Scott D. Sather, 29 • Maj. Gregory Stone, 40 • Maj. William R. Watkins III, 37 **MARINES:** Cpl. Daniel R. Amaya, 22 • Lance Cpl. Brian E. Anderson, 26 • Lance Cpl. Levi T Angell, 20 • Chief Warrant Officer Andrew Todd Arnold, 30 • Staff Sgt. Jimmy J. Arroyave, 30 • Maj. Jay Thomas Aubin, 36 • Lance Cpl. Aaron C. Austin, 21 • Lance Cpl. Andrew Julian Aviles, 18 • Pfc. Eric A. Ayon, 26 • Pfc. Chad E. Bales, 20 • Lance Cpl. Aric J. Barr, 22 • Capt. Ryan Anthony Beaupré, 30 • Sgt. Michael E. Bitz, 31 • Lance Cpl. Thomas A. Blair, 24 • Gunnery Sgt. Jeffrey E. Bohr Jr., 39 • Pvt. Noah L. Boye, 21 • Cpl. Travis J. Bradach-Nall, 21 • Cpl. Andrew D. Brownfield, 24 • Lance Cpl. Cedric E. Bruns, 22 • Lance Cpl. Brian Rory Buesing, 20 • Lance Cpl. Jeffrey C. Burgess, 20 • Pfc. Tamario D. Burkett, 21 • Pfc. Benjamin R. Carman, 20 • Lance Cpl. James A. Casper, 20 • Staff Sgt. James W. Cawley, 41 • Cpl. Kemaphoom A. Chanawongse, 22 • Chief Warrant Officer Robert William Channell Jr., 36 • Lance Cpl. Marcus M. Cherry, 18 • Second Lt. Therrel S. Childers, 30 • Lance Cpl. Donald J. Cline Jr., 21 • Pfc. Christopher R. Cobb, 19 • Capt. Aaron J. Contreras, 31 • Pfc. Ryan R. Cox, 19 • Lance Cpl. Kyle D. Crowley, 18 • Lance Cpl. Andrew S. Dang, 20 • Cpl. Nicholas J. Dieruf, 21 • Cpl. Jason L. Dunham, 22 • Cpl. Mark A. Evnin, 21 • Cpl. Tyler R. Fey, 22 • Capt. Travis A. Ford, 30 • Lance Cpl. Phillip E. Frank, 20 • Lance Cpl. David K. Fribley, 26 • Capt. Richard J. Gannon II, 31 • Cpl. José A. Garibay, 21 • Pfc. Juan Guadalupe Garza Jr., 20 • Lance Cpl. Cory Ryan Geurin, 18 • Cpl. Christopher A. Gibson, 23 • Pvt. Jonathan L. Gifford, 30 • Lance Cpl. Shane L. Goldman, 20 • Cpl. Armando Ariel Gonzalez, 25 • Cpl. Jesus A.

Gonzalez, 22 • Cpl. Jorge A. Gonzalez, 20 • Cpl. Bernard G. Gooden, 22 • Lance Cpl. Torrey L. Gray, 19 • Pfc. Christian D. Gurtner, 19 • Lance Cpl. José Gutierrez, 22 • Pfc. Deryk L. Hallal, 24 • Sgt. Nicolas M. Hodson, 22 • Pvt. Nolen R. Hutchings, 19 • Cpl. Evan T. James, 20 • Pfc. Ryan M. Jerabek, 18 • First Lt. Oscar Jimenez, 34 • Staff Sgt. Phillip A. Jordan, 42 • Cpl. Brian Matthew Kennedy, 25 • Lance Cpl. Nicholas Brian Kleiboeker, 19 • Cpl. Kevin T. Kolm, 23 • Sgt. Bradley S. Korthaus, 28 • Lance Cpl. Jakub Henryk Kowalik, 21 • Sgt. Michael V. Lalush, 23 • Lance Cpl. Alan Dinh Lam, 19 • Sgt. Jonathan W. Lambert, 28 • Capt. Andrew David La Mont, 31 • Pfc. Moises A. Langhorst, 19 • Lance Cpl. Travis J. Layfield, 19 • Pfc. Christopher D. Mabry, 19 • Lance Cpl. Gregory E. MacDonald, 29 • Lance Cpl. Joseph B. Maglione, 22 • Cpl. Douglas José Marenco Reyes, 28 • Pfc. Francisco A. Martinez-Flores, 21 • Cpl. Matthew E. Matula, 20 • Staff Sgt. Donald C. May Jr., 31 • Sgt. Brian McGinnis, 23 • First Lt. Brian M. McPhillips, 25 • Cpl. Jesus Martin Antonio Medellin, 21 • Gunnery Sgt. Joseph Menusa, 33 • Pfc. Matthew G. Milczark, 18 • Cpl. Jason David Mileo, 20 • Lance Cpl. Jason William Moore, 21 • Capt. Brent L. Morel, 27 • Pfc. Geoffery S. Morris, 19 • Pfc. Rick A. Morris Jr., 20 • Maj. Kevin Nave, 36 • Cpl. Patrick R. Nixon, 21 • Lance Cpl. Patrick T. O'Day, 20 • Lance Cpl. Eric J. Orlowski, 26 • Lance Cpl. David Edward Owens Jr., 20 • Sgt. Fernando Padilla-Ramirez, 26 • First Lt. Joshua M. Palmer, 25 • Pfc. Chance R. Phelps, 19 • Second Lt. Frederick E. Pokorney Jr., 31 • Pfc. Christopher Ramos, 26 • Sgt. Brendon C. Reiss, 23 • Sgt. Duane R. Rios, 25 • Lance Cpl. Anthony P. Roberts, 18 • Pfc. José Franci Gonzalez Rodriguez, 19 • Cpl. Robert M. Rodriguez, 21 • Cpl. Randal Kent Rosacker, 21 • First Lt. Timothy Louis Ryan, 30 • Capt. Benjamin W. Sammis, 29 • Pfc. Leroy Sandoval Jr., 21 • Pfc. Dustin M. Sekula, 18 • Lance Cpl. Matthew K. Serio, 21 • Lance Cpl. Brad S. Shuder, 21 • Cpl. Erik H. Silva, 22 • Lance Cpl. John T. Sims Jr., 21 • Lance Cpl.

Thomas J. Slocum, 22 • Pfc. Brandon C. Smith, 20 • First Sgt. Edward Smith, 38 • Lance Cpl. Matthew R. Smith, 20 • Lance Cpl. Michael J. Smith Jr., 21 • Cpl. Michael R. Speer, 24 • Sgt. Kirk Allen Straseskie, 23 • Lance Cpl. Jesus A. Suarez del Solar, 20 • Staff Sgt. Riayan A. Tejeda, 26 • Lance Cpl. Jason Andrew Tetrault, 20 • Cpl. Jesse L. Thiry, 23 • Master Sgt. Timothy Toney, 37 • Pfc. George D. Torres, 23 • Lance Cpl. Elias Torrez III, 21 • Lance Cpl. Ruben Valdez Jr., 21 • Lance Cpl. Gary F. VanLeuven, 20 • Cpl. David M. Vicente, 25 • Cpl. Scott M. Vincent, 21 • Lance Cpl. Michael B. Wafford, 20 • Staff Sgt. Allan K. Walker, 28 • Lance Cpl. Christopher B Wasser, 21 • Staff Sgt. Kendall Damon Waters-Bey, 29 • Staff Sgt. Aaron Dean White, 27 • Lance Cpl. William W. White, 24 • Cpl. Joshua S. Wilfong, 22 • Lance Cpl. Michael J. Williams, 31 • Lance Cpl. William J. Wiscowiche, 20 • Second Lt. John T. Wroblewski, 25 • Lance Cpl. Robert P. Zurheide Jr., 20 **COAST GUARD:** Damage Controlman Third Class Nathan B. Bruckenthal, 24

'One of the hardest parts of my job is to console the family members who have lost their life.'

– GEORGE W. BUSH, April 2004

'Victory means exit strategy, and it's important for the President to explain to us what the exit strategy is.'

– GEORGE W. BUSH, April 1999

This list of war dead was compiled with the help of U.S. military sources and *Army Times*.

2

THE MILITARY

'In the councils of government, we must guard against the acquisition of unwarranted influence, whether sought or unsought, by the military-industrial complex. The potential for the disastrous rise of misplaced power exists and will persist.

We must never let the weight of this combination endanger our liberties or democratic processes. We should take nothing for granted. Only an alert and knowledgeable citizenry can compel the proper meshing of the huge industrial and military machinery of defense with our peaceful methods and goals, so that security and liberty may prosper together.'

– PRESIDENT DWIGHT D. EISENHOWER, farewell speech to the nation, January 17, 1961

'We ought to have a commander in chief who understands how to earn the respect of the military, by setting a clear mission, which is to win and fight war, and therefore deter war.'

– GEORGE W. BUSH, January 2000

WE rule, right?

We do. The latest budget proposal asks for nearly half a trillion dollars a year for defense, more than the next fifteen most powerful countries in the world combined. The defense budget accounts for almost half of all discretionary government spending. (Discretionary spending is everything except Social Security, Medicare, and Medicaid, which are theoretically separate and sealed funds.) U.S. defense spending accounted for 43 percent of the entire world's military spending in 2002 – the year *before* the invasion of Iraq.

The 'coalition forces' the president pulled together for the invasion of Iraq were hardly the Allied nations of World War II. The forty-nine nations strongarmed into supporting the United States – including Eritrea, Palau, Latvia, Rwanda, and Tonga – were mostly window dressing for the president. They were a face-saving way of showing the rest of the world that we weren't completely going it alone. The truth is, the United States is covering the vast majority of expenses in Iraq. By contrast, America's share of the $61 billion Gulf War in 1991 was only about 20 percent, according to the Congressional Research Service, the rest split among wealthy allied countries like Saudi Arabia, Kuwait, and Germany. (In 2004, as the insurgency has grown, the 'coalition' has shrunk. Spain, Honduras, and the Dominican Republic have decided to withdraw, and Poland and Thailand might be next.)

The Department of Defense was allocated $401.3 billion for 2004. That's about $1,370 for every man, woman, and child in America. If you include the supplemental funds for the forces in Iraq, the budgeted defense spending of other government agencies, and interest on past debt-financed military spending, the true defense budget comes to roughly $754 billion, according to Robert Higgs, senior fellow in political economy at the Independent Institute. That's about $2,570 for every man, woman, and child in the country.

As Fred Kaplan pointed out in *Slate*, adjusted for inflation and including Bush's May 2004 request for an additional $25 billion for the wars in Iraq and Afghanistan, the Pentagon's budget for 2005 will be the largest since the peak of the Korean War in 1952, and the second biggest since the Second World War:

A total of about 1.4 million men and women are serving in active duty. According to the Department of Defense, there are

- 482,000 in the army. Defense Secretary Donald Rumsfeld, however, invoked emergency powers in early 2004, authorizing the force to expand temporarily to 512,000 troops. An additional 360,000 serve in the Army National Guard.
- 380,000 in the navy.
- 376,000 in the air force.
- 177,000 in the marines.
- 38,000 in the Coast Guard, counted as part of homeland security.
- There are more than 500,000 serving in the reserves, spread over all branches of the military.

So what else are we spending all that money on?

The wrong things, it would seem. According to many military experts, we're paying for antiquated, cold war thinking and weaponry to fight a virtual, post-9/11 enemy. Remember, we're not at war with other countries. Were that the case, we would have gone into Saudi Arabia, where fifteen of the nineteen September 11 hijackers came from. No, if it's the war on terror you're talking about, the enemy isn't Iraq or Iran or Syria. It's a rootless army of enraged Islamicist fanatics, moving about in the world's shadows. And they're *everywhere*. Taking over a country and expecting that to eliminate the terrorist threat is as outmoded a military plan of action as the British Square was during the Boer War.

As David Wood wrote in *The San Diego Union-Tribune*, 'While

American infantrymen hunt guerrillas in the back alleys of Iraq and Special Forces foot soldiers track terrorists in Afghanistan and Indonesia, the Pentagon is spending billions on supersonic jets like the new F-22 Raptor, which moves too fast to identify ground targets.' Robert Killebrew, a retired army colonel and strategy consultant to the Defense Department, told Wood, 'We are buying a military designed to fight short blitzkrieg wars, but that is a flawed concept.' In fact, 75 percent of the Defense Department budget goes to the same sorts of things it did pre–September 11, says Wood.

The Pentagon puts its faith and its money in big-scale weapons systems because they're easy to get through Congress. In 2002, Bill Keller wrote in *The New York Times* that Boeing, for instance, spread the subcontracting work on the dual-use F/A-18E tactical fighter-bomber to forty-six states, which makes a lot of House members very happy. There's also the matter of simple expediency. If you're doling out billions upon billions of dollars in contracts, it's much easier giving it out to a few companies than to thousands.

The most recent Defense bill includes

- $878 million for five D-5 Trident II nuclear missiles. Each Trident II typically carries eight warheads. The most powerful has an explosive yield of 475 kilotons, so a loaded missile usually packs 3,800 kilotons. 'Little Boy,' the bomb dropped on Hiroshima, exploded with a force of about 14 kilotons, killing around seventy thousand people instantly and ultimately about two hundred thousand. As of January 2003, the U.S. military had 288 Trident II missiles already deployed, enough to eradicate life on earth at least twice.
- $2.6 billion for a Virginia-class submarine designed to hunt Soviet subs in the 1980s. The navy already has more than fifty perfectly capable nuclear-powered attack subs.
- $3.6 billion for three new navy destroyers. The navy already

has a surface combatant force of well over one hundred ships, including fifty-six destroyers.

- $1.5 billion for the new DD(X) surface combat ship, which will be outfitted with stealth technology.

- $1.8 billion for the Marine Corps V-22 Osprey. It sounds great – it takes off and lands like a helicopter but flies like a plane – but it's never been battle tested. Indeed, in twenty years of research testing, at a cost of more than $12 billion, there have been four crashes, resulting in thirty deaths. Long term, the Pentagon wants to buy 458 Ospreys at a total cost of $48.3 billion. When Dick Cheney was secretary of defense under George H. W. Bush, he tried to kill the Osprey program, arguing that it was too costly.

- $12.4 billion for the F/A-18E Super Hornet fighter-bomber, the new Joint Strike Fighter, and the F-22 air superiority fighter. The Joint Strike Fighter is expected to be the Pentagon's most expensive weapons program ever. Experts predict that the Pentagon will eventually buy up to five thousand of these planes, at an ultimate cost of more than $200 billion. As for the F-22s, they will run about $300 million each. The Pentagon intends to buy 278 of them, for a total cost of more than $83 billion. According to *The New York Times*, 'The Pentagon plans to spend hundreds of billions of dollars over the next two decades on these planes, which are designed to replace older models that are already superior to anything any other country can put in the air . . . in real places like Afghanistan and Iraq, they have serious disadvantages. Unlike helicopters, they cannot hover over battlefields. Unlike unpiloted drones, they place fliers' lives at risk. They have restricted flying ranges and require expensive airborne tankers for refueling. The Air Force's excessive dependence on short-range fighters also forces Washington to cut deals with dubious allies for bases near shifting combat zones.'

- $643 million for the Patriot missile system. During a visit to a Raytheon missile plant during the first Gulf War, President George H. W. Bush told an audience of the defense contractor's employees that the 'Patriot works because of patriots like you, and I came again to say thank you to each and every one of you . . . 42 SCUDs engaged, 41 intercepted.' During the Gulf War, Raytheon's 'miracle' missiles had achieved worldwide fame as 'SCUD Busters,' scoring a near-perfect record. But when Congress appointed Joseph Cirincione, an expert on proliferation and security issues, to investigate the Patriot, he found that the Patriot had made only two to four successful intercepts out of forty-four attempts. Most of the dazzling explosions shown on TV in the first Gulf War and reported as SCUD intercepts were actually Patriots blowing up in midflight, Cirincione told *60 Minutes* in February 2004. He says the military had known of the Patriot's problems since 1991.

But money poured into the Patriot program after the Gulf War, and it wasn't until 2001 that the Pentagon admitted that the Patriot had not worked. Nonetheless, the Patriots were sent back to Iraq for the administration's Operation Iraqi Freedom. Of the Patriot's twelve intercepts this time, three were with coalition planes. 'It's clear that the failure to correct some of the problems that we've known about for 10, 12 years led to soldiers dying needlessly, to flyers dying needlessly,' Cirincione told *60 Minutes*. But he added, 'You don't get promoted for reporting bad news.'

▪ $10 billion for missile defense. This represents a more than 50 percent increase in missile defense spending since Bush took office. By 2002, more than $120 billion had been spent over the last fifty years trying to develop a workable missile defense system, with virtually nothing to show for it. Finally taxpayers got *something* for their money – the opportunity to pitch their own missile defense ideas. In early 2002, the Pentagon invited the public to submit 'new and innovative' concepts for consideration. About two hundred proposals were received within a year, according to *The Washington Post*, detailing plans for everything from a stealth jet carrying Special Forces soldiers ready to ambush would-be missile attackers, to satellites that would zap incoming missiles with X-ray lasers from space. 'I tell my folks, for the initial round of peer review, if the ideas violate no more than two laws of physics, we'll keep them,' Gary Payton, director of advanced concepts at the Missile Defense Agency, told *The Post*. 'The one on X-ray lasers violated several laws of both physics and economics.'

In a 2003 conversation with former Pentagon budget analyst Chuck Spinney, PBS's Bill Moyers asked if it was okay to put up with a bit of waste in the Pentagon budget, as long as it made the country safer.

SPINNEY: Oh, absolutely . . . It gets really out of control when you have a political system that caters to fear, which is what I think is going on now.

MOYERS: But the fear is legitimate today, given 9/11 and the war on terror?

SPINNEY: . . . The problem is that if you start thinking about how you deal with these kinds of threats, you don't need B-2's. You don't need ballistic missile defense. You don't need Comanche helicopters. Basically what you need are really highly trained individuals that basically understand economics, anthropology . . . as well as fighting, particularly in close quarters combat, which is the most difficult form of fighting . . . And my point here is those kinds of solutions don't generate big budgets. And that's the problem.

MOYERS: So we keep spending big money on those old systems . . .

SPINNEY: For the wrong threat.

MOYERS: But America has just won a war against Iraq. I mean, some people would say, look, somebody must be doing something right.

SPINNEY: Well, the first thing I would say is Iraq has been under sanctions for ten years or so. They have a defense budget of $1.8 billion. Most of their equipment is vintage Soviet equipment. They're untrained. We spend $460 billion when you count the supplemental [money] for fighting the war to take out Iraq in a month. If you can't do that for $460 billion what can you do?

What about the actual troops, the ones on the ground?

'My attitude is, any time we put one of our soldiers in harm's way, we're going to spend whatever is necessary to make sure they have the best training, the best support and the best possible equipment.'

– COMMANDER IN CHIEF GEORGE W. BUSH, September 2003

Forget expensive weapons systems. Ground troops in Iraq reported shortages of more quotidian elements of war, everything from ammunition, protective gear, and armored vehicles to walkie-talkies, which often couldn't reach from point to point. When they failed, units would try to contact each other by cell phone or e-mail.

Bush has made more flashy press appearances using U.S. soldiers as a public relations backdrop than any president in modern memory. Indeed, by landing on the USS *Abraham Lincoln* in a borrowed flyboy rig or posing in Baghdad with a decorative Thanksgiving turkey that the troops couldn't eat, he seems actually to have convinced himself he's one of them, with the troops punctuating his pep talks with rowdy 'Hooahs!' Actual soldiers have put a brave face on most of this posturing. But when Bush taunted insurgent Iraqis from the safety of the White House to 'Bring 'em on!' many troops on the ground in Iraq – some of them still lacking essential safety items – were incensed.

Presidential hopeful Dick Gephardt echoed the feelings of soldiers and their families when he urged the president to stop the 'phony, macho rhetoric. We should be focused on a long-term security plan that reduces the danger to our military personnel. We need a serious attempt to develop a postwar plan for Iraq and not more shoot-from-the-hip one-liners.'

The fact is that the Bush White House, in its frenzied rush to take over Iraq in early 2003, paid little or no attention to the needs of the young men and women who would shed their blood to get the job done. The forty-four-day war was one thing. The ill-thought-out aftermath (more U.S. soldiers died in April 2004 than in April 2003, the war's heaviest month of casualties) has been fairly catastrophic in terms of lives lost due to troops lacking basic equipment. These shortages fall into four basic areas:

- Kevlar vests
- Biochemical gear
- Armored Humvees
- Troop transportation

VESTS FIRST

Seven months after the start of the Iraq war, there were still approximately forty thousand soldiers – nearly a third of the troops there – without Interceptor vests, designed to stop a round from an AK-47, the most common automatic rifle in the world. (In some units, one vest was being shared among several soldiers.) Most U.S. troops were supplied with vests, but many of them were Vietnam-era flak jackets designed to protect the wearer from shrapnel, not modern ammunition. Interceptors are made of Kevlar. They're a third lighter than the old ones and have pockets for ceramic plates to protect vital organs. The difference between having a vest and not having one, Ben Gonzalez, chief of the emergency room at the Twenty-eighth Combat Support Hospital in Baghdad, told *The Washington Post*, is 'between being hit with a fist or with a knife.'

The vests are credited with saving the lives of at least twenty-nine soldiers in Afghanistan alone. And in a near half-trillion-dollar defense budget, one would think that at a time of war the Pentagon would have spent the estimated $60 million to provide safe, modern vests for those forty thousand soldiers who didn't have them.

In wars past, parents of soldiers sent their kids chocolate bars, cookies, photos, and other mementoes of home. In the wake of the Iraq invasion, parents of American soldiers scoured the Internet looking for Interceptor vests (about $1,500 retail) they could send overseas.

One mother, Suzanne Werfelman, an elementary school teacher in Sciota, Pennsylvania, bought one for her son, Army Spc. Richard Murphy, who was spending twenty months in Iraq. As Jonathan Turley recounted the story in *USA Today*, Murphy and his unit had been given the old flak jackets. Murphy's reserve unit 'was eventually given some Interceptor vests weeks after they arrived in Iraq, but [they] were missing the essential ceramic plates. That is when Werfelman went out and bought some plates for $650 – more than her weekly salary – and sent them to her son so he'd have basic protection. Workers at one armor company she called said that they had been deluged with calls from parents trying to buy vests and plates for their sons and daughters over-seas.'

In the *Los Angeles Times*, Turley told the story of Sergeant Zachariah Byrd, a soldier with the Third Armored Cavalry Regiment, 'who was shot four times with AK-47 bullets (twice in the chest and twice in his arms) when his unit was ambushed. The [Interceptor] vest protected his chest and he survived.' Except that 'Byrd had been issued a standard flak jacket and, if he had been wearing it during the attack, he'd probably be dead. However, at the beginning of the patrol, his buddy who was driving that night gave his . . . vest to Byrd, a passing kindness that saved Byrd's life.'

When Turley, a George Washington Law School professor, called the Pentagon to talk about the vests, a procurement officer told him that the Interceptor vests were ' 'non-priority' items, like tents.'

FORGET THE VEST, WHERE'S MY CHEM/BIO GEAR?

In late 2002, as the White House was steamrolling the United Nations to jump-start an invasion of Iraq by spring, army investigators discovered that 62 percent of its gas masks didn't work properly. And an incredible 90 percent of its chem/bio detectors, which give early warning of a chemical or biological weapons attack, were found to be defective. As Bush sent American forces off to the Middle East in preparation for war in a country believed to have huge and threatening stores of biochemical weapons, *60 Minutes* reported that tens of thousands of soldiers were equipped with defective chem/bio suits, some with holes and ripped seams. As retired U.S. Army Colonel David Hackworth told Mike Wallace, 'When the Pentagon tried to trace down these bad suits, they couldn't find them at all. So a trooper out in the . . . middle of a desert is putting on a suit, [and] he doesn't know if he's got a good one or a bad one. It's, it's, kind of like Russian roulette.'

During a House Subcommittee on National Security hearing in March 2003, Congressman Dennis Kucinich testified that the General Accounting Office 'discovered amazingly that some military units were selling their protective suits on the Internet for three dollars while other units were desperately clamoring for these critical items.' Congressional investigators, reported

60 Minutes, said that the Defense Department had sold 429 of its $200 protective suits on eBay – for $3 each. This was a situation only Joseph Heller, author of *Catch-22*, could have fully appreciated.

Kucinich testified that 'one military wing . . . had only 25 percent of the protective masks required . . . In fact, the Pentagon's own Inspector General raised these concerns, stating that . . . "420,000 suits were not on hand as recorded in the inventory ballots." . . . For these reasons, Congresswoman Jan Schakowsky, a former member of this subcommittee, wrote to Defense Secretary Rumsfeld to ask him, 'Do the troops going to Iraq have the minimum required levels of chem/bio protective equipment?' She asked him to certify this to Congress.

'On February 27th, just three weeks before the war in Iraq began, she got her answer and that answer was *no*. The Defense Department refused to certify to Congress that it had provided to troops in Iraq the minimum levels of chem/bio equipment as these levels were established by the Pentagon itself.'

As if that's not bad enough, don't forget the heat in Iraq, where midday temperature can soar to 130 degrees. Even far from the battlefield, the chem/bio gear is hard to wear. When Defense Department officials gave journalists a demonstration of the suits with members of the army's Tactical Escort Unit, 'One of the group wearing the deluxe 'decontamination' suit fainted from the heat of the TV lights and pitched into the gallery of reporters,' reported Judith Coburn in *LA Weekly*.

NEVER MIND THE VESTS AND THE CHEM/BIO SUITS. DUDE, WHERE'S MY ARMORED HUMVEE?

'We're kind of sitting ducks in the vehicles we have.'

– LIEUTENANT COLONEL VINCENT MONTERA,
310th Military Police Battalion, Iraq

By the end of 2003, about nine months after the start of the war in Iraq, *Newsday* reported that less than 13 percent of the Humvees – essentially Hummers built for military purpose – being used by American forces were outfitted with armor capable of stopping AK-47 rounds and protecting against roadside bombs and land mines. The other 87 percent of the Humvees being used were essentially desert-camouflaged pleasure vehicles, many with fabric roofs and doors that would have trouble withstanding a rock attack let alone rounds from an AK-47. (Soldiers, never at a loss for humor, call these 'soft tops.') Troops from the 310th Military Police Battalion told *Newsday* that they made do with their eighty unprotected Humvees by hanging their vests on the doors and lining the floors with sandbags.

The military doesn't put out figures for Humvee casualties, but as 2003 drew to a close, more than seventy troops had been killed in vehicles since the end of the war, at that point, according to *Newsday*, almost a quarter of all postwar military deaths. Most of those lives could have been saved if the troops had been riding in armored vehicles. Those are the dead. Add to this many times the number of young soldiers returning home wounded, many minus arms and legs, because they were traveling in unarmored vehicles when they were attacked.

During a hearing of the House Armed Services Committee in late 2003, Victor Snyder, a Democratic congressman from Arkansas, and Neil Abercrombie, a Democratic congressman from Hawaii, quizzed Lieutenant General Richard Cody about the shortage of armored Humvees.

> SNYDER: If I might bring this question home. We had dinner a couple of times with soldiers from our home states and I met with Arkansans, and a couple of young soldiers in order to understand what their daily life has been like. In order to have them drive with me for 30 minutes, they were putting their life at risk . . . it would be a lot less

risky if they had the up-armored Humvee. This is a very important question.

CODY: . . . [in Iraq] the requirement that we received was for about 235 additional up-armored Humvees [in August 2003]. Once the commander came back . . . they came in for a requirement of another 1,233. That grew to 1,407 six months later and now we just received a request for another 1,500 from the combatant commander . . . We anticipate to meet the 1,407 initial requirement here soon. The 1,500 we're going to have to go back and look for more money . . . Even when we do this, we will not have every soldier in an up-armored Humvee.

SNYDER: . . . What you're telling me [is] you do not have a calculation of how much additional money you need, is that what you're saying?

CODY: Not right now, no, sir, I don't . . .

ABERCROMBIE: . . . Surely, surely we know how much 1,280 [sic] of them are.

CODY: Yes, sir.

ABERCROMBIE: Well, how much?

CODY: Sir, I do not have the figure. It changes.

ABERCROMBIE: How much is *one*?

CODY: Sir, I do not have that figure.

In fact, the Pentagon's full complement of armored Humvees is not expected to arrive in Iraq until the summer of 2005, more than two years after the end of the war. As replacement troops prepared to head off to Iraq in early 2004, some hometowns were taking matters into their own hands. The Associated Press wrote that at least twenty-nine vehicles being used by the National Guard's 711th Signal Battalion from Mobile, Alabama, were fitted with steel plating by members of the community, including technical school students, just before Christmas 2003. The story quoted Keith Langham, a local metal shop teacher who helped with the plating: 'It doesn't give you 100% coverage, but it gives you a lot more than zero.' Because the army turns a gimlet eye on equipment it doesn't provide itself, the soldiers who would be using the Humvees were reluctant to talk to the AP reporter.

Marines may be short of armored personnel carriers, but they were sent something from an evangelical group they probably weren't expecting – It was a pamphlet called 'A Christian's Duty in Time of War,' requesting leathernecks to: pray for the president, and fill in a tear-out page and send it to the White House, saying that they had.

> 'Many of our troops are listening tonight. And I want you and your families to know: America is proud of you. And my administration, and this Congress, will give you the resources you need to fight and win the war on terror.'
> – GEORGE W. BUSH, State of the Union, 2004

VETERANS RETURNING HOME ON LEAVE OR AFTER THEIR TOUR OF DUTY DISCOVER THERE ARE BATTLES STILL TO FIGHT

> 'The people who serve in the military are giving their best for this country, and we have the responsibility to give them our full support.'
> – GEORGE W. BUSH, March 2003

> 'Congress is to receive a $75 billion war supplemental request from the president. Why is there not a single dime for veterans' health benefits in that $75 billion?'
> – DENNIS KUCINICH AT A HEARING OF THE HOUSE SUBCOMMITTEE ON NATIONAL SECURITY, March 2003

As soldiers, reservists, and National Guard members return home from their long, exhausting tours of duty in the Middle East, they do not discover cheering throngs and an appreciative government.

For battle troops, the second phase of their own private war begins when they hit U.S. soil.

- When the Pentagon flew soldiers back from Afghanistan and Iraq for home leave, it pretty much dumped them at airports in a handful of cities in Germany and the United States. From there, soldiers had to make their own way home on their own dime. Because leaves are short and handed out at the last minute, full-fare airline tickets to hometowns had to be bought on the same day, making the last leg brutally expensive to most soldiers, many of whom live paycheck to paycheck.
- Shamed by a number of mothers – as well as air carriers that offered frequent fliers the chance to donate their miles to returning troops – the Pentagon said in December 2003 that it would budget $55 million to pay for the last part of a soldier's journey home.

'The willingness with which our young people are likely to serve in any war, no matter how justified, shall be directly proportional to how they perceive the veterans of earlier wars were treated and appreciated by their nation.'

– GEORGE WASHINGTON

According to a study by the American Legion cited in *The Wall Street Journal*, the average wait to get a medical appointment at a Veterans' Affairs hospital was seven months – and this was *before* the invasion of Iraq. Some 280,000 veterans are waiting to hear about their disability ratings, which will determine how much they receive in benefits. Another 108,000 vets who've appealed their ratings are waiting to hear back on those decisions, according to the *Journal*. The Department of Veterans' Affairs believes that as many as 25 percent of America's homeless are veterans.

So the system is already strained. If the percentage of Gulf War veterans who returned home disabled is any indication, the military can expect a further fifty thousand soldiers from the war in Iraq to file disability claims in coming years.

One element that could escalate this number considerably is uranium 238, or depleted uranium, which is used in munitions carried by the A-10 Warthogs, Abrams battle tanks, Bradley Fighting Vehicles, and other weapons systems. It is an effective addition to antitank and anti-bunker weaponry because it's able to slice through armor that would repel conventional shot. In *Weapon of Mass Deception: What the Pentagon Doesn't Want Us to Know About Depleted Uranium*, Frida Berrigan, a senior research associate at the World Policy Institute who focuses on nuclear weapons policy, wrote, 'When a DU shell hits its target, it burns, losing anywhere from 40 to 70 percent of its mass and dispersing a fine dust that can be carried long distances by winds or absorbed directly into the soil and groundwater.'

Because of uranium 238's toxicity and radioactivity, many experts believe it is one of the contributing factors to Gulf War syndrome. During that conflict, the United States used approximately 320 tons of depleted uranium.

While the European Union parliament has called for a moratorium on DU weapons, the Pentagon continues to insist that DU doesn't pose a serious health risk to troops in Iraq. In late 2003, nine soldiers from a New York National Guard company who'd returned from Iraq sought treatment for what they believed to be symptoms of DU contamination. They asked the army to test them. The army said no to six of them and were slow to produce results for the other three. So the soldiers called the *Daily News*, which arranged for them to be tested by Dr. Asaf Durakovic, a nuclear medicine expert. 'Four of them "almost certainly" inhaled radioactive dust,' the paper reported. Pentagon spokesman Michael Kilpatrick told the *News* that the air force and army had used at least 127 tons of DU rounds in 2003 (DU use by other branches of the military hasn't been revealed).

'America's veterans honored their commitment to our country through their military service. I will honor our commitment to them with a million-dollar increase to ensure better access to quality care and faster decisions on benefit claims.'

– GEORGE W. BUSH, State of the Union, 2001

How has the Bush administration actually prepared for the onslaught of returning heroes from Iraq? By slashing budgets for programs intended to ease the suffering of veterans as well as active soldiers, including trying to cut the pay of the troops currently in Iraq.

Here is what Bush has offered:

- He wanted to charge some returning troops a first-ever $250 fee to enroll in the VA medical plan. Congress blocked him. (Congressman Kucinich testified that Bush's cuts would ultimately force an estimated 1.25 million enrolled veterans out of the VA health-care system.)
- He was opposed to a plan to expand health care for returning reservists and National Guard troops, 20 percent of whom, according to the General Accounting Office, have no health coverage. The White House then compromised with Congress and dropped its opposition.
- Disabled American Veterans, an association that helps returning soldiers sort through the morass of forms needed for disability claims, has been severely restricted by the Pentagon from visiting soldiers in the hospital. They were told the reasons were 'security' and 'privacy.' When they are granted visitation with soldiers, DAV meetings are closely monitored. As David W. Gorman, executive director of the Washington office of DAV, wrote to Defense Secretary Rumsfeld, 'The American people would be outraged if these restrictions became public knowledge.'
- Most humiliating of all, hospitalized soldiers were being

charged $8 a day for their food until Congress voted to stop it.

> 'Our men and women in uniform deserve the best weapons, the best equipment, the best training – and they also deserve another pay raise.'
> – GEORGE W. BUSH, State of the Union, 2002

The Bush administration tried to cut the 'imminent danger' pay soldiers in battle zones receive from $225 to $150 a month.

The Bush administration tried to cut the extra $250 a month the families of combat soldiers received to $100, calling the additional money 'wasteful and unnecessary.'

The administration failed on both counts when Congress balked.

The Washington Post reported in December 2003 that the Bush administration was spending $1.6 billion to study the closing of fifty-eight schools it runs on military bases. In total, the Defense Department runs sixty-nine such schools, educating around thirty-three thousand students for $363 million a year.

In October 2003, the following morning conversation took place on a C-SPAN call-in show. The edited transcript:

MODERATOR PETER SLEN: Miami Beach, Good morning.
CALLER: I would just like to say I had occasion the other day to spend the entire day with the troops that have come back from Iraq and had been wounded and – I also visited troops during the Vietnam era – but the thing that I was most shocked by, as I was walking into the hospital, the first person I ran into was a boy about . . . 19 or 20 years old who'd lost both of his arms. And when I walked into the hospital and visited all these boys all day long – everyone had lost either one limb, or two limbs . . . and there were a lot of legs that seemed to be missing. And a couple of the boys told me it was because . . . the rockets

pierce their vehicles so much, he said it's like being kind of in a tin can . . . Three guys in the same vehicle had [each] lost a leg. And another thing that I saw was that if they'd lost one leg, that the shrapnel that had hit the other leg had been so devastating that they were having to pull, like, the thigh – you know, the muscle and the thigh – around the bottom of the calf to try to make the leg workable . . .

SLEN: Where did you spend the day?

CALLER: Walter Reed [Army Medical Center, in Washington, DC].

SLEN: . . . What were you doing at Walter Reed? Are you a volunteer?

CALLER: No, I was just asked to come and spend the day. I was working that day in Washington, D.C., and . . .

SLEN: What kind of work do you do?

CALLER: Um, I'm an entertainer.

SLEN: What kind of entertaining? Are you USO?

CALLER: No, I actually was called by the USO but I'm, I'm just an entertainer. And I really don't want to go much past that, but um . . .

SLEN: Is this *Cher*?

CALLER: Yeah.

SLEN: OK. And you spent the day at Walter Reed.

CALLER: Yeah. And I spent the day with – I mean they were great guys . . . They had the most unbelievable courage. It took everything that I have as a person to – to not, you know, break down while I was talking to these guys . . . I wonder why Cheney, Wolfowitz, Bremer, the president – why aren't they taking pictures with all these guys? . . . Talking about the dead and the wounded, that's two different things. But these wounded are so devastatingly wounded . . . It's unbelievable. You know, if you're going to send these people to war, then don't hide them . . . Have some news coverage where people are sitting and talking to these guys and seeing how they are and seeing their spirit. It's just – I think it's a crime.

Surely the war dead are treated with some degree of dignity?

That depends on your definition of dignity.

'For the brave Americans who bear the risk, no victory is free from sorrow.'

– GEORGE W. BUSH, State of the Union, 2003

The Bush administration has refused to allow media coverage of dead soldiers arriving at U.S. military bases. No video or photographs from the bases show the American public the nearly daily arrival of lines of flag-draped coffins. Nothing, really, for the nation to see. No public forum for the nation to grieve.

By the end of January 2004, the Pentagon had managed essentially to 'smuggle' five hundred dead American soldiers into the country without the watchful eyes of the media recording even one arrival. (That is until April 2004, when *The Seattle Times* published a photograph of flag-draped coffins taken by a private contractor aboard a cargo plane in Kuwait. She was subsequently fired for violating military and company regulations. As was her husband. Later that week, the air force released more than three hundred photos of flag-draped caskets at Dover Air Force Base, giving in to a Freedom of Information Act request by First Amendment advocate Russ Kick. The Pentagon wasn't pleased and called the decision a mistake.)

The Bush administration being the Bush administration, this was all thought out in advance. In March 2003, as U.S. troops were preparing for the invasion of Iraq, American military bases received the following directive from the Pentagon: 'There will be no arrival ceremonies for, or media coverage of, deceased military personnel returning to or departing from Ramstein [Germany] airbase or Dover [Delaware] base, to include interim stops.'

The ban had been put in place by the senior Bush at the time of the first Gulf War, but it was not strictly enforced until the start of the Iraq war. During Vietnam, the military took to returning dead bodies in the middle of the night to avoid press scrutiny. As Joe Lockhart, former White House press secretary to Bill Clinton, told *The Washington Post*, 'This administration manipulates information and takes great care to manage events, and sometimes that goes too far . . . I'm outraged.'

More than five hundred dead and twenty-five hundred injured (many of them amputees) by the first month of 2004, and neither the president, the vice president, nor the secretary of defense had attended a single public military funeral. Reagan, the senior Bush, and Clinton all attended military funerals or memorials during their terms. The only flag-draped coffin George W. Bush has been photographed with, was that of former president Reagan. For that matter, Bush. has yet even to visit the troops in Afghanistan.

As former Clinton foreign policy official Susan Rice told *The Boston Globe* at the end of 2003, 'If [Bush] spent a tenth of the time he spends at fund-raisers at funerals or with families, that would make a difference. You can't pretend it's not happening. The American people know it's happening. They're not stupid. Every morning, when you turn on the TV or read the newspaper, you see it.'

'Apart from a flurry of ceremonies on Veterans Day,' wrote Andrew Rosenthal in November 2003, in *The New York Times*, 'this White House has done everything it can to keep Mr. Bush away from the families of the dead, at least when there might be a camera around.' And as Rosenthal points out, 'Along with coverage of these casualties, the coverage of combat in Iraq has virtually ceased. The "embedded" correspondents who reported on the stunningly swift march to Baghdad during the invasion are gone. The Pentagon has ended the program. The ever-upbeat Mr.

Rumsfeld likes to say that the attacks on American soldiers are brief and relatively few in number.' Which is, of course, not true. In April 2004, almost a year after the official hostilities in Iraq had ended, more than 130 Americans died, more than in any month during the war.

More upbeat yet was Rumsfeld's deputy, Paul Wolfowitz. At a House Appropriations Subcommittee hearing on April 29, when Ohio representative Marcy Kaptur asked Wolfowitz how many soldiers had died up to that point, he replied, 'It's approximately 500, of which – I can get the exact numbers – approximately 350 are combat deaths.' In fact, at that time the true number was 722, of which 521 were combat deaths. That Wolfowitz, the son of a famed mathematician and one of the principal architects of the war, could be off the mark by more than 30 percent reflects an astonishingly insensitive attitude toward young American lives.

Those are the dead. But as *The Washington Post* reported the same week, there are many whose injuries are so severe they're never expected to regain consciousness. While accurate statistics are not available, *The Post* reported that doctors in Baghdad were dealing with 'wounds they used to see once or twice in a military campaign but now treat every day.' The wounded are flown back to the United States, where families are left with the difficult decision of whether, or when, to turn off life support. 'I'm actually glad I'm here and not at home,' Lieutenant Colonel Robert Carroll, a surgeon, told *The Post*, 'tending to all the social issues with all these broken soldiers.' Many of the wounds are far worse than those seen during previous wars because of roadside bombs that send debris upward, causing severe injuries to the head and face. 'We're saving more people than should be saved, probably,' said Carroll.

As Bob Woodward claims in *Plan of Attack*, preparing troops for guerrilla warfare clearly wasn't part of the administration's plan (or else the Pentagon might have provided all the troops with Interceptor vests and armored Humvees, as opposed to only those in the forward units). But as Undersecretary of Defense for Policy

Douglas Feith told *The Atlantic Monthly*, Rumsfeld is 'death to predictions . . . nobody will find a single piece of paper that says, "Mr. Secretary or Mr. President, let us tell you what postwar Iraq is going to look like, and here is what we need plans for." If you tried that, you would get thrown out of Rumsfeld's office so fast . . . you wouldn't get to your next sentence!' For the families of the returning dead and wounded, this attitude must offer little in the way of consolation.

VERSAILLES ON THE POTOMAC

Defense Secretary Donald Rumsfeld declared war on the Pentagon bureaucracy and its budget, calling it 'a matter of life and death.' That was on September 10, 2001.

The next day he changed his mind.

The thing is, he was right the first time. The scandals of the past few years at companies like Enron and WorldCom pale in comparison to the situation at the Pentagon. The senior Bush attempted to get a handle on runaway spending and accountability when he signed the Chief Financial Officers Act of 1990 into law. Simply put, it requires the inspectors general of each government department to produce an audit each year, much as corporations are required to do.

How many times has Pentagon passed a company wide audit? Not once.

We've heard the stories about the Pentagon waste. You know, $640 for a toilet seat, $1,800 for a pillow, that sort of thing. September 11 did little to help Rumsfeld's war on waste. A clip from *CBS Evening News*, January 29, 2002:

> VINCE GONZALEZ REPORTING: And in a rush to fund the war on terrorism, the war on waste seems to have been forgotten.

PRESIDENT BUSH: [January 23] My '03 budget calls for more than $48 billion in new defense spending.

GONZALEZ: More money for the Pentagon when its own auditors admit the military cannot account for 25 percent of what it already spends.

RUMSFELD: According to some estimates, we cannot track $2.3 trillion in transactions.

GONZALEZ: $2.3 trillion with a 'T'; that's $8,000 for every man, woman and child in America.

The White House did, however, name former federal investigator L. Jean Lewis to be chief of staff of the Defense Department's 1,240-employee office of the inspector general, which, with a $160 million budget, is charged with auditing the department's contracts for waste and fraud. The job is supposed to be non-partisan. Lewis, however, was a driving force in the Whitewater investigation into the Clintons' real estate investments that helped form the basis for the investigation that led to the Starr Report. Political columnist Gene Lyons wrote in 2003, 'It's a $118,000-a-year job for a woman who once proposed peddling "Presidential BITCH" T-shirts and coffee mugs mocking Hillary Clinton out of her government office at the now defunct Resolution Trust Corp. . . . Of much greater concern was Lewis' bizarre testimony. Under oath, she swore the "Presidential BITCH" T-shirts signified no political bias and that she personally didn't mind being called a bitch.'

All of this is great news for defense contractors – and their CEOs. Bill Moyers in 2002 looked into the matter. A quick run-down of how they've done since Bush came into office:

- In 2000, Kent Kresa, CEO of Northrop Grumman, earned $7.3 million; by 2002, he was making $9.2 million. (Kresa left Northrop Grumman in April 2003 and joined the Carlyle Group later that year.)

- In 2000, Nicholas Chabraja, CEO of General Dynamics, earned $5.7 million; by 2002, he was making $15.2 million.
- In 2001, Vance Coffman, CEO of Lockheed Martin, earned $5.8 million; by 2002, he was making $25.3 million.

Compare that to the annual salary for a private first class in the army: base pay plus housing and food allowances and a military tax break – starts at $29,794 and tops out at $31,936. Sergeants fare only slightly better: salaries start at $35,231.

WELCOME TO THE DEPARTMENT OF DEFENSE INC. HAVE A NICE DAY!

By the middle of its second year, the Bush White House, according to William Hartung, the author of *How Much Did You Make on the War, Daddy?*, writing in the *Los Angeles Times*, had 'named 32 appointees to top policymaking positions who were former executives, paid consultants or major shareholders of top defense contractors.' There were so many hires from the private sector that a commentator in the press referred to the Pentagon as the 'Department of Defense Inc.'

Abuse was rampant. In 2003, Boeing CEO Phil Condit took the honorable route and stepped down when it was discovered that officials at his company had dangled a job before Darleen Druyun, an air force procurement official, while she was still negotiating with Boeing over a $20 billion deal to supply the military with up to one hundred 767s to use as refueling tankers. Druyun pleaded guilty to conspiracy in April 2004. What made it even worse, wrote Hartung, was that buying the planes outright – instead of leasing some or all of them as originally planned – would have saved the Pentagon $4 billion on the planned deal. We might as well have put Tyco CEO Dennis Kozlowski in charge of the arrangements.

Richard Perle, one of the neocon architects of the Iraq invasion, had argued for leasing the planes from Boeing. Perle is not only close to Rumsfeld, he also was a member of the Pentagon's hugely influential advisory panel, the Defense Policy Board, until he resigned in February 2004. He had been the chairman of the board until March 2003 but stepped down from that role due to his controversial dealings with private companies – including his firm Trireme, a venture-capital group that chiefly invests in companies dealing with homeland security and defense.

And there's this: A year before Perle began lobbying in favor of the Boeing lease, Boeing had committed to invest $20 million in Trireme.

There's this too: As Hartung pointed out, two other members of the Defense Policy Board, retired admiral David Jeremiah and retired air force general Ronald Fogelman, also argued for the Boeing lease. Nothing wrong with that – except that both men had consulting contracts with Boeing at the time.

And before I drop the subject: According to the Center for Public Integrity in December 2002, nine of the Defense Policy Board's thirty members at that time were directors or officers of companies that won $76 billion in defense contracts in the first two years of the Bush administration. That's $76 *billion.*

One last thing about this, then I promise I'll move on: Dick Cheney is still getting paid by Halliburton, one of the Defense Department's biggest contract partners, even while he's a sitting vice president. He gets just under $180,000 a year in deferred compensation for the Chief Executive post which he quit to run for public office in 2000.

We're spending all this money. We must be staffed up to the gills, right?

Maybe. Maybe not. Although Rumsfeld has downplayed the need for a bigger army, in January 2004 he approved a temporary increase of thirty thousand soldiers. In Congress there is growing support for a permanent increase in the size of the army by at least ten thousand soldiers. Army Lieutenant General John M. Riggs, however, told the *Baltimore Sun*, 'You probably are looking at substantially more than 10,000. I have been in the Army 39 years, and I've never seen [it] as stretched . . . as I have today . . . It's not my intent to be provocative but to be intellectually honest with my feelings on the strategy and the commitments of the Army.'

So how will the Pentagon fill the vacancies once the troops in Iraq are allowed to come home? Four ways:

- Extend troops' tours
- Enlist more soldiers
- Outsource the work
- Hire Canadians (I'm serious)

EXTEND TROOPS' TOURS

The best way to fill vacancies is to prevent them from happening in the first place. So the Pentagon issued 'stop loss' orders for the Iraq war to prevent troops from leaving Iraq at the end of their tour or quitting the military altogether after their contracted term of service. In April 2004, the Bush administration ordered twenty thousand troops to stay in Iraq for at least another three months. Secretary of Defense Donald Rumsfeld acknowledged that he had not expected American casualties to be as high as they had become and said troop levels had to be kept high to quell the continued violence.

One-quarter of those forced in April to serve extended tours were members of the National Guard and reservists, who make up 40 percent of the total force in Iraq. The extended tours have exacerbated the financial havoc suffered at home by many reservists and their families due to payroll problems. In November 2003, the General Accounting Office issued a report stating that some National Guard troops hadn't received payments after six months in Iraq. 'This is exactly the kind of thing that servicemen and women, especially those dealing with the heightened anxiety of life in a war zone, do not need,' wrote Bob Herbert in *The New York Times*. 'Major Kenneth Chavez of the Colorado National Guard told a Congressional committee of the problems faced by the unit he commanded: "All 62 soldiers encountered pay problems . . . During extremely limited phone contact, soldiers called home only to find families in chaos because of the inability to pay bills due to erroneous military pay."'

When they finally do get paid, it's often too little, too late. 'It's been hell,' Brandie Broersma told *The New York Times* in April 2004, as her husband served in Iraq. 'I don't think National Guard families were prepared for such long deployments.' The Broersmas filed for bankruptcy and lost their mobile home after their income fell while Mr. Broersma was in Iraq.

THE PENTAGON CAN ENLIST MORE SOLDIERS

Here the Bush administration's dismal employment figures play right into its own hand. Jobs are hard to come by, and the opportunity to train for months, get paid less than $30,000 a year, and head into the heat and danger of the Iraqi desert is to many young men and women now a viable career opportunity.

Many of those answering the call to serve are immigrants. There are about thirty-seven thousand noncitizens serving in the military. Those eager to begin the process of becoming citizens can avoid the usual five-year wait by joining up – immigrants can begin the application process after one year of service. It was in the summer of 2002 that Bush called for the expediting of citizenship requests for immigrants on active duty since 9/11. Dan Kane of the Bureau of Citizenship and Immigration Services told the *Houston Chronicle* in April 2003 that the fifty-five hundred applications for citizenship received from service members in the nine months following Bush's directive 'could be the highest in the decade.' There is one sure way to get your application fast-tracked: get killed. *Newsday* reported in January 2004 that a recently signed bill grants citizenship to immigrants killed while fighting for the United States in Iraq or Afghanistan.

OUTSOURCE THE WORK

The Brookings Institution estimated that during the buildup, for every one hundred soldiers, the United States had outsourced work to ten others in the field who work for private contracting firms like Halliburton, Bechtel, Blackwater, and the Carlyle Group. By 2004, there were more outsourced American civilians on the ground in Iraq than there were British soldiers.

This privatization of war is a relatively new concept. The firms do many things soldiers used to do, plus everything from security work and training the new police, to building latrines, hospitals, dorms, and prisons, to rebuilding Iraq's oil and electrical infrastructure. According to Ian Traynor in *The Guardian*, 'The private sector is so firmly embedded in combat, occupation and peacekeeping duties that the phenomenon may have reached the point of no return: the US military would struggle to wage war without it.'

Traynor says that 'the battleships in the Gulf [during the invasion] were manned by US navy personnel. But alongside them sat civilians from four companies operating some of the world's most sophisticated weapons systems. When the unmanned Predator drones, the Global Hawks, and the B-2 stealth bombers went into action, their weapons systems, too, were operated and maintained by non-military personnel working for private companies.'

To Defense Department mandarins, outsourcing is most certainly one of those ideas that spark why-didn't-we-think-of-this-before? conversations. The advantages are threefold:

- Outsourced employees are largely overlooked in reports about the number of troops engaged in conflict.
- Outsourced employees killed in the field don't wind up on official Pentagon casualty lists.
- Outsourced employees can engage in the sorts of activities the Pentagon knows Congress wouldn't approve of. In *The New York Times Magazine*, Dan Baum reported that Congress has mandated that the Defense Department be limited to four hundred soldiers in Colombia. 'But for years, civilian pilots employed by DynCorp . . . have been flying what amount to combat missions in Colombia under contract to the State Department to spray coca crops with defoliant and occasionally getting shot at.' And three Americans who work for a Northrop Grumman subsidiary were kidnapped after their plane crashed in Colombia. Because they're not 'prisoners of war,' however, they're not protected by the Geneva Conventions, nor do they receive much help from the U.S. government.

The spoils of war are staggering. During the U.S. action in Bosnia and Kosovo in the late 1990s, nearly $15 of every $100 the Pentagon spent went to Halliburton, wrote Baum. Of the $87 billion the Pentagon was granted in the 2004 war supplement to spend in Iraq and Afghanistan, about $20 billion was budgeted for reconstruction work that will mostly go to private firms, *The Seattle Times* reported in late 2003. And since there are only so many companies expert at doing the jobs the Pentagon wants done but can't do itself, the war in Iraq was and is a seller's market. 'All I can say is it's mind-boggling,' James Lyons, a former military subcontractor, told *The Washington Post*. 'People must be drooling.'

It's no surprise that huge, politically connected conglomerates like Houston-based Halliburton and San Francisco-based Bechtel are well nourished from feeding at the Pentagon trough.

Halliburton's subsidiary, Kellogg, Brown & Root, won the $1.7 billion worth of contracts last year from the Army Corps of Engineers to rebuild Iraq's oil infrastructure. It didn't even have to bid for the job. Bechtel Corp., one of the United States' other chief outsourcing behemoths, has a lock on most of the other reconstruction work on Iraq's infrastructure.

KBR has a particularly dodgy reputation when it comes to over-charging.

- The company is under investigation for charges that, through a Kuwaiti sub-contractor, it overbilled the government $61 million for fuel in Iraq. KBR charged an average of $2.64 per gallon to import gasoline to Iraq from Kuwait, more than twice the going rate.

- In 2002, without admitting liability, the company agreed to pay a $2 million settlement to the U.S. government to resolve a lawsuit relating to overcharges on an army contract in California. According to Peter W. Singer, a fellow at the Brookings Institution, during the Balkans conflict, KBR 'is alleged to have failed to deliver or severely overcharged the U.S. Army on four out of seven of its contractual obligations.' The company nevertheless was handed a $1 billion contract to work alongside U.S. forces in Kosovo, wrote Singer in 2001.

- It allegedly overcharged more than $16 million for meals at a single U.S. military base, Camp Arifjan, in Kuwait. During the first seven months of 2003, according to *The Wall Street Journal*, KBR billed for four million meals that were never served. Halliburton said it took improper conduct seriously and was investigating it.

- In February 2004, a former Halliburton employee told a Democratic panel of lawmakers about rampant waste at the firm. Among his allegations were that Halliburton had spent up to $7,500 a month to rent cars and trucks that could have been rented for less than $2,000, and had bought monogrammed towels for $7.50 apiece when regular bath towels could have been purchased for $2.50. Because Halliburton was allowed to charge the Pentagon a fixed percentage fee on top of what it paid for goods, there was an incentive to pay more. 'They did not want to control costs at all,' a former employee told the *Los Angeles Times*. 'Their motto was, "Don't worry about costs, it's cost plus."'

Before the war even ended, Bechtel had already won contracts ultimately worth about $1 billion to repair Iraq's ports, electrical grid, and more than twelve hundred schools. No sooner had Bechtel gotten to work on the schools than complaints started pouring in. In response, army officials visited twenty of the schools Bechtel had worked on and found nine of them in 'poor' condition, in some cases lacking electricity or even working bathrooms. The Scripps-Howard News Service reported that army officials found that 'the subcontractors Bechtel hired left paint everywhere – on the floors, on desks, all over windows. The classrooms were filthy, the school's desks and chairs were thrown out into the playground and left, broken. Windows were left damaged, and bathrooms that were reportedly fixed were left in broken, unsanitary condition.'

Bechtel reportedly spent about $48 million 'renovating' the schools, or nearly $40,000 each. 'For that much money we can build a new school,' an Iraqi regional planning director in Baghdad told *The Boston Globe* in December 2003. Bechtel said it was working in extreme conditions in which employees' lives were at risk, and that only a few schools were involved.

Food, lodging, mail delivery – that and more is being outsourced to private contractors in Iraq. 'The result? Months into the war,' wrote David Morse in *Salon*, troops 'were still camped out, still eating the loathed MREs [meals ready to eat], and are still without adequate water. Mail is backlogged for weeks.'

(For defense contractors there's even better news. In many conflicts, they arm *both* sides. The United States not only leads the world in weapons sales, most of the weapons not sold to the Pentagon go to developing countries and to countries we eventually wind up in.)

Nations previously ineligible but now permitted to buy U.S. weapons include Armenia, Azerbaijan, India, Pakistan, Tajikistan, and Yugoslavia, wrote Rachel Stohl for the Center for Defense Information in January 2003. 'Since September 11, the United States has made billions of dollars' worth of arms deals to strategic countries,' Stohl says, 'including a $1.2 billion sale of fighter jets and missiles to Oman and nearly $400 million worth of missiles to Egypt.'

Indeed, our very success in taking out our enemies during the initial 'shock and awe' firepower strikes serves as a Super Bowlworthy ad campaign for U.S. military superware once the fighting stops. 'I'd be surprised if countries like Pakistan and Jordan weren't stocking up on U.S. gear,' retired air force general David Baker told *The Boston Globe*. The Bush administration is already paving the way for American arms manufacturers to sell their goods to Iraq. Rachel Stohl told *The Globe* that she didn't understand the White House's hurry to sell the country arms before it has established itself politically. 'We could be sending them more weapons even before we know who's really on our side.'

UNCLE SAM WANTS YOU, EH?

Not my headline. It appeared in *The Village Voice* over a story by James Ridgeway in late 2003. He discovered that Pentagon recruiters had been trolling southern Canada hoping to sign up First Nations people – Canada's term for what we call Native Americans – for active service. And they're legally allowed to, wrote Ridgeway, according to 'a Canadian Defense Ministries report [that] said the U.S. claimed that under the 1794 Jay Treaty, it had the right to recruit Canadian native inhabitants for its military because aboriginal Canadians held dual U.S.–Canadian citizenship.'

When the Canadians complained to Washington, the recruiters were returned home. 'The way some Canadians see it,' says Ridgeway, 'the U.S. has already stolen their oil and gas, metals, diamonds, and water, and owns much of their industry. Now their manpower? Even the most laid-back of our neighbors to the north think this is going a bit far.'

A SITUATION WHERE EXPERIENCE HELPS

Retaliating against an out-and-out attack, as we did against the Japanese during World War II, is one thing. Waging a preemptive war – a 'war of our choosing' – against another country, like Iraq, is quite another.

It would be helpful if the commander in chief had served in battle. But he did not. Bush got out of fighting in Vietnam by serving in the National Guard.

It would even help if Vice President Cheney had fought in combat. But he didn't. He avoided the draft during Vietnam by getting five student and marriage deferments.

Barring actual military service on the parts of the president and vice president, what about their children? Men and women who see nothing wrong with sending others' children off to war should volunteer their own kids for active duty. This would have considerably slowed the panic to go to war with Iraq. According to Mark Weisbrot of the Center for Economic and Policy Research in Washington, only 2 out of the 535 members of Congress had children who fought in the Gulf War. A dozen years later, the situation isn't much different. The congressional newspaper *The*

Hill lists only eight members of Congress, as of April 2004, who have children in the military – less than half of them serving in the White House's Operation Iraqi Freedom.

As Chuck Hagel, a Republican senator from Nebraska and a Vietnam veteran, put it, 'Many of those who want to rush this country into war . . . don't know anything about war. They come at it from an intellectual perspective versus having sat in jungles or foxholes and watched their friends get their heads blown off.'

'The best military in the world must have every adequate advantage required to defend the peace of the world.'

– GEORGE W. BUSH, October 2002

3

.

SECRECY

'Everybody knows that corruption thrives in secret places, and avoids public places, and we believe it a fair presumption that secrecy means impropriety.'

— PRESIDENT WOODROW WILSON, 1912

'Since I've been here, I have never known an administration that is more difficult to get information from.'

— SENATOR PATRICK J. LEAHY, first elected in 1974

'I kind of like ducking questions.'

— GEORGE W. BUSH, April 2004

BUSH Nominee For Archivist Is Criticized For His Secrecy' read a headline in the April 20, 2004, edition of *The New York Times*. The report, by Sheryl Gay Stolberg and Felicia R. Lee, said that earlier that month, the White House had made moves to replace the incumbent national archivist (a Clinton appointee) and nominated in his place someone who shared the administration's overarching operational philosophy – secrecy. The archivist's job involves not only preserving the nation's historical records but also deciding which documents should be made available to historians, journalists, and the public. Secrecy is precisely the quality you don't want in an archivist.

In creating the position, Congress specifically stated that it expects any nomination for the post 'will be achieved through consultation with recognized organizations of professional archivists and historians.' The Bush administration did nothing of the sort – it consulted not a single professional before releasing the name of the nominee. The reaction from historians and archivists was polite – they are historians and archivists, after all – but they were outraged. Nine organizations representing archivists and historians issued a joint comment. They said it was the first time since the position was created in 1934 that a nominee had been put forward without consulting outside experts. 'There is a protocol and procedure, and this kind of came out of the blue,' Nancy Beaumont, executive director of the Society of American Archivists, said at the time.

Why bring in a new national archivist? It's perhaps no coincidence that the papers of Bush's father's administration were due to be released in January 2005. Or that sensitive documents of the 9/11 Commission were due to be turned over. Or that it would be wise for an administration like Bush's to take measures while still in office to protect the papers it has been so closely guarding, in case of an election defeat.

The nominee for the post, Allen Weinstein, had been head of the Center for Democracy, a Washington-based think tank with a board loaded with Republican mandarins, including Henry Kissinger and Texas senator Kay Bailey Hutchison.

As a historian, Weinstein is the Bush administration's kind of guy. In 1978 he published *Perjury: The Hiss-Chambers Case* about the accused American traitor Alger Hiss. When critics asked to see the interviews and notes he collected for the book – a request supported by the Standards of the American Historical Association – he refused. Alexander Vassiliev and Weinstein's 1999 book *The Haunted Wood*, about Soviet spies in the American government, came under similar fire when it was discovered that although his publisher had paid for access to files from the archives of the old Soviet Union, Weinstein failed to share them with fellow scholars. This appeared to be a violation of the International Council on Archives code of ethics.

'His history of sharing his information is not all that great,' Anna K. Nelson, a professor of history at American University, told *The New York Times*. 'We don't know how he would run the archives. We ought to find out. How would he balance the public's right to know versus the president's right to protect his papers?'

Early on, the Bush White House was considered by many presidential historians to be the most secretive administration in modern history. On December 12, 2000, the day the Supreme Court issued a decision favorable to presidential candidate George Bush on the Florida vote recount, he quietly arranged for all the records from his term as governor of Texas to be boxed up. Then, according to former Nixon White House counsel John Dean in his book *Worse than Watergate*, they were 'placed on sixty large pallets, shrink-wrapped in heavy plastic, and, with no announcement, quietly shipped off to his father's presidential library at Texas A&M University.'

Peggy Rudd, the head of the Texas State Library and Archives Commission, filed a formal complaint. Texas law dictates that documents, letters, and so forth from a governor's term be indexed and then made available to the public. Appeals for access to documents were brushed aside. The new administration argued that because the papers were now in a presidential library, they were therefore under the authority of the National Archives and Records Administration – in other words, it was now a federal rather than a state matter. Appellants were told, Dean says, 'that the federal archivists were too busy with the father's papers to process the son's.' Rudd persevered, and in May 2002, the Texas attorney general ordered Bush's papers returned to Austin, the Texas capital, where they are still being catalogued, Dean says, 'slowly.'

Reagan's White House papers were due to be released in January 2001 in accordance with the Presidential Records Act. Included in the records were documents from Reagan's second term that could prove embarrassing to Bush and his father. George W. Bush instructed the White House lawyers to ask for an extension in order to review the 'many constitutional and legal questions' involved. The administration was granted the extension. The White House requested two more; both were granted. Early in 2002, 8,000 pages were cleared for release by the National Archives. In March 2002, 59,850 pages were subsequently released, leaving approximately 150 pages sealed.

On November 1, 2001, even while the west side of the Pentagon was under reconstruction and the crater where the World Trade Center towers had stood was a mountain of twisted, smoking steel, the administration did not lose its focus as far as secrecy was concerned. On that day, Bush issued Executive Order 13223, establishing a new set of guidelines for the release of presidential papers.

As Dean lays out in *Worse than Watergate,* the order gives former presidents the power to keep their papers sealed indefinitely. In the past, presidents had to offer reasons why certain papers should not be released. Under the new rules, the person *seeking* the papers must give reasons why the documents should be released. Access to a president's papers must be approved not only by the sitting president but also by the former president in question. If the former president is dead, it's up to his or her family or representatives to decide. The new order also gives vice presidents – Cheney, for instance – the same rights as presidents to classify information.

Bush, who holds the record for the fewest solo press conferences by a president since the beginning of the television age, has made secrecy an endemic and systematic part of his administration.

Bush sees himself as a CEO-type president. But no chief executive can possibly be successful if he's surrounded by wall upon wall of secrecy. Those walls stop not only the decision-making process and the dialogue leading to decisions from being disseminated to the shareholders of the enterprise – in a president's case, the taxpayers – they also stop outside opinions and arguments from filtering in. The virtual gag order the administration has placed on how it goes about its business has created in the Bush White House an intemperate, imperial presidency. 'What has stunned us so much,' Gary Bass, executive director of the public interest group OMB [Office of Management and Budget] Watch, told *U.S. News & World Report*, 'is how rapidly we've moved from a principle of "right to know" to one edging up to "need to know."'

Columnist David S. Broder of *The Washington Post* calls the Bush White House 'an organization with great discipline and a strong belief in orderly structures and articulated concepts and policies. But it is also a top-down bureaucracy, with little capacity for hearing variant viewpoints or testing its theories against the practical wisdom of front-line operatives.'

Mary Graham, a fellow in governance studies at the Brookings Institution, told Adam Clymer of *The New York Times*, 'What are often being couched as temporary emergency orders are in fact what we are going to live with for 20 years, just as we lived with the cold war restrictions for years after it was over. We make policy by crisis, and we particularly make secrecy policy by crisis.'

The Bush administration is also selective in its secretiveness. That is to say, secretive when it is helpful to the White House to do so, open when it could prove harmful to others. A case in point: Once in office, the administration wanted to capitalize on Clinton's controversial last-minute pardon of fugitive financier Marc Rich. The administration provided Dan Burton, chairman of the House Committee on Government Reform, with selectively edited transcripts of phone conversations between Clinton and Israeli prime minister Ehud Barak, who had lobbied on Rich's behalf. As Dean reports in his book, 'Burton, in turn, publicly released the transcripts. Clinton was angry when he read them, for they were incomplete. When Clinton requested that all of the relevant passages in the conversations between himself and Barak be released, Bush's White House said no, claiming the material was classified.'

What is curious is that a White House so obsessed with carrying out its affairs in private demands so much transparency on the part of its opponents and in the private lives of its citizens.

'When you're in this type of conflict, when you're at war, civil liberties are treated differently.'

      – SENATE MINORITY LEADER TRENT LOTT, September 2001

'To those . . . who scare peace-loving people with phantoms of lost liberty, my message is this: Your tactics only aid terrorists, for they erode our national unity and diminish our resolve. They give ammunition to America's enemies, and pause to America's friends.'

      – ATTORNEY GENERAL JOHN ASHCROFT, December 2001

'The Constitution just sets minimums . . . Most of the rights that you enjoy go way beyond the Constitution.'

      – SUPREME COURT JUSTICE ANTONIN SCALIA, explaining the administration's ability to scale back civil liberties in times of war, March 2003

'. . . the Western world, the free world, loses what it cherishes most, and that is freedom and liberty we've seen for a couple of hundred years in this grand experiment that we call democracy.'

      – GENERAL TOMMY FRANKS, explaining that the United States might revert to a military form of government if weapons of mass destruction are used on American civilians, November 2003

This is how fragile our grip on democracy and civil liberties has been in the age of the Bush administration. Throughout this period, members of the administration regularly dropped veiled and not-so-veiled hints that America is one attack away from delivering to the commander in chief unprecedented powers over the rights and freedoms of U.S. citizens. In a way, the terrorists have already won the war: Americans have allowed the administration to come closer to an imperial presidency than was ever thought possible.

With God on their side, Bush and Ashcroft have stripped away the rights of prisoners of war, civilians arrested for possible involvement in terrorism, and even American citizens abroad. The president has used the attacks of September 11 to concentrate authority in the executive branch, giving himself unilateral power to detain anyone he deems to be an 'enemy combatant.' And under the broad umbrella of national security, the White House has erected laws to go after peace protesters, hospitals and patients, universities and students, libraries and book borrowers.

As an editorial in the Fort Wayne, Indiana, *Journal Gazette* said, 'In the name of national security, President Bush, Attorney General John Ashcroft and even Congress have pulled strand after strand out of the constitutional fabric that distinguishes the United States from other nations . . . Actions taken over the past year are eerily reminiscent of tyranny portrayed in the most nightmarish works of fiction. The power to demand reading lists from libraries could have been drawn from the pages of Ray Bradbury's *Fahrenheit 451* . . . The Bush–Ashcroft explanation that restricting freedom will enhance freedom echoes the Big Brother proclamations in George Orwell's *1984* . . . The sudden suspension of due process for immigrants rounded up into jails is familiar to readers of Sinclair Lewis' *It Can't Happen Here.'*

The cornerstone of the administration's grab for power over the rights of citizens is the USA Patriot Act. It's an abbreviation, by the way, for Uniting and Strengthening America by Providing Appropriate Tools Required to Intercept and Obstruct Terrorism Act. The 342-page act was hurried into law just forty-five days after the September 11 attacks and just as the anthrax scare was paralyzing Washington and many legislators didn't have access to their offices. Congress voted 357 to 66 for it. The Senate vote was 98 to 1, with Wisconsin Democrat Russ Feingold the lone hold-out. The Patriot Act, which is in violation of the First, Fourth, Fifth, Sixth, Eighth, and Fourteenth amendments to the U.S. Constitution, was passed without debate or public hearings. 'The final version of the Patriot Act that was passed into law was rewrit-ten between midnight and 8 o'clock in the morning behind closed doors by a few unknown people, and it was presented to Congress for a one-hour debate and an up or down vote,' Democratic congressman Peter DeFazio told *The Sacramento Bee*. 'It was hun-dreds of pages long, and no member of Congress can tell you they knew what they were voting for in its entirety.'

A USA Patriot Act primer (as outlined by the American Civil Liberties Union):

- The Patriot Act grants the attorney general the right to jail or detain noncitizens based on mere suspicion.
- The Patriot Act grants the attorney general the right to deny readmission to the United States of noncitizens (including those with visas or green cards) for engaging in free speech as protected by the First Amendment to the Constitution.
- The Patriot Act grants the attorney general the right to detain non-Americans, if the government determines that there are 'reasonable grounds to believe' they may be threats to national security. Suspects can be detained for seven days before criminal or deportation charges are brought. After that, they can be detained indefinitely in six-month increments without a proper court hearing.
- The Patriot Act grants law enforcement agencies sweeping powers to tap into phone lines or the Internet, without getting a warrant from a judge.
- The Patriot Act grants the government the power to engage in 'sneak-and-peek' and 'black bag' secret searches of

people's homes, without notifying the suspects. These provisions are applicable in both antiterrorism investigations and routine criminal investigations.

- The Patriot Act permits law enforcement to investigate American citizens for criminal matters without establishing probable cause if they designate that the investigation is for 'intelligence purposes.'

- The Patriot Act grants the CIA the authority to perform intelligence surveillance on U.S. citizens.

- The Patriot Act grants the administration broad leeway in its definition of 'domestic terrorism.' This grievous attack on free speech is so vaguely defined that legal advocacy groups such as Greenpeace and People for the Ethical Treatment of Animals could be defined as terrorist organizations by law enforcement and therefore subject to wiretaps, surveillance, and infiltration.

- The Patriot Act grants the FBI and other law enforcement and intelligence agencies access to medical, financial, mental health, and academic records, with minimal judicial oversight, more specifically:

- Under Section 215 of the Patriot Act, the FBI can request a court order to seek 'any tangible thing (including books, records, papers, documents and other items)' from anyone, including a third party. All the FBI has to do is specify that the items being sought are related to an investigation of suspected terrorism.

- According to Dahlia Lithwick and Julia Turner in *Slate*, 'Third party holders of [personal] financial, library, video rental, phone, medical, and church, synagogue and mosque records can be searched without [an individual's] consent or knowledge.'

- Under Section 215, there is virtually no restriction on the records or tangible items the FBI can seek, from suspects or just citizens. According to ACLU, these include:

- Personal belongings, such as books, letters, journals, or computers, which can be taken directly from one's home.
- A list of people who have visited a particular Web site.
- Medical, including psychiatric, records.
- A list of people who have borrowed a particular book from a public library.
- The membership lists of advocacy groups like the League of Conservation Voters or the ACLU.
- A list of people who worship at a particular church, mosque, temple, or synagogue.
- A list of people who subscribe to a particular periodical.

During a House Judiciary Committee meeting in June 2003, the following exchange took place between Ashcroft and Democratic congresswoman Tammy Baldwin:

BALDWIN: Now, under section 215 of the USA Patriot Act, now the government can obtain any relevant, tangible items. Is that correct?

ASHCROFT: I think they are authorized to ask for relevant, tangible items . . .

BALDWIN: Genetic information?

ASHCROFT: . . . I think [we] probably could.

An interim regulation enacted in October 2001 all but eliminates the clause in the Sixth Amendment to the Constitution dealing with the right to assistance of counsel. Federal agents are allowed to monitor conversations between attorneys and prisoners whenever, the regulation states, 'reasonable suspicion exists to believe that a particular inmate may use communications with attorneys or their agents to further or facilitate acts of terrorism.' The regulation furthermore says that neither client nor lawyer need be informed of the monitoring if a court order has been obtained. This means in any case involving a suspected terrorist, no lawyer or prisoner can ever be sure that he or she is not being taped. Without a recognition of the principle of attorney-client privilege, the Sixth Amendment's right to assistance of counsel becomes meaningless.

There is a growing groundswell of opposition to the Patriot Act, in whole or in part. One movement, led by Vermont congressman Bernard Sanders, would exempt bookstores and libraries from the reach of the act. In the Senate, Idaho Republican Larry Craig is trying to get the law changed so that the FBI would have to show 'specific and articulable facts giving reason to believe that the person to whom the records pertain is a foreign power or an agent of a foreign power.' Four states and 325 cities and counties representing more than fifty million Americans have passed initiatives or resolutions to protect their civil liberties and oppose the Patriot Act.

Under Ashcroft's orders, the Justice Department drafted an even more intrusive sequel to the act, the Domestic Security Enhancement Act of 2003. Dubbed the USA Patriot Act II, it was prepared in secret and was obtained in February 2003 by the Center for Public Integrity. The organization posted the draft on its Web site, and public and legislative outcry forced the Justice Department to withdraw the plan. This is what the administration wanted to do:

- Create new authority for secret arrests
- Reduce judicial oversight over surveillance, or eliminate it altogether
- Give law enforcement and intelligence-gathering agencies more leeway
- Create a database of the DNA of people the executive branch considers suspicious
- Create a wider range of crimes that would be punishable by the death penalty
- Create the authority to take American citizenship away from citizens who belong to, or just support the legal activities of political groups the administration considers 'terrorist'

The administration then took many of the proposals in the Domestic Security Enhancement Act and added them to the Intelligence Authorization Act for 2004, which the president signed into law the week Americans were distracted by the capture of Saddam Hussein. This gives intelligence authorities the right to examine travel agency records, as well as the records of casinos, pawnshops, and car dealerships. Even eBay transactions.

> 'History teaches that grave threats to liberty often come in times of urgency, when constitutional rights seem too extravagant to endure. The World War II relocation-camp cases . . . and the Red Scare and McCarthy-era internal subversion cases . . . are only the most extreme reminders that when we allow fundamental freedoms to be sacrificed in the name of real or perceived exigency, we invariably come to regret it.'
> – SUPREME COURT JUSTICE THURGOOD MARSHALL, 1989

It could fairly be assumed that Bush's passion for secrecy goes back to his time at Yale and his being tapped for Skull and Bones. Elitist, secretive, and a path to all manner of later establishment connections, the club admits only fifteen members a year. Bush was a third-generation Bonesman. According to one Bonesman in a *Vanity Fair* article by Alexandra Robbins, 'For some people, Skull and Bones becomes the most important thing that ever happened to them, and they tend to stay involved.' Novices are given nicknames like the ones the fraternity inductees received in the movie *Animal House*. Democratic presidential nominee John Kerry was a Bonesman two years ahead of Bush. His nickname is unknown. Bush was given the name 'Temporary.' He was unable to come up with an alternate, and so he is still called Temporary by fellow Bonesman. According to Robbins, ten of Bush's administration appointments are members of Skull and Bones, including SEC head Bill Donaldson and Associate Attorney General Robert McCallum Jr.

As emblematic as anything about the Bush administration's secretive operations was Cheney's closed-door Energy Task Force and the vice president's almost fanatical desire for the meetings to be kept private. (See also chapter 4, 'The Environment.') A brief history:

- January 2001. Bush creates the national Energy Policy Development Group. Chaired by the vice president, it meets in complete secrecy with four hundred experts, almost all of them from the energy industry, a large source of Republican campaign dollars.
- Not one member from an environmental group is interviewed by Cheney. (Environmental representatives are eventually brought in. They are interviewed as a group by task force aides in a single sitting. The meeting lasts just forty minutes.)
- April 2001. Congressmen John Dingell and Henry Waxman ask the General Accounting Office to investigate the activities and makeup of Cheney's task force. Cheney refuses to cooperate.
- May 2001. The task force releases its 170-page report. In August 2001, the *Los Angeles Times* reports that, without any scientific reason, the White House deleted sections from the White House Energy Policy criticizing an oil- and gas-recovery technique pioneered by Halliburton.
- David Walker, chief of the General Accounting Office (GAO), begins his inquiries. The White House responds testily that Walker's questions 'intrude into the heart of Executive deliberations, including deliberations among the President, the Vice President . . .'
- January 2002. Walker tells Congress that the White House's stonewalling has forced the GAO's hand. For the first time in its history, the agency decides to 'file suit to enforce access rights against a federal official.' (In July 2001 the conservative

government watchdog Judicial Watch and the Sierra Club filed what was essentially the same suit Walker filed.)

- January 2002. White House Press Secretary Ari Fleischer claims that Cheney's secret meetings were no different from those leading up to the drafting of the Constitution. As Joe Conason points out in *Big Lies*, the meetings of the Founding Fathers were indeed held in secrecy. Once the Constitution had been completed, however, 'the founders immediately published every document associated with the drafting . . . revealed the names of everyone who had been involved . . . and kept nothing secret, including the minutes of the debate over its provisions.'

- August 2002. The U.S. District Court for the District of Columbia orders Cheney to produce the requested documents in the Judicial Watch case. Cheney refuses and eventually appeals the decision.

- December 2002. The same District Court dismisses Walker's suit on the grounds that the GAO had not received sufficient injury to sue for information.

- July 2003. The DC Court of Appeals in the Judicial Watch case orders Cheney to turn over the documents relating to the task force.

- December 2003. Cheney appeals to the Supreme Court.

- January 2004. Cheney goes duck hunting in Louisiana on an oil-services entrepreneur's land with Justice Antonin Scalia. Scalia denies impropriety and rebuffs suggestions that he recuse himself from the Court during the Cheney decision. 'Quack, quack,' he tells reporters.

- April 2004. The Supreme Court hears Cheney's appeal.

- June 2004. The Supreme Court refuses to order the administration to make public the details of the Energy Task Force documents. Instead, they send the case back to the Lower Court to decide.

So you have the most secretive president in generations. And you have the most secretive vice president in generations. Which not surprisingly creates the most secretive administration in generations. A Bush White House secrecy sampler, by year:

2000

- The relative health of candidates for high public office is information vital to the electorate. The Bush–Cheney campaign thinks otherwise. Cheney had suffered three heart attacks before being named as Bush's running mate. His doctors said he was fit enough to campaign. When pressed to provide more detailed information about his health, the campaign promises to do so. It never does.
- November. Cheney suffers another heart attack. Dr. Lawrence K. Altman, medical reporter for *The New York Times*, reviews the records Cheney's doctors had released and finds them incomplete.

2001

- October. Although the previous administration released pretty much all government documents under the Freedom of Information Act – unless there was a threat to the nation's security – Attorney General John Ashcroft does the opposite. He orders all departments to release nothing unless they absolutely have to.
- November. Bush signs an executive order giving him unprecedented power over presidential papers.
- December. Dan Burton, chairman of the House Government Reform Committee, requests documents that might show that FBI agents had allowed informants to

commit serious crimes. Bush tells Ashcroft to reject the request, saying it threatens the 'national interest' because it would give Congress a window into 'prosecutorial decision making.' When House members from both sides express outrage, the White House quietly caves.

2002

- February. The Department of Agriculture announces strict controls over information it releases. Scientists at the department's Agricultural Research Service are told to seek prior approval before releasing anything having to do with 'sensitive issues.'
- November. The Homeland Security Act declares that companies that voluntarily submit information to the Department of Homeland Security regarding infrastructure will be exempt from civil litigation in those areas. *U.S. News & World Report* says, 'Some critics see this as a get-out-of-jail-free card, allowing companies worried about potential litigation or regulatory actions to place troublesome information in a convenient "homeland security" vault.'
- December. In the lead-up to war, Iraq delivers 11,800 pages of documents relating to its weapons to the United States. The British press reports that before turning the information over to the UN Security Council, the administration removed 3,200 pages from the dossier.

2003

- March. Bush enforces a ban on news coverage of military funerals as well as arrivals of coffins at Dover Air Force Base in Delaware.

- March. Bush signs Executive Order 12958, delaying the declassification of millions of documents twenty-five years old, for another three years. He gives Cheney power to issue similar declarations.

- March. The White House's Office of Management and Budget ceases issuing its annual Budget Information for States report. (The BIS is the document that puts in writing what each state receives from federal programs.)

- March. According to Ohio congressman Sherrod Brown's time line, the administration begins passing a series of controversial bills either late at night or early in the morning. At 2:54 a.m. on a Friday, the House cuts veterans' benefits just as the White House is launching its war against Iraq.

- April. At 2:39 a.m. on a Friday, the House cuts education and health-care funding.

- May. At 1:56 a.m. on a Friday, the House passes its tax cut bill.

- June. At 2:33 a.m. on a Friday, the House passes the sweeping Medicare privatization and prescription drug bill.

- July. At 12:57 a.m. on a Friday, the House reduces funding for Operation Head Start.

- October. At 12:12 a.m. on a Friday, the House passes legislation giving the administration $87 billion toward the war in Iraq.

- November. At 5:55 a.m. on a Saturday, the House passes the new Medicare bill.

- June. *The New York Times* reports that the White House edited an EPA draft report on the state of the environment, eliminating references to studies showing industrial pollution and automobiles as chief contributors to global warming. The original draft of the report included the following sentence: 'Climate change has global consequences for human health and environment.' The White House deleted it.

- November. Bush puts official limits on questions congressional Democrats can ask the administration. House members must now put them in writing to Republican committee chairmen.
- December. *The Washington Post* reports that the White House made a change in its Web site, inserting the word 'Major' in a May 1 headline that had said 'President Bush Announces Combat Operations in Iraq Have Ended.'
- December. New auto and tire safety regulations had been passed by Congress back in October 2000 following the massive Ford-Firestone recall. The National Highway Traffic Safety Administration said that the data from the tire and auto manufacturers would be made public. In December 2003, NHTSA rescinds that promise. The data, including important safety information, are not made public.

2004

- February. Bowing to pressure from news organizations, Bush says he will release all the records of his years in the National Guard. On *Meet the Press*, he tells Tim Russert that these will prove that he completed his tour. The records are incomplete.
- March. Richard S. Foster, Medicare's chief actuary, informs Congress that he told the White House the year before that the prescription drug plan they were preparing would cost 25 percent to 50 percent more than the administration was telling the House and the public. The real numbers were concealed, and Foster was told he would be fired if he informed lawmakers of the true costs.
- March. The inspector general of the Department of Health and Human Services begins an inquiry into whether the

White House acted illegally when it withheld the true cost of the drug prescription bill. As *The New York Times* notes, 'Mr. Foster's figures do have significance. The Medicare bill was President Bush's highest legislative priority going into the election year, and Congressional forecasts about its cost were highly uncertain. At the same time, conservative lawmakers were up in arms over the expense, and were threatening to vote against the measure.'

- March. When the supplemental budget estimates are due from the administration, the White House says that Pentagon analysts can't say what the costs of the wars in Iraq and Afghanistan will be. Bush says he can't provide the full estimates until January 2005, three months after the election.

- April. In Hamburg, Germany, a judge releases an Al Qaeda member who was accused of assisting the September 11 hijackers. The reason: The United States refused to share testimony from one of its own terrorist suspects.

- April. House Republicans overrule Democrats, shutting down an inquiry into whether the White House acted illegally when it withheld the true cost of the drug plan from them.

- April. Bob Woodward reports in his book *Plan of Attack* that in 2002 Bush diverted $700 million from the funds appropriated for the war in Afghanistan to pay for preparations for a war in Iraq without Congress's knowledge. 'Congress was totally in the dark on this,' says Woodward.

The most secretive administration in the modern age has been feverish in its attack on transparent governance. In 1999, there were eight million reports or documents classified as official secrets. By 2002, there were twenty-three million. According to John Podesta, now head of the Center for American Progress, the cost to the nation is twofold. First are the actual bureaucratic costs involved. The clerical expenses to classify just those twenty-three million documents will cost taxpayers $5.7 billion. The second, more intangible cost to the nation is that of nontransparency. And this is of far greater import. As David Broder says, weaknesses in the administration are hidden from public view – as are its strengths.

Secrecy leads to unaccountability, and unaccountability in a democracy leads to something approaching an elected dictatorship.

> 'The true threats to stability and peace are these nations that are not very transparent . . . that don't let people in to take a look and see what they're up to.'
>
> – GEORGE W. BUSH, March 2001

> 'If this were a dictatorship, it'd be a heck of a lot easier, just so long as I'm the dictator.'
>
> – GEORGE W. BUSH, December 2000

4

◼

THE ECONOMY

'It's clearly a budget. It's got lots of numbers in it.'
                                    – GEORGE W. BUSH, May 2000

THE Bush administration's relentless assault on the finances of the nation has proved not only injurious to the U.S. economy in the short run but may prove catastrophic over time. A report and subsequent follow-up released by the International Monetary Fund's Western Hemisphere Department in early and mid-2004 showed growing concern over the American economy, putting the United States in the company of nations that have also caused significant alarm, such as Argentina and Haiti. 'In most countries, the I.M.F. is often viewed as America's agent, preaching the inconvenient gospel of fiscal discipline and austerity,' said an editorial in *The New York Times*. 'There is a certain poignancy now in having the I.M.F. preach the so-called "Washington consensus" to Washington . . . No wonder the rest of the world is appalled.'

The IMF derided the 'complicated and nontransparent manner' in which the Bush administration's tax cuts were made. It also noted that the enormous deficits Washington has run up, combined with its mushrooming trade imbalance, have given foreign investors pause, thus weakening the dollar against other global currencies. 'We feel there is a substantial risk that foreign investors' appetite for U.S. assets . . . will, over time, diminish,' Charles Collyns, deputy director of the IMF's Western Hemisphere Department, said at a news conference in January 2004. Because the United States is the turbine that all but powers the rest of the world's economy, the administration's actions could well affect the wealth of nations; the IMF report stated that in a matter of years, America's net financial obligations to the rest of the world could amount to 40 percent of the U.S. economy, calling the current debt 'unprecedented . . . for a large industrial economy.'

The White House's reaction to the IMF's warnings? It dismissed them as alarmist.

The fact is that Republicans as well as Democrats *are* alarmed. Tax-cutting, free-spending ideologues such as the president, the vice president, and House Majority Leader Tom DeLay should begin looking over their shoulders. (DeLay's not a fan of *all* tax cuts – he was the leading outspoken voice against giving families making between $10,500 and $26,625 an increase in the child tax credit.) In January 2004, the heads of six major conservative organizations declared that they were making a 'major break' with both the administration and the Republican-controlled Congress over what they consider 'drunken sailor' spending habits during Bush's first three years. The groups, including the National Taxpayers Union and the American Conservative Union, objected, among other things, to the president having increased discretionary federal spending by up to 35 percent in his first three years in office. When you compare this increase to the total value of the goods and services produced in the United

States, or gross domestic product (GDP), which is seen as the more accurate way to measure areas of our economy, a different picture emerges. Economist and *New York Times* columnist Paul Krugman points out that 'the bulk of this increase has been related to national security. Traditional budget measures distinguish between defense and nondefense discretionary spending. Even by these measures, defense accounts for most of the increase in recent years. But a better measure would group homeland security and other costs associated with 9/11 with defense, not domestic programs. The Center for American Progress – confirming related work by the Center on Budget and Policy Priorities – estimates that from 2000 to 2004 security-related discretionary spending rose to 4.7 percent of GDP from 3.4 percent, while non-security spending rose to only 3.4 percent from 3.1 percent. In other words, the role of non-security spending in the plunge into deficit is trivial, compared with tax cuts and security spending.'

Former Reagan commerce secretary Pete Peterson, in an essay in *The New York Times Magazine* in June 2003, acknowledged it didn't have to be this way: 'Coming into power, the Republican leaders faced a choice between tax cuts and providing genuine financing for the future of Social Security. They chose tax cuts. After 9/11, they faced a choice between tax cuts and getting serious about the extensive measures needed to protect this nation against further terrorist attacks. They chose tax cuts. After war broke out in the Mideast, they faced a choice between tax cuts and galvanizing the nation behind a policy of future-oriented burden sharing. Again and again, they chose tax cuts.' Those tax cuts are the single greatest reason that the United States has run up such enormous deficits during the Bush years, as well as burgeoning national debt.

- When Bush came into office, under the laws and policies then in effect, the ten-year forecast was for the national debt to be eliminated and replaced with a projected surplus of $5.6 trillion.

▪ By the end of Bush's second year in office, the ten-year surplus was projected downward to $1.3 trillion.

▪ After the sweeping Bush tax cuts and an optional war, the ten-year forecast didn't indicate a surplus at all but rather, a $4.3 trillion *deficit*. (More on this later.)

Going from a forecasted surplus of $5.6 trillion to a deficit of $4.3 trillion? Forget about searching for WMDs in Iraq. Where did our almost $10 trillion go?

The Center on Budget and Policy Priorities (CBPP) reports, 'Approximately 35 percent of this stunning $9.3 trillion deterioration is due to the tax cuts enacted over the past three years . . . In terms of legislation since 2001, tax cuts are the single most important factor in explaining the move from surpluses to deficits.'

Bill Clinton, distractions aside, managed three surplus years in his eight years at the White House – the highest being $236 billion in 2000. (Remember the campaign line, 'It's the economy, stupid'?) Then, according to the Office of Management and Budget, this happened:

▪ In February 2000, the Clinton administration predicted a 2003 surplus of $185 billion.

▪ In February 2001, the Bush administration increased Clinton's forecast to an annual operating surplus of $242 billion for 2003.

▪ In February 2002, it revised that figure to a *deficit* of $80.2 billion.

▪ In October 2003, the deficit for 2003 was calculated to be $375.3 billion.

▪ In early 2004, depending on which governmental agency you trust the most, there was a forecasted deficit of $521 billion (OMB) or a deficit of $477 billion (Congressional

Budget Office). A source at the CBO says that the OMB numbers are higher because 'they pump it up so the administration can claim they cut the deficit more than they had expected.'

The deficits for 2003 and 2004 are the biggest in U.S. history, besting the previous record of $290 billion. That was the 1992 deficit, when the senior Bush had the job. Never let it be said that the son hasn't lived up to the accomplishments of the father.

By the end of February 2004, unemployment had risen 33 percent from when the Bush administration came into office, and there were more than 2.3 million fewer Americans with jobs. That's more net job losses during a single administration than in any since the Hoover White House during the Great Depression.

During the 2000 campaign, Bush advertised himself to voters as a 'compassionate conservative.' It was a tagline Karen Hughes had coined to win over the moderate Republicans who had been put off by the antigovernment extremism of House Speaker Newt Gingrich's coup of the party in the mid-1990s. As Joe Conason wrote in *The Nation*, ' "Compassionate" softens "conservative," a word that tends to be associated with smug stinginess rather than benevolence or mercy.'

Yoshi Tsurumi, professor of international business at Baruch College in Manhattan, taught the young Bush at the Harvard Business School in the 1970s. This is what he recalled of the future president in those days, according to an essay he wrote for the Japanese Institute of Global Communications:

- 'He declared that "people are poor because they are lazy."'
- 'He was opposed to labor unions, Social Security, environmental protection, Medicare, and public schools.'
- 'To him, the antitrust watchdog, the Federal Trade

Commission, and the Securities and Exchange Commission were unnecessary hindrances to "free market competition."'

■ 'To him, Franklin Roosevelt's New Deal was "socialism."'

Has George W. Bush handled our money well? A report card:

THE TAX CUTS

'By far the vast majority of my tax cuts go to the bottom end of the spectrum.'

– GEORGE W. BUSH, presidential candidate

Once the Bush administration got into office, it pushed through a profound long-term plan that would lower income tax rates across the board, abolish the estate tax, gradually double the child tax credit, and end the so-called marriage penalty. A one-time rebate check – married couples would receive $600, single parents $500, and individuals $300 – would be mailed out by midfall 2001. Total cost: $1.35 trillion over ten years. Bush stressed that this tax relief package was needed to jumpstart our 'faltering economy.' Yet, other than the rebate checks, economists noted that the short-term stimulus would be minimal since most of the cuts wouldn't take effect until the second half of the ten-year period. Furthermore, in year eleven, all the cuts would disappear, and taxes would revert back to their 2000 levels. In 2002, Congress passed Bush's second tax cut, which largely favored businesses. The stimulus bill, introduced shortly after September 11, 2001, and passed more than a year later, granted businesses three years of tax breaks for investments in new equipment – worth more than $100 billion. In 2003, a booster to the 2001 tax cut was passed. The major parts of this plan – to cost $350 billion over ten years – included reducing the tax rate on dividend income and capital gains, and accelerating the reductions of the income tax rates. Bush has pushed Congress to make his tax cuts permanent. Analysts estimate that making the tax cuts permanent will cost nearly $2 trillion over the next ten years. All combined, the tax cuts enacted have caused the federal government's revenues from taxes as a percentage of the overall economy to fall to their lowest level since 1950. In May 2004, a *New York Times* editorial reported, 'Even if the economy recovers fully, the country would have to revert to a 1957-era government to break even. In 1957, the Interstate System was just getting under way, and Medicare did not exist, much less a war on terrorism.'

When Bush was running for office, he pitched the 2001 tax plan to middle-income Americans and small businesses, assuring them that they would be the principal beneficiaries of the cuts. Not surprisingly, the exact opposite is true. The 2001 and 2003 tax bills enacted by the Bush White House were written almost exclusively for the wealthy. A tax program that gets rid of capital gains and estate taxes is hardly in the interests of the working class. When it comes down to it, there really is only one piece of evidence necessary to demonstrate that the Bush cuts were created to favor the wealthy but not the working: *Payroll taxes were not included in the cuts*. (The payroll tax, which funds Social Security and Medicare among other programs, is paid by all Americans who receive a paycheck. And as Paul Krugman has noted, it 'is the main tax paid by about four out of five families . . . The payroll tax is regressive: it falls much more heavily on middle- and lower-income families than it does on the rich. In fact, according to Congressional Budget Office estimates, families near the middle of the income distribution pay almost twice as much in payroll taxes as in income taxes.'

For 2001, the Citizens for Tax Justice found that 'the middle 20% of the income distribution, with average incomes of $35,300, got an average of about $400 from the Bush tax cuts.' As for those lauded rebate checks, 26 percent, or an estimated thirty-four million taxpayers, received no rebate check at all.

Data from the Urban Institute–Brookings Institution Tax Policy Center illustrate the effects in 2004 of the tax cuts already enacted. The following are highlights:

- In 2004, the middle 20 percent of U.S. households will receive 8.9 percent of the tax cuts.
- By contrast, millionaires – comprising just 0.2 percent of U.S. households – will receive 15.3 percent of the tax cuts. In other words, the tiny group of millionaires will receive total tax cuts much greater than those received by the middle 20 percent of American households.
- The tax cuts will bestow more than $30 billion on the nation's 257,000 millionaires in 2004 alone.
- By the time the tax cuts are completely phased in, the wealthiest 1 percent of U.S. citizens will be rewarded with 39 percent of the total tax savings. The Bushes, for instance, received $30,858 from his tax plans in 2003. Campaign Money Watch estimated that Pfizer CEO Henry McKinnell (who donated more than $200,000 to the Bush campaign) saved an estimated minimum of $244,214 on his taxes in 2003 alone.

The result is that America is well on its way to having a flat tax. *The New York Times* Pulitzer prize-winning financial reporter David Cay Johnston says that 'the most important measure of tax burden is how many pennies out of each dollar go to taxes. The top 400 taxpayers in 2000 had an average income of $174 million, yet they paid just 22 cents on the dollar in federal income taxes . . . Had the 2003 tax cuts been in effect, the top 400 would have paid just 17.5 cents on the dollar, not much more than the overall national average of 15.3 cents that Americans actually paid that year.' He says that when all other taxes are included (state, local, and so forth), 'The top fifth of Americans pays just a penny more out of a dollar in taxes overall than the poorest fifth, 19 cents versus 18 cents.'

A flurry of surveys and studies released in early 2004 were troubling indicators of the White House's dogged mission to reward the rich. An Associated Press/Ipsos Poll released in April 2004 found that only 13 percent of Americans found that their taxes had decreased, and 49 percent found that their taxes had actually gone up since the Bush administration took office. A CNN/*Money* poll that came out at the same time found that 60 percent of Americans said they did not benefit from the tax cuts. Furthermore, it appears that a balanced budget is of greater concern to citizens than it is to their president – 61 percent of those interviewed in the AP poll said they preferred it to tax cuts. And in early 2004, a report released by the General Accounting Office included a statistic that truly floored most Americans: 60 percent of large U.S. companies *paid no federal taxes whatsoever* between 1996 and 2000. And according to an independent study of new Internal Revenue Service data released in 2004, tax enforcement prosecutions against big tax avoiders have fallen by half over the past decade.

From the start, Bush pledged that his tax cuts would be good for the economy and would stimulate economic growth and create jobs. Yet Economy.com found that the tax cuts 'will have accounted for less than one third of real economic growth over the years of the Bush presidency.' And worse, the CBO has concluded that the Bush tax cuts 'will probably have a net negative effect on saving, investment, and capital accumulation over the next 10 years.'

THE DEFICIT

'We cannot go down the path of soaring budget deficits.'

– GEORGE W. BUSH, August 2002

'My Administration firmly believes in controlling the deficit and reducing it.'

– GEORGE W. BUSH, February 2003

In fact the deficit, as reported by the CBPP in early 2004, will exceed $400 billion every year for the next ten years, and by 2014 it will reach $708 billion. The potential effect of these escalating deficits on our long-term economic stability is frightening. 'Right now the U.S. government is running deficits bigger, as a share of [gross domestic product], than those that plunged Argentina into crisis,' said Paul Krugman. 'The reason we don't face a comparable crisis is that markets, extrapolating from our responsible past, trust us to get our house in order.'

In a joint report released in January 2004, former treasury secretary Robert Rubin, Peter Orszag of the Brookings Institution, and Allen Sinai of Decision Economics cautioned that 'the U.S. federal budget is on an unsustainable path . . . The inability of the federal government to control the budget deficit could be interpreted as a broader failure of the nation to address its economic problems, and thus prompt a loss of business and consumer confidence, which would undermine capital spending and real economic activity.' Future generations of Americans could be confronted with an even weaker job market than the current one and suffer a deterioration in their standard of living. The Brookings Institution calculated that 'by 2014, the average family's income will be an estimated $1,800 lower because of the slower economic growth' caused by the budget deficits. A family with a $250,000 thirty-year mortgage will be paying $2,000 more per year in interest payments alone. Even Federal Reserve Chairman Alan Greenspan is speaking out. Early in May he told a banking conference in Chicago that 'our fiscal prospects are, in my judgment, a significant obstacle to long-term stability.'

These annual deficits will have a nightmarish effect on our national debt too. (The national debt is the difference between all money the government has ever spent and all the revenue it has ever collected.) As the total increases by much more than a billion dollars a day, our national debt of $7.1 trillion (or 37 percent of our GDP) is likely to hit $9.7 trillion by 2014. Each American's share of the $7.1 trillion is more than $20,000. An editorial in *The New York Times* said that this dramatic swing into the red has increased America's dependence on foreign nations to serve as our creditors. Foreign governments, institutions, and individuals, over the last few years, have financed an astounding 80 percent of our deficit.

UNEMPLOYMENT

The tax cuts, which created the biggest deficits in U.S. history, were intended to boost employment. They did anything but. During the Clinton administration, 22 million new jobs were created. During the Bush administration, as of late May 2004, 1.5 million jobs have been lost. By early 2004, the unemployment rate hit 5.6 percent, down from its high of 6.3 percent in June 2003. The Economic Policy Institute (EPI) considers the rate to be 7.4 percent when you factor in the 'missing labor force,' those who have become so discouraged with the job market that they are no longer looking and are therefore no longer figured into unemployment rolls.

This wasn't meant to happen. In 2001, the Bush administration boldly announced that its first tax cut package would create 800,000 new jobs by the end of 2002. The next year, Bush claimed that there would be 3.4 million more jobs in 2003 than there were in 2000. Neither figure proved accurate. The economy *lost* 1.7 million jobs during that period. The overreaching estimate was, according to *The Washington Post*, the largest forecast error in at least fifteen years. In May 2003, the administration's second tax cut package, which the White House euphemistically called the 'Jobs and Growth Plan,' was passed. In it, the administration predicted that 5.5 million new jobs would be created by the end of 2004. To hit this number, a total of 306,000 new jobs would have to be created every month beginning in July 2003. For the first eight months, job gains fell noticeably short of the administration's projected figures. In fact, just 21,000 jobs, all government hires, were added in February 2004. So it was welcome news when job gains for March climbed to 337,000 – comfortably above the projected monthly 306,000 figure – followed by a further 288,000 jobs in April. Encouraging, depending on how you look at it. The war in Iraq may be one reason for this sudden growth spurt. Defense contractors had been taking on new workers in early 2004 to meet increased demand. The White House projected that more than three million jobs would be created between July 2003 and April 2004. As it turned out, a little more than one million were created.

A week after releasing the 2004 Economic Report of the President, members of the Bush administration attempted to distance themselves from the report's bullish job growth forecasts which, according to the CBPP and EPI, 'predicted that employment will average 132.7 million in 2004, reflecting a 2.6 million increase in jobs over its average in 2003. To achieve this estimate an average of 460,000 jobs a month would need to be created from February through December 2004.'

Members of the administration, including Treasury Secretary John W. Snow, Commerce Secretary Donald L. Evans, and Press Secretary Scott McClellan, made statements indicating it was backing off its own Council of Economic Advisers figures. According to McClellan, 'The president is not a statistician.'

Unwilling to stand by a benchmark of its own making by which to measure the success of its own economic policies, the administration resorted to downright dishonesty. When Bush was asked about the 2004 Economic Report of the President, he had Secretary of Labor Elaine Chao tell legislators that he hadn't signed it. In fact, his signature appears on page four of the report.

Billowing unemployment figures month after month are, it goes without saying, not the sort of news administrations like seeing bandied about. So what did the Bush White House do when the job figures weren't going its way? On Christmas Eve 2002, it stopped issuing the traditional monthly Bureau of Labor Statistics report – known as the Mass Layoff Statistics program – which tracks closings of workplaces with a firing of more than fifty employees. The administration hoped nobody would notice. Unfortunately, *The Washington Post* picked up on it, and the White House – which had claimed the report's demise was due to budget cuts – was forced to begin releasing the report again, albeit revised. A footnote to the report reveals that, 'Extended Mass Layoffs, has been redefined to cover only the private nonfarm economy. Quarterly information on layoff events in agriculture and government will no longer be collected.' It turns out that the president was carrying on a tradition. Bush's father stopped releasing the Mass Layoffs report in 1992 after a slew of job losses, and it was not restored until Clinton's presidency.

Since the Bush administration came into office, the manufacturing sector has lost more than 2.8 million jobs. And when manufacturing jobs go, they tend to stay gone.

▪ Bush's solution 1: Appoint a 'jobs czar.' This didn't go over too well. Anthony Raimondo, a Nebraska businessman, was the president's pick to be assistant secretary of commerce for manufacturing. Problems arose when it was discovered that Raimondo had laid off seventy-five employees two years before and was putting $3 million into building a new factory in China. Mr. Raimondo's job offer in Washington was withdrawn. In April 2004, Bush nominated California businessman Alfred A. Frink for the post.

▪ Bush's solution 2: Reclassify 'manufacturing' jobs. This one didn't go over too well either. The 2004 Economic Report of the President – the one he signed but said he didn't – attempted to classify jobs in fast-food restaurants as manufacturing jobs. Congress was not amused.

The unfortunate Americans who found themselves out of work, found themselves out of work for an average of 19.2 weeks in 2003, longer than at any time in the past twenty years. By mid-2004, the Labor Department expected two million people to exhaust their unemployment benefits. In March alone, more than 350,000 individuals lost their benefits, an all-time monthly high. When a popular program to provide thirteen weeks of additional benefits to laid-off workers who had exhausted their twenty-six-week unemployment insurance came before the Senate in May, it was voted down by the Republicans.

In his 2004 State of the Union address, Bush announced a program he called 'Jobs for the 21st Century' that would earmark $500 million for job training. It sounds worthy, except that according to the Center for American Progress, over the previous three years, Bush had already proposed at least $1 billion in cuts for job training and vocational education. Bush did, however, ask Congress for a $1 million job-training allowance for the new hires who would be joining his second administration. The presumptive request was the first in American history.

Vast waves of unemployed people mean that employers feel little need to increase wages or maintain benefits. Despite corporate profits rocketing 87 percent from the third quarter of 2001 to the end of 2003, wages and salaries grew a paltry 4.5 percent – a figure that decreases to 1.1 percent when inflation is factored in. By contrast, average compensation of CEOs at the largest U.S. corporations jumped from $3.6 million in 2002 to $4.6 million in 2003.

The quality of work being added to the economy is also declining. According to the EPI, 'In 48 out of 50 states, jobs are shifting from higher-paying industries such as manufacturing and information to lower-paying industries such as retail and hospitality.' Even the Department of Labor reports that 70 percent of the new jobs created through 2012 will be in low-wage service fields including janitorial, retail, food service, and hospital care.

For those who have jobs, but low-paying ones, the 'compassionate conservative' opposed efforts to increase the minimum wage, despite the fact that polls show that 90 percent of Americans want it raised. It has stood at $5.15 per hour since 1997. This means that somebody who works at that rate for forty hours a week for fifty-two weeks makes a total of $10,712 per year. Democrats wanted a boost to $7 per hour over a two-year period. This would have given that person $14,560 per year – and even this figure is below the federal government's definition of poverty. According to the U.S. Census Bureau's 2003 numbers, the federal poverty level for a family of three – a single parent with two children – is $14,824.

Corporations, on the other hand, were treated more compassionately. The Bush administration proposed new legislation that could have prevented an estimated eight million employees from receiving overtime pay. Facing a deluge of criticism, the administration scaled back its proposal in late April 2004, just four months after the AP reported that the Labor Department began 'giving employers tips on how to avoid paying overtime.' In May 2004, the Senate voted against Bush's overtime proposals for the second time in a year.

The White House also embraced outsourcing jobs overseas. In February 2004, the *Los Angeles Times* quoted N. Gregory Mankiw, chairman of Bush's Council of Economic Advisers, as saying, 'Outsourcing is just a new way of doing international trade.' His comment came less than two months after analysts had predicted that two million white-collar jobs would be exported during a time of significant unemployment. When Bush's spokesman was asked whether Mankiw should resign over his insensitive remarks regarding outsourcing, Scott McClellan called the mere suggestion 'laughable.'

When members of the Bush White House extol the country's 'high productivity,' they mean that employers are increasing output with fewer employees. As Nobel prize-winning economist Joseph

Stiglitz remarked, corporations are 'trying to squeeze more and more work out of workers.'

When the jobless figures for February 2004 were released – twenty-one thousand jobs were added, all of them from government, remember – Bush paid a visit to Bakersfield, California, a hardscrabble city with a brutal 13.6 percent unemployment rate. Ever the upbeat economic warrior, the president said he was happy that Les DenHerder, a local stock car chassis manufacturer, was adding new employees. The number of employees Les DenHerder was adding? Two or three. Bush pronounced these hires as 'really good news' and went on to say, 'A lot of people are feeling confident and optimistic about our future so they can say, "I'm going to hire two more." They can sit here and tell the president in front of all the cameras, "I'm going to hire two more people." That's confidence!' When reached for comment in May 2004, Mr. DenHerder relayed that he had hired only one employee, but 'we're accepting résumés.'

AMERICA'S POOR

'First, let me make it very clear, poor people aren't necessarily killers. Just because you happen to not be rich doesn't mean you're willing to kill.'

– GEORGE W. BUSH, May 2003

The United States is the wealthiest, mightiest country in all of human history, and yet it has a higher percentage of poor or, worse, hungry citizens than almost every other industrialized nation. The situation was not George Bush's doing – he just made it worse. In comparison to other countries, U.S. poverty rates have reached alarming proportions. The Luxembourg Income Study, which has been tracking household incomes of twenty-five countries for more than twenty years, recently compared nations' relative poverty rates. 'Relative' poverty is defined as a household making less than 50 percent of the national median income. In Finland, Norway, and Sweden, poverty rates range between 5.4 percent and 6.5 percent. Of our two neighbors, Canada and Mexico, the United States' poverty rate is much closer to Mexico's – Canada has an 11.4 percent poverty rate; Mexico, 22.1 percent. The U.S. poverty rate is 17 percent, according to the Luxembourg study, only 1.8 percent lower than Russia's.

We also have one of the worst child poverty rates among industrialized nations. Studies show that children growing up in Sweden, France, or Germany have a six times better chance of escaping from poverty than American kids do.

There are 34.6 million officially poor Americans – one in eight of the population. That's more people than the entire population of Canada. And the number rises by about 1.7 million every year. There are 3 million more Americans living in poverty now than when the Bush administration took office.

How poor is poor? It's really poor. Once again, the federal definition of poverty is $14,824 for a single parent with two children; $18,660 for two adults with two children. That means that the national poverty figures above don't even count single parents earning, say, $17,000 a year, or working couples making $20,000.

There are the poor and then there are the outright hungry. According to the Department of Agriculture, there are thirty-five million 'food insecure' adults and children in the United States – people who can't count on their next meal. The 'food insecure' are still better off than the 9.4 million Americans who experience regular 'hunger' – people whom the government defines as suffering from an 'uneasy or painful sensation caused by lack of food and recurrent, involuntary lack of access to food.' Every day a number of Americans equal to the entire population of Sweden are 'hungry.' Food stamps are a help for some – 23.5 million Americans use them, up from 17 million when the Bush administration came into office.

Ohio, one of the states Bush carried in the 2000 election, has lost more than 17 percent of its manufacturing jobs, or 168,000 positions. Hunger has become a major issue. The number of people in the state on food stamps has risen nearly 50 percent since January 2001. Of Ohio's eleven million residents, almost one million are so poor that they rely on handouts from food charities.

In May 2004, Timken, a large manufacturing employer, announced that it was closing its steel and ball-bearing plants in Canton, Ohio, putting a further thirteen hundred out of work. Back in April 2003, Bush visited Timken (its chairman is a large Republican and Bush donor) and boldly predicted that 'the future of employment is bright for the families that work here.' He said that the White House's plan to eliminate the double taxation of stock dividends would mean 'companies like Timken have got a better capacity to expand, which means jobs.'

After the tax cuts, which so rewarded the rich, the administration 'is threatening to make up some of the difference by cutting desperately needed programs aimed at the poor,' *The New York Times* reported in January 2004. 'One candidate for the chopping block is Section 8, the federal rent-subsidy program whose main purpose is preventing low-income families from becoming homeless . . . At the moment, the program covers about 2.1 million households. Most of these families include minor children; 40 percent include elderly or disabled people.' The federal government used to fund the entire cost of the 1.9 million vouchers given to poor tenants under the Section 8 program. Then, in April 2004, the Department of Housing and Urban Development informed local housing agencies that it would pay only the cost of the vouchers as it stood in August 2003, with adjustments for inflation. This could result in a national budget shortfall of hundreds of millions of dollars for the current fiscal year and will have a serious impact on poor Americans living in areas where rent increases outpace inflation. According to *The New York Times*, this 'shortfall . . . may force housing agencies to freeze the number of vouchers, demand more money from tenants or do something that has never happened in Section 8's three-decade history: evict tenants from federally subsidized housing because of insufficient funding.' The cuts to housing agencies could cost 250,000 families their homes in 2005, and 600,000 by 2009.

The White House also decided to trim costs by making it tougher for the working poor to receive child-care aid. Reductions in this program could affect between 200,000 and 365,000 children over the next five years. When the Senate voted for increasing child-care payments to welfare recipients and low-income wage earners, the White House howled, arguing that the increase was unnecessary. 'The day care issue has become even more crucial now that Congress is expected to increase the number of hours that welfare recipients must work in exchange for benefits,' wrote *The New York Times* in March 2004.

To shave $3.5 billion off the budget, the Bush administration dropped the child tax credit for twelve million children of low-income workers. The cost of the child tax credit represented a tiny fraction of the overall budget, and there were a range of measures that could have been taken to accommodate it. The legislative proposal to close abusive corporate tax shelters is an example. This cause was close to President Bush's heart in 2002, when he promised in a speech on Wall Street that his administration would crack down on corporate criminal activity and 'end the days of cooking the books, shading the truth and breaking the law.' Bush called for 'a new ethic of personal responsibility in the business community,' vowing that 'we will use the full weight of the law to expose and root out corruption.' According to *The Washington Post*, the Senate bill for the 2004 budget 'included provisions to crack down on abusive tax shelters, combat some accounting scams such as those pursued by Enron Corp., prevent U.S companies from moving their headquarters to Post Office boxes in offshore tax havens such as Bermuda and limit grossly inflated deferred compensation plans for corporate executives.' The cost saving, had those Senate provisions passed, would have totaled some $25 billion, more than enough to pay for the child tax credit. Yet despite the president's tough talk on corporate reform, every single one of the provisions was dropped in conference.

The attack against the poor continued in Bush's 2005 budget. There is a proposal to cut $3 billion in funding for the Earned Income Tax Credit, which lowers taxes for working parents whose combined income is less than $35,000. The IRS – the same IRS that lets 60 percent of all U.S. companies get away without paying taxes – announced that it would be auditing more families who claim the Earned Income Tax Credit.

The rich–poor divide in the United States is now more unequal than in any other democratic country. In America, 40 percent of the wealth is held by 1 percent of the population. (In Britain, by comparison, the richest 1 percent control 18 percent of the wealth, according to *The Guardian*.)

THE TRADE DEFICIT

'Ours is an administration dedicated to free trade. Free trade is good for America.'

– GEORGE W. BUSH, March 2001

In addition to its unease over America's budget deficit, the International Monetary Fund's reports issued in early 2004 exhibited concern over America's enormous trade deficit, which soared to a record $489.4 billion in 2003. This meant that the United States imported $489.4 billion more goods and services in 2003 than it exported. In 1983, America was the world's largest creditor nation; by 2003, we stood as the world's largest debtor nation. According to *The New York Times* in January 2004, the IMF warned, 'With its rising budget deficit and ballooning trade imbalance, the United States is running up a foreign debt of such record-breaking proportions that it threatens the financial stability of the global economy.'

Even more troubling than the IMF concerns is the fact that Warren Buffett is nervous. In his 2003 annual report to stockholders, the investment legend announced that he was buying foreign currencies because he felt that the flood of U.S. dollars out of the country to rectify the deficit would further drive down the dollar's value against other currencies. This is the sort of progression of events Buffett worries about:

Currency traders begin selling dollars and buying other currencies.

▼

Foreign investors, anxious over the state of the U.S. economy and its dollar, sell their American assets.

▼

To win back those investors, interest rates are forced up.

▼

Indebted Americans have trouble maintaining the higher payments on their debt.

▼

Bankruptcies and inflation ensue. (The president is eager to sign a bill that would make it more difficult for families and individuals to declare bankruptcy. This piece of legislation would benefit credit card giants like MBNA America, the country's largest credit card issuer – and also the largest financial services campaign donor to the Republicans. MBNA stands to earn almost $100 million more in revenues each year if the measure passes and is signed into law.)

As a presidential candidate, George Bush campaigned as an advocate of free trade and continued to do so while in office. His actions, of course, are somewhat different. In January 2004, at a summit of Latin American leaders in Mexico, Bush promoted open trade as a certain path to long-term prosperity. Delegates at the talks were skeptical. A Zogby International Poll of Latin

American opinion formers released before the summit showed respondents giving Bush an 87 percent negative rating.

A brief history of the Bush White House's adventures in the trade game:

- November 2001. At a meeting of the World Trade Organization in Qatar, the administration promises to ease up on pharmaceutical patents to allow developing countries access to less expensive drugs.
- March 2002. As the midterm elections near, Bush hopes to win favor with several key swing states by imposing up to 30 percent tariffs on most imported steel. The tariffs are deemed to be illegal, and Britain and the European Union threaten to retaliate.
- May 2002. Bush gives American farmers what he calls a 'generous' $180 billion in subsidies.
- August 2002. Congress bestows trade promotion authority to the president. This gives Bush the power to negotiate trade agreements that cannot be changed by Congress – only accepted or rejected.
- December 2002. At a meeting of the World Trade Organization (WTO) in Geneva, Bush's people, under pressure from American pharmaceutical giants, renege on the administration's November 2001 promise to ease up on pharmaceutical patents to allow some developing countries access to less expensive drugs.
- September 2003. At a meeting of the WTO in Cancún, delegates from twenty-one developing nations walk out when the United States goes back on its promise to lower subsidies for American farmers.
- November 2003. In the midst of the rift over the steel tariffs, Britain's *Evening Standard* reports that Bush is offering compensation to U.S. companies in Britain that relocate jobs back to America. The White House also places

limits on some Chinese textile imports, including apparel and brassieres.

- December 2003. Bush rolls back the steel tariffs.
- February 2004. The European Union imposes $4 billion in retaliatory sanctions against the United States for its refusal to eliminate overseas tax shelters for American exporters. The WTO had approved the sanctions in May 2003, but the EU delayed their implementation, hoping that Congress would eliminate the tax shelters. American business interests manage to delay congressional passage of the reforms until May 2004, at which point the Corporate Tax Reform bill is passed – replacing export subsidies with another giveaway: $170 billion in U.S. corporate tax breaks.

SOCIAL SECURITY

The truth about Social Security is that it's in pretty good shape. Over the past twenty years, the plan essentially brought in an estimated $1.7 trillion more than it paid out. So there is a surplus. In 2004, for instance, the amount coming in is projected to be $653 billion and the amount going out $500 billion. There are nevertheless dramatic forecasts from fanatical right-wing Republicans and those in the administration that the plan will be bankrupt at any moment. These worries, however, are political and not based on any economic model. According to the 2004 annual Social Security Trustees Report, the program has enough money to pay retirees until 2042, when it will be 'exhausted.' After that – or unless Social Security taxes rise – it can handle 73 percent of the currently scheduled benefits. In May 2004, a *New York Times* editorial pointed out that 'if the tax cuts are not made permanent, as Mr. Bush intends, the revenue from those taxes would cover the increased cost of Social Security, without reducing benefits.'

The Social Security surplus is supposed to be held in a trust fund, or 'lockbox,' and is technically off-limits to Congress and presidents who want to borrow from it and have the money repaid later. 'In my economic plan, more than $2 trillion of the federal surplus is locked away for Social Security,' Bush said during the 2000 campaign. 'For years, politicians in both parties have dipped into the trust fund to pay for more spending. And I will stop it.'

In March 2001, Bush said that 'another priority is retirement systems of Americans. And so the budget I set up says that payroll taxes are only going to be spent on one thing, and that's Social Security – that the Congress won't be using the payroll taxes for other programs. So – Lock-box, I think, is the terminology they like to use up here.'

In February 2002, *The Wall Street Journal* reported that the opposite was true. Bush's budget, the paper said, uses 'all the Social Security surpluses . . . to fund the government for the next two years, and to spend well over $100 billion of Social Security funds in each of the following three years.' While the administration distanced itself from the president's earlier promises not to dip into the Social Security nest egg, the Republican-led Congress raided it to replace the necessary government funding that the tax cuts took away. The administration replaced the borrowed money as others have been doing since the Johnson administration – with treasury notes.

If politicians keep their hands out of the cookie jar, Social Security is fine for a good long time. During the 2000 campaign, Bush told the *NewsHour*'s Jim Lehrer, 'It's more likely' that younger workers would 'go to Mars than to receive a check from the Social Security system.' So why did the Bush administration embark on a public relations campaign to make the situation look more dire than it is? Because it wants to privatize a portion of America's Social Security payroll taxes into individual accounts of stocks and bonds. (The performance of their private investments determines how much money the retirees would receive.). Why would it want to do that? Because it will put billions of dollars into the hands of big banks and brokerages, both of which are serious Republican donors. David Langer, a specialist in retirement benefit planning, wrote in *The Christian Science Monitor*, 'Assuming 2 percent of workers' taxable pay goes into individual accounts, the financial community's gross income could be augmented by more than $100 billion in the next decade and escalate rapidly from there . . . many of the financial companies have made a big investment to promote the privatization. They have paid more than $60 million to the political campaigns of the president and numerous members of Congress [as of 2001]. They have also given a tidy sum to conservative think tanks to come up with and heavily publicize messages that I call "think bombs," which worry the public about the soundness of Social Security and which are largely untrue.'

5

■

THE ENVIRONMENT

'I'm confident that the environmental path that I announce will benefit the entire world.'

– GEORGE W. BUSH, February 2002

GEORGE Bush began implementing his crimes against America's air, water, and land – his crimes against nature – on January 20, 2001. The president called in Andrew Card, his chief of staff, and told him to send directives to every executive department with authority over environmental issues, ordering them to immediately put on hold more than a dozen new regulations left over from the Clinton administration. The regulations included everything from lowering arsenic levels in drinking water to reducing releases of raw sewage. There were rules setting limits on logging, drilling, and mining on public lands; increasing energy efficiency standards; and banning snowmobiles in Yellowstone and Grand Teton National Parks.

That is what President Bush – the man whom Robert F.

Kennedy Jr., among many others, has called the worst environmental president in U.S. history – did on his first day in the White House.

This is what Texas governor Bush left behind on December 21, 2000, his last day in Austin. According to a 2000 report by the Republicans for Environmental Protection (REP), Texas was

- the #1 state in the nation in manufacturing plant emissions of toxic and ozone-causing chemicals.
- the #1 state in the nation in the discharge of carcinogens harmful to the brain and central nervous system of small children.
- the #1 state in the nation in the release of industrial airborne toxins.
- the #1 state in the nation in the number of hazardous waste incinerators.
- the #1 state in the nation in the production of cancer-causing benzene and vinyl chloride.
- the #1 state in the nation in violations of clean water discharge standards.
- the #1 state in the nation in the release of toxic waste into underground wells.

Furthermore:

- A third of the state's rivers were, by the time he left office, so polluted that they were unfit for recreational use.
- While Bush was Texas governor, Houston passed Los Angeles as the city with the worst air quality in America.

The REP study could find not a single initiative by Bush during his term as governor that sought to improve either the state's air or its water.

Bush, the presidential candidate, announced, 'Prosperity will mean little if we leave to future generations a world of polluted air, toxic lakes and rivers, and vanished forests.'

Bush, as president, has dedicated his energies and those of his administration to rolling back more than two hundred rules and regulations involving clean air and water, protected lands, and endangered species – thereby undoing much, if not most, of the framework for environmental protection legislation that had been fought so hard for since the first Earth Day in 1970.

Two and a half years after the REP released its report on Bush's record as governor of Texas, the same organization produced an environmental report card on his term as president. The results were even worse than his grades at Yale: one B minus, six Ds, and an F. This study, remember, wasn't done by a group of tree-hugging liberals – it was done by old-fashioned Republicans.

In his 2004 State of the Union address, Bush did not once mention global warming, clean air, clean water, pollution, or environment. (The last president to go through an entire State of the Union address without mentioning the environment was Bush's father, in 1992.) The current Bush has had far greater luck than his father in dismantling the nation's environmental laws. Never before has a president so willfully delivered the government departments and agencies responsible for safeguarding America's air, water, and public lands into the hands of antiregulatory zealots, many of whom came from the same polluting industries they're charged with regulating. In most recent administrations, Congress provided a safety net when a president went too far. The Republican-controlled Congress has done little in the way of providing a check to his antiregulatory ideology.

When members of the White House began to worry that the public was getting wise to their environmental agenda and that it might become an election issue, the Bush administration didn't change its attitude toward deregulation. It changed its message.

Enter Frank Luntz, the Republican pollster who helped orchestrate House Speaker Newt Gingrich's 1994 Contract with America.

The White House's communications shaman was given the Herculean task of producing a program of propaganda that would gloss over the Bush administration's disastrous record on the environment. In a sixteen-page memo obtained by *The New York Times*, Luntz confronted the fact that the White House's record on the environment 'is probably the single issue on which Republicans in general – and President Bush in particular – are most vulnerable.' He warned them to avoid hostile language when discussing environmental issues. 'Indeed,' he said, 'it can be helpful to think of environmental issues [and other] issues in terms of a "story." A compelling story, even if factually inaccurate, can be more emotionally compelling than a dry recitation of the truth.'

Luntz also urged administration members to speak in soothing tones, using words that disguise their actual meaning. For instance, when Bush and Cheney say they want to 'provide a little balance' to environmental protection, that's the administration's code for continuing to ease regulations in favor of big Republican campaign donors who want to go on polluting. When James Connaughton, the chairman of the White House Council on Environmental Quality, says that the administration is making 'significant steps forward in all areas of environmental policy,' what he really means is that regulations will continue to be rolled back. Similarly:

- 'Commonsense approaches' is another exercise in Bushspeak that really means regulatory rollbacks.
- 'Climate change' means global warming. As Luntz puts it, 'While global warming has catastrophic connotations attached to it, climate change suggests a more controllable and less emotional challenge.'
- 'Sound science' means nonscience or religion-based science.
- 'Healthy forests' means opening up America's public forestland to private logging interests.
- 'Information quality' means obfuscation.
- 'Clear skies' means polluted air. In the spring of 2003, Bush

made the following announcement: '[I] do hereby proclaim April 21 through April 27 . . . as National Park Week.' That he made the statement with a straight face is commendable. Because even then his Clear Skies initiative was slashing regulations that forced power plants that contributed to the haze in the country's national parks to reduce their emissions. He was also pushing for increased highway building in national parks and expanded snowmobile use in Yellowstone National Park.

The Bush White House's assault on the environment has received little public scrutiny, which is especially remarkable considering the devastating effects its initiatives will have on America's land, air, and water for generations to come. Reports or programs the administration must by law announce, but would rather go unnoticed, are given to low-level officials to deliver. These disclosures are often made on days and at times inconvenient to the national news media and the public. As Robert Perks, coauthor of the Natural Resources Defense Council's ongoing *The Bush Record*, said in the online environmental magazine *Grist*, 'Without fail, they announce their most controversial rollbacks just before the holidays, when most reporters are unavailable, or on Friday evenings at 5:00, after the network news has [been taped] and everybody's heading home; we call it the Friday Night Follies.' More than fifty initiatives or changes to existing regulations injurious to the environment have been announced by the Bush administration either on a Friday, just before a major holiday, or during a holiday weekend.

- On the evening of December 23, 2002, for instance, the Bush administration announced plans that would allow the paving over of hiking trails, dry streambeds, animal crossings, and old wagon paths to convert them into roads for moving heavy industrial equipment.

- On New Year's Eve, 2002, the Bush administration announced a change in the requirements that tuna canners must meet in order to put the 'dolphin-safe' guarantee on their products. *The New York Times* consigned its coverage to page four of the business section on New Year's Day.

- On Friday, August 22, 2003, the White House disclosed that it had finalized regulations allowing the nation's most polluting coal-fired power plants and refineries to upgrade their facilities without installing modern air quality controls. As Joel Connelly reported in the *Seattle Post-Intelligencer*, the original 'announcement of the plan came from an underling just before Thanksgiving . . . New rules formally easing the requirements were issued on New Year's Eve.'

- On October 10, 2003, the start of the Columbus Day weekend, the Department of the Interior quietly announced that it was overturning regulations that severely limited the amount of public land that can be used by mining companies for dumping their waste, thereby eliminating the restrictions on what is the largest volume of toxic material released in the United States each year.

- On Friday, January 23, 2004, the Bush administration reversed a Clinton-era rule designed to safeguard hundreds of rare animal and plant species from logging in national forests.

Fridays are also good days for releasing news antithetical to the Bush administration's antienvironmental mission.

- On Friday, September 26, 2003, the administration quietly released an Office of Management and Budget study that determined that environmental rules are good for the economy and well worth the costs they impose on industry and consumers, resulting in major public health benefits and other improvements.

Writing in *The Philadelphia Inquirer*, Walter Cronkite said that the major news organizations are complicit in this process. 'This slow death of our environment is a constant, ongoing threat. Every second of every minute of every day, our Earth is literally wearing out because of our mistreatment of it. Most of the more popular news media report on this piecemeal deterioration only when the environment suffers a dramatic blow – a major oil spill, for instance, or when a dense smog threatens the health of an entire region.' Fox News's Roger Ailes's response when Robert Kennedy Jr. asked why his network doesn't report on the environment more often was, 'If you release toxics into the air, people don't get sick for 20 years. We need something that is happening this afternoon. The polar ice caps melting – that's just too slow for us to cover.'

With the notable exception of the Reagan presidency, not since the administration of President Warren Harding in the 1920s – which resulted in Teapot Dome, the most damning political scandal of the last century – has a White House so staffed its departments with people who used to represent the corporate interests they now have jurisdiction over. It could fairly be said that the only green things the president and the people he has put in charge of our environment cherish are printed at the U.S. Mint. The nation's biggest polluters not only donated $44 million to the Bush–Cheney 2000 campaign and the RNC, they also provided a virtual hiring pool for the incoming administration. These are the people Bush has put in charge of taking care of America's air, land, and water:

Dick Cheney, vice president and head of the White House's Energy Task Force

- He is the former CEO of the oil-service contractor Halliburton.
- Halliburton is under investigation by the Justice Department, the SEC, and a French court for several of its

business dealings. One that could come back to haunt Cheney is France's investigation in particular. A judge there is examining whether he can be held accountable for alleged bribes of $180 million made by Kellogg, Brown & Root, a subsidiary, and its partner in a consortium to secure a contract to build a natural gas complex in Nigeria, even if Cheney wasn't aware that some of the alleged bribes were made while he was CEO.

▪ He convened the Energy Task Force – and in complete secrecy (more on this later).

Spencer Abraham, energy secretary

▪ As a senator from Michigan in the 1990s, he introduced legislation that sought to abolish the very government department he now heads.

▪ As a senator, he also backed legislation that would have allowed drilling in the Arctic National Wildlife Refuge.

▪ According to the League of Conservation Voters, in 2000, Abraham's re-election campaign accepted more campaign contributions from the automotive industry than any other congressional candidate – over $700,000.

▪ As energy secretary, he was one of the principal architects of a White House initiative that, although raising certain SUV standards by just 1.5 miles per gallon (by 2007), will allow more SUVs to qualify for lower standards by increasing their weight. He then actively promoted tax incentives for purchasers of the largest and least fuel-efficient of these vehicles.

Gale Norton, secretary of the interior

▪ As a lawyer, she represented oil, logging, and mining interests and challenged the constitutionality of the Endangered Species Act.

- As a lobbyist, she represented the lead paint industry.
- She was a protégé of Reagan interior secretary James Watt, who resigned under pressure in 1981. The Sierra Club considered him 'public enemy No. 1' and collected more than one million signatures calling for Watt's dismissal. Watt once said that 'the only way to eliminate pollution is to eliminate people and I'm opposed to that.' He produced an offshore leasing plan that offered more than one billion acres – practically the entire U.S. coastline – for oil and gas drilling. He also brokered the largest coal lease sale in history, auctioning off more than a billion tons of coal in the Powder River Basin of Montana and Wyoming.
- Rodger Schlickeisen, president of the conservationist organization Defenders of Wildlife, has called Norton 'the greatest threat to America's wildlife and natural heritage today.'
- The National Center for Policy Analysis reported, 'Another position that puts Gale Norton firmly outside the mainstream is her belief that polluters should be allowed to police themselves . . . and when Norton implemented this "self-policing" scheme as Attorney General of Colorado, she let polluters keep their criminal confessions a secret, a move that was denounced by the EPA.'
- Norton is charged with protecting not only America's wildlife but also the nation's 507 million acres of public land.

J. Steven Griles, deputy secretary, Department of the Interior

- As an executive, he was a senior vice president of United Company, an international gas, oil, and coal development concern.
- He was, like Norton, a Watt protégé.

- As a lobbyist, he represented the National Mining Association, Shell Oil, Chevron, and Occidental Petroleum. In 2001, after his confirmation, Griles sold his client list for $1.1 million to National Environmental Strategies in which he maintained a principal interest. Since the arrangement was for Griles to receive four payments of $284,000 over four years, the interior deputy secretary was, in effect, receiving income from his former clients.
- As Norton's deputy, he has met with former clients and industry lobbyists dozens upon dozens of times, including fifteen sit-downs with representatives of the National Mining Association, after which, according to Schlickeisen, he 'then helped clear the way for more coal mining in wetlands.'
- He fought for oil drilling off the coast of California, thereby benefiting former client Shell Oil.

Rebecca Watson, assistant secretary for land and minerals management, Department of the Interior
- As a lawyer, her firms represented coal-bed methane-drilling companies and mining interests, including Glamis Gold, Ltd.
- In her Interior job, according to *Mother Jones*, she signed off on a decision to allow a mining company to dig for gold on a sacred Native American site in California. The mining company: Glamis Gold, Ltd.

David Bernhardt, director of congressional and legislative affairs, Department of the Interior
- As a lawyer, he represented oil, mining, and chemical interests.
- In his job at Interior, he has dismissed the environmental concerns of the government's own scientists regarding drilling in the Arctic National Wildlife Refuge.

Allan Fitzsimmons, wildland fuels coordinator, Department of the Interior

- As a consultant, he wrote, 'The main problem is that ecosystems are not real . . . [they are] only mental constructs, not real, discrete or living things on the landscape. The second problem is that even if they were real, we have no idea of what their "health" or "integrity" might mean.'

- Fitzsimmons is the man in charge of Bush's Healthy Forests initiative.

Bennett Raley, assistant secretary for water and science, Department of the Interior

- As lawyer and lobbyist, he represented water utilities and property-rights groups, and in testimony he gave to a congressional committee, he advocated repeal of the Endangered Species Act.

- In his job at Interior, in 2002, 'he allotted water from Oregon's Klamath River to irrigators rather than to endangered fish, leading to a massive salmon die-off,' according to a report in *Mother Jones*.

Patricia Lynn Scarlett, assistant secretary for policy, management and budget, Department of the Interior

- She was president of the Reason Foundation, a libertarian organization funded by industry groups such as the American Petroleum Institute, the American Forest and Paper Association, Shell Oil, and Union Carbide.

- Scarlett has interesting views about the environment, to say the least. She thinks disposable products are not harmful to the ecosystem. She says that the United States is not running out of resources. She says that Americans are not wasteful. She says, in fact, that all three of these issues are myths.

- She is the architect of the White House's plan to privatize

National Park Service jobs and the administration's opposition to turning the Gaviota Coast of California into a national seashore.

William G. Myers, former solicitor general, Department of the Interior

- As a lawyer and lobbyist, he represented the National Cattlemen's Beef Association, Kennecott Energy, and the National Mining Association.
- Even during his nomination process, he continued to represent ranching and banking interests in a legal case involving the rights of ranchers to use public grazing land permits as collateral for loans.
- He resigned as solicitor general in October 2003 while under investigation for ethics violations by the department's inspector general. (He was eventually cleared.)
- He was nominated by Bush to the Ninth Circuit Court of Appeals, which has jurisdiction over 485 million of America's 507 million acres of public land.

Ann M. Veneman, agriculture secretary

- When Abraham Lincoln created the USDA, he called it the 'People's Department.' The agency is steward of 192 million acres of national forests and rangelands. The USDA is also responsible for maintaining food safety standards for all U.S. citizens.
- Veneman served on the board of Calgene, a pioneer in genetically modified foods that was later bought by Monsanto, which itself was later purchased by Pharmacia.
- According to Earthjustice, a public interest law firm, while campaigning for Bush before the 2000 election, Veneman assured California farmers that with Bush in the White House, they would no longer be subjected to 'unnecessary and burdensome' environmental regulations.

- The Madison, Wisconsin, *Capital Times* reported farm activist Mark Ritchie as describing Veneman as having a notably 'pro-agribusiness, pro-pesticide company, pro-pharmaceutical company positions.'

Mark Rey, undersecretary for natural resources and environment, Department of Agriculture

- As a lobbyist, he spent two decades working for logging interests.
- As the Bush administration's top forestry official, he has been instrumental in the White House's Healthy Forests initiative that promotes increased logging in public forests.

Mike Leavitt, administrator, Environmental Protection Agency

- As former governor of Utah, he left the state in only slightly better environmental shape than Bush left Texas.
- Texas is the #1 state for poor air quality and toxic releases. Utah is #2.
- A 2003 EPA report on how states measured up in six key areas under the Clean Water Act found Utah to be the worst in the nation, tied with Ohio and Tennessee.
- As governor, Leavitt worked out a deal with Gale Norton that stripped away protections for 2.5 million acres of Utah public land – much of it red rock country – under consideration for wilderness designation.
- Leavitt now oversees the agency charged with safeguarding the environment and protecting U.S. citizens from the effects of toxins and pollutants.

James L. Connaughton, chairman, White House Council on Environmental Quality

- As a lobbyist, he acted on behalf of utilities and corporations fighting Superfund cleanup regulations.

- As the president's senior environmental adviser, Connaughton's strategy has been to ignore global warming and ease air-quality regulations.

Jeffrey Holmstead, assistant administrator, air and radiation, Environmental Protection Agency

- As a lawyer, he fought the EPA on pesticide control on behalf of the American Farm Bureau Federation.
- In the Senior Bush's administration, Holmstead served as an assistant to presidential counsel C. Boyden Gray. The two opposed William Reilly, Bush's EPA chief, who in 1990 pushed for adjustments to strengthen the Clean Air Act. Holmstead is now in charge of the nation's Clean Air Act.

Elsewhere in the administration there are dozens of others with backgrounds in the energy industries. 'Thirty-one of the Bush transition team's forty-eight members had energy-industry ties,' Robert Kennedy Jr. wrote in *Rolling Stone*. 'Bush's cabinet and White House staff is an energy-industry dream team – four cabinet secretaries, the six most powerful White House officials and more than twenty high-level appointees are alumni of the industry and its allies.'

At the Environmental Protection Agency, Bush's appointments and initiatives proved to be so ideological, antienvironmental, and overtly political that there has been a flurry of resignations and retirements. These include EPA administrator Christine Todd Whitman (resigned May 2003); Jeremy Symons, a climate policy adviser and a member of Cheney's Energy Task Force (April 2001); Eric Schaeffer, director of the Office of Regulatory Enforcement (February 2002); Sylvia Lowrance, acting director of the Office of Enforcement and Compliance (August 2002); Bruce Boler, a biologist (October 2003); Bruce Buckheit, director of the Air Enforcement Division (December 2003); Rich Biondi, associate director of air enforcement (December 2003); John Suarez, the EPA's top enforcement official (January 2004); Marianne Lamont Horinko, assistant administrator for the Office of Solid Waste and Emergency Reponse (April 2004).

Big Republican donors expected a return on their investment following the 2000 presidential election, and Bush was more than willing to deliver. Koch Industries, the country's largest privately held oil-gas-chemicals conglomerate, donated $800,000 to the Republicans in 2000. When the Bush team came into office, Koch faced a ninety-seven-count felony indictment and '$357 million in fines' for, as Kennedy put it, 'knowingly releasing ninety metric tons of carcinogenic benzene and concealing the releases from federal regulators.' The Department of Justice dropped many of the charges. The court accepted a guilty plea to one count of concealment of information from a Koch subsidiary that had also been charged. Koch also agreed to pay US $10 million in criminal fines and the same amount for community service programs

In 2001, Peabody Energy, the world's largest coal company, proposed construction of the biggest coal-fired power plant in America in decades. Peabody wanted to build the plant just sixty miles from Kentucky's Mammoth Cave National Park, which already has the worst visibility of any U.S. national park. After the Fish and Wildlife Service questioned the plan, Peabody met with Fran Mainella, director of the National Park Service.

Around the same time, Peabody and one of its subsidiaries forwarded $300,000 in soft money to the Republican Party. The process to approve the permit for the plant was put into high gear. Peabody then made a $50,000 donation. The permit was granted. Two weeks later, Peabody kicked in an additional $100,000.

So the Republican Party got $450,000 and Peabody got its plant. This chain of events, from the meeting with Mainella to the approval of the plant, took less than three months, though

Peabody claims the money was pledged earlier and was not related to the plant. Never let it be said that the wheels of government move slowly.

A prime impediment to the administration's goal of paying back its 'investors' is the National Environmental Policy Act, which was signed into law by President Richard Nixon in 1970. It's considered to be America's environmental Magna Carta. The NEPA's mission is eloquent and simple: 'To declare a national policy which will encourage productive and enjoyable harmony between man and his environment; to promote efforts which will prevent or eliminate damage to the environment and biosphere and stimulate the health and welfare of man; to enrich the understanding of the ecological systems and natural resources important to the Nation . . .'

How has the Bush White House treated this document? According to Michigan representative John Dingell, who wrote the original statute, 'The Bush administration has undertaken a full frontal assault on this bedrock environmental law. Almost immediately after he was elected, President Bush appointed a NEPA task force. The goal of this task force, in the words of administration officials, is to "get faster decisions."' It should be noted that when it comes to the environment, 'faster decisions,' 'streamlining,' and 'modernizing' are Bush administration code words for excluding public discourse on environmental decisions and for scaling back impact analysis prior to initiating legislation. In its first two years in office, the Bush White House was the instrumental force in ninety-four court cases that pursued outcomes actively hostile toward the NEPA.

Environmental enforcement at the EPA has plunged under Bush. Since 2001, monthly violation notices – the most important tool against polluters – are down 58 percent from Clinton's monthly average.

The Bush administration has also taken the antienvironment fight beyond American shores, not only causing damage to global ecosystems but also further eroding America's already spotty reputation as a responsible superpower. In its first three years in office, the Bush White House rejected, undercut, or ignored many of the world's international environmental treaties, including

- The Kyoto Protocol, the 1997 international agreement ratified or accepted by 122 nations that requires cuts in greenhouse gas emissions from industrialized countries. 'Kyoto is not acceptable to the administration or Congress . . . Kyoto is dead,' National Security Adviser Condoleezza Rice told fifteen ambassadors from nations in the European Union. (See also Chapter 10, 'Reputation.')
- The Montreal Protocol, the 1987 treaty signed by more than 150 nations that sought to limit production of substances harmful to the ozone layer.
- The Stockholm Convention on Persistent Organic Pollutants, the 2001 treaty signed by more than 150 nations that put limits on the production of twelve toxic, decay-resistant chemicals including dioxins, polychlorinated biphenyls, and pesticides.

Bush convened his National Energy Policy Development Group nine days after taking office. This was the panel that came to be known as the vice president's Energy Task Force. For almost four months, Cheney, Energy Secretary Abraham, and other cabinet secretaries and their deputies formulated the nation's energy policy behind the closed doors of the vice president's office and the Cabinet Room. *The New York Times* reported that eighteen of the Republicans' top twenty-five donors from the energy industry were invited in and asked to contribute to the plan. Kenneth Lay of Enron, who had loaned Bush his company jet during his presidential campaign, met with the group numerous times. Executives from such companies and organizations as Chevron, Exxon-Mobile, the Nuclear Energy Institute, Westinghouse, Edison

Electric Institute, and the American Petroleum Institute consulted with the committee between six and nineteen times. The administration even used access to the task force to strong-arm energy interests to chip in more to the Republicans. As Robert Kennedy Jr. reported, 'When Westar Energy's chief executive was indicted for fraud, investigators found an e-mail written by Westar executives describing solicitations by Republican politicians for a political action committee controlled by Tom DeLay as the price for a "seat at the table" with the task force.' DeLay said the allegations had no substance and would be dealt with by the Ethics Committee.

Upward of 400 executives from 150 corporations and trade associations met with the task force from February to May 2001. And yet the Cheney group did not speak to a single environmentalist during the meetings. Abraham said he didn't have time to meet them, and Cheney's office denied their requests for inclusion.

Cheney demanded that the meetings and records of the task force be kept confidential and safely away from the prying eyes of legislators, journalists, environmentalists, and the public. The move prompted David M. Walker, the comptroller general and head of the General Accounting Office, to take the vice president to court to force him to release the names and affiliations of the people he met with, as well as the cost of the task force. As Don Van Natta Jr. wrote in *The New York Times*, 'For the first time in the 81-year history of [the GAO], the auditing arm of Congress, the comptroller general of the United States went to federal court to ask a judge to order a member of the executive branch to turn over records to Congress.'

The U.S District Court in Washington DC dismissed the GAO suit. But Judicial Watch and the Sierra Club also filed a suit with the DC District Court. After the court ruled against the vice president he appealed to the Supreme Court. In June 2004, the Supreme Court handed Cheney a partial victory when it ordered the Lower Court to look at the case again. The ruling allows Cheney's task force documents to be kept secret until there is a final decision.

Cheney and his colleagues emerged with a National Energy Plan in May 2001. It included one hundred proposals and led to a massive energy bill with tax breaks for U.S. energy interests estimated by Congress's Joint Committee on Taxation at $23.5 billion, a 53,300 percent return on the $44 million it had donated to the Republicans during the previous year's election.

The day of the announcement, Bush flew to Minnesota and Iowa for photo ops of him visiting a plant and a research center looking into new ways of producing cheaper or alternative forms of energy. He said that his sweeping plan was built on a philosophy of conservation. 'I've laid out an initiative that said first and foremost, we better be conservationists in the country.' But Cheney had already preempted him. 'To speak exclusively of conservation is to duck the tough issues,' the vice president said earlier. 'Conservation may be a sign of personal virtue, but it is not a sufficient basis, all by itself, for a sound, comprehensive energy policy.'

So much for conservation.

In fact, there wasn't a single line in the energy bill requiring an increase in the fuel efficiency of the nation's 204 million passenger vehicles. (Nor, for that matter, was there any mention of global warming.) The plan did, however, include proposals that would have a new power plant built every week for the next twenty years. Senator John McCain, the Arizona Republican who joined the Democrats in eventually getting the legislation watered down, called the bill the 'Leave-No-Lobbyist-Behind Act.' Haley Barbour, a former Republican National Committee chairman and a leading lobbyist for the electricity industry, certainly earned his keep during Cheney's closed-door meetings. Barbour had urged Cheney to convince the president to abandon his campaign promise to regulate CO_2 emissions at power plants. And he succeeded. When asked about the turnaround, the president glibly said that he was 'responding to realities.' Five days after the energy plan was announced, Peabody Energy – whose CEO had met with the task force – issued a public stock offering that raised $60 million more than expected.

The president valiantly tried to sell Congress and the country on the urgency of the bill. 'If we fail to act, Americans will face more, and more widespread blackouts,' he said, adding that the United States also needed 'to come up with additional supplies.' The warnings of an 'energy crisis,' however, were less a call to arms than a covert way to get Congress to relax environmental regulatory laws that attempt to keep energy companies from polluting. Much of the urgency in the task force's report was pinned on California's energy crisis, which was later found to be a crisis of that state's energy industries' own making in order to drive up prices. And 'additional supplies' was code for opening up public lands to oil and gas concerns. According to the *Los Angeles Times*, in March 2001, a briefing paper prepared for a task force meeting with Bush stated that 'on the whole, U.S. energy markets are working well, allocating resources and preventing shortages.' But the Cheney task force's report said something completely different, claiming on its first page that 'America in the year 2001 faces the most serious energy shortage since the oil embargoes of the 1970s.'

The oil and gas industries got just about everything they wanted in the White House's energy bill.

- The bill offered incentives for deep offshore drilling and waived royalties for drilling on public land.
- The bill not only eliminated the secretary of the interior's authority to deny permits to oil companies wanting to drill on public land but also stated that oil and gas companies would be reimbursed for the costs of environmental impact studies – a gift that the Congressional Budget Office estimated would cost taxpayers $330 million over the next decade.
- All oil and gas companies were to be given exemption from the Clean Water Act for construction activities.
- Oil and natural gas companies involved in hydraulic fracturing, a drilling technique that can contaminate

groundwater, were granted exemptions from the Safe Drinking Water Act. According to a report from California Democratic congressman Henry Waxman, when congressional staff members pointed out the environmental dangers of hydraulic fracturing during the committee meetings, the White House and the EPA refigured the data on the drilling technique so that it appeared more ecologically inoffensive. (Cheney's old alma mater Halliburton is one of the nation's leading suppliers of hydraulic-fracturing services.)

▪ The bill addressed the petroleum industry's concern over an estimated $29 billion in lawsuits and cleanup costs resulting from a cancer-causing gasoline additive called methyl tertiary butyl ether, or MTBE, that has poisoned the water supplies of hundreds of communities nationwide. Lyondell Chemical Corp., the largest producer of MTBE in the country, happens to be located near House majority leader Tom DeLay's home district in Texas and is a major donor to Republican campaigns. Following an incredible Republicans-only private conference committee session, DeLay got a provision written into the energy bill giving companies like Lyondell legislative protection from a range of lawsuits. This provision, which could have potentially saved the companies as much as $1 billion in cleanup fees, proved to be too much for even some Republicans to support – six joined the Democratic opposition. With the bill's passage seemingly doomed, Bush phoned DeLay and asked him to drop the MTBE provision. DeLay's response to Bush: no.

There were other little add-ons to the bill that had almost nothing to do with energy and everything to do with getting wayward representatives on the bus. One called for a set of five development projects to be financed by tax-exempt bonds at a cost to taxpayers of $350 million. The projects included the construction of a $2.2 billion shopping mall in Syracuse, New York, three times the cost of Minnesota's Mall of America. Another involved an urban renewal project in Bossier City, Louisiana, that included construction of a Hooters restaurant.

With DeLay's refusal to remove the MTBE provision, the bill had little chance of passing, and in November 2003 the Senate blocked the vote. The bill's backers forged ahead, and in May 2004 a package of $14 billion in tax breaks from the stalled energy bill was attached to an unrelated bill on corporate tax reform. The Senate approved the tax reform legislation, which awarded the bulk of the tax breaks to the oil and gas industries. After its passage, Senator John McCain, who had lobbied to remove the energy tax cut package from the bill, said, 'with a half-trillion dollar deficit, we're giving tax credits, for guess who, the [oil] industry in America, which last time I checked was doing really well.'

The White House's National Energy Plan aside, the administration has produced legislation and regulations actively hostile to the nation's environment. A report card:

THE CLEAN AIR ACT

Three decades after the passage of the Clean Air Act, almost one in three Americans still breathes air filled with nitrous oxide, sulfur dioxide, carbon dioxide, coal dust, mercury, and hundreds of other toxic pollutants. They cause everything from headaches and breathing problems like bronchitis to premature death and spine and brain damage in young children. The pollution comes from myriad sources, but within the energy business, the prime culprit is coal, which powers half of America's electricity and causes 90 percent of the electric power industry's pollution. Two years after Bush took office, the rollbacks of pollution regulations had caused sales of pollution-control equipment for coal plants to drop dramatically. According to an article in the *Los Angeles Times,* the firms belonging to the Institute of Clean Air Companies, a trade group comprising a third of the industry, saw their sales decline from $1 billion in 2001 to $75 million in the first half of 2003. 'Orders for the future are almost non-existent,' David Foerter, the executive director of the eighty-member association, told the *Times.* 'It's like falling off a cliff.'

The Bush administration's attack on the Clean Air Act was fought on three fronts:

- Rolling back New Source Review regulations
- Promoting its Clear Skies initiative
- Weakening mercury emissions standards

New Source Review

New coal plants have to meet Clean Air Act standards. A goal of the Clinton administration was to get old coal companies to add new pollution controls anytime they upgraded or enlarged their facilities. The New Source Review passed by Congress in 1977 made this a requirement by altering the grandfather clause in the Clean Air Act that old plants invoked when they performed their upgrades – their argument being that they shouldn't have to spend the extra money modernizing their pollution controls because they weren't 'new' coal plants. New Source Review treated all major upgrades or expansions of old plants as new energy sources and therefore accountable to Clean Air Act standards. Full implementation would, according to the Department of Energy, lower sulfur dioxide emissions from roughly 10 million to around 3 million tons a year, and nitrous oxide emissions from 4.5 million to 1.6 million tons a year.

In February 2000, when he was running for president, Bush told Tim Russert on *Meet the Press,* 'I'm the first person to say,

'We're going to stop this grandfathering business. We're going to bring plants into compliance.' '

In September 2000, according to a report by the Public Interest Research Group, he reiterated this promise. 'With the help of Congress, environmental groups, and industry, we will require all power plants to meet clean air standards in order to reduce emissions of sulfur dioxide, nitrogen oxide, mercury and carbon dioxide within a reasonable period of time, and we will provide market-based incentives such as emissions trading to help industry achieve the required reductions.'

Then, in November 2003, Bush did the exact opposite of what he had promised as a candidate. He announced that the administration was watering down the New Source Review program so that aging, dirty coal plants that upgraded their facilities would not necessarily also have to upgrade their pollution-control equipment. The rollback covers more than just coal plants; it eases restrictions on more than twenty-two thousand utilities, industrial concerns, and refineries. The details of the announcement:

- It was made on a Friday.
- Bush was out of the country at the time.
- An assistant EPA administrator delivered the briefing.
- No cameras or film crews were allowed.

The effects of the decision are quantifiable. Reports by both the GAO and the Rockefeller Family Fund calculated that an additional 1.4 million tons of air pollution would be released in twelve states, though many more will be affected. The National Academy of Sciences estimates that the change in the law will result in thirty thousand American deaths. In December 2002, an alliance of attorneys general from twenty-four states and attorneys from thirty cities and municipalities sued the EPA, arguing that the new rules would violate the Clean Air Act. In December 2003, the DC Circuit Court agreed for now and issued a temporary injunction preventing the EPA from implementing the new rules until the case is settled.

Clear Skies

In July 2002, Bush announced that his Clear Skies initiative would lower most power plant emissions by 70 percent by the year 2018. 'In the next decade alone,' he said, 'Clear Skies will eliminate 35 million more tons of pollution than the current Clean Air Act, bringing cleaner air to millions of Americans.'

In fact, the Natural Resources Defense Council (NRDC), the Sierra Club, and other environmental groups all say that Clear Skies targets are dramatically lower than those of the existing Clean Air Act. Also

- Clear Skies includes no regulation of carbon dioxide emissions, 40 percent of which come from power plants.
- Clear Skies allows for 68 percent more nitrous oxide by the end of the decade than the Clean Air Act.
- Clear Skies allows for 225 percent more sulfur dioxide emissions by the end of the decade than the Clean Air Act.
- Clear Skies allows for 520 percent more mercury releases by the end of the decade than the Clean Air Act.

The EPA produced its own program for reducing power plant emissions, which was much tougher than the White House's plan. It also did an analysis of its program, which was obtained by *The New York Times*. 'The documents say that the agency's proposal would prevent at least 19,000 premature deaths, 12,000 new cases of chronic bronchitis, and 17,000 hospitalizations and would save about $154 billion in annual health care costs by 2020.'

According to papers obtained by Henry Waxman, of the sixty-six people who met with Deputy Energy Secretary Francis S. Blake to talk about clean air rules, sixty-five were from the energy industry.

The White House rejected the EPA's proposal. And Congress rejected the Bush administration's plan. For now. In May 2004, Clear Skies legislation remained stalled in Congress.

In a study released in June 2004, Abt Associates, a research firm that the Bush administration commissioned to analyze Clear Skies, compared the Bush plan with two other proposed legislative plans to cut power plant emissions and found Bush's to be the least effective, eliminating 32 percent fewer deaths per year than the best of the three measures. In addition, the estimated value of health benefits of the White House initiative was $62 billion lower than the top plan, which is being sponsored by Senator James Jeffords, Independent of Vermont. Not surprisingly, the Bush plan would cost the industry the least amount of money.

Mercury Emissions Standards

Coal-fired power plants produce almost 40 percent of the mercury pollution in the United States – an estimated forty-eight tons annually – and are the largest single source of mercury pollution. The Natural Resources Defense Council has estimated that mercury pollution has contaminated '12 million acres of lakes, estuaries and wetlands, and 473,000 miles of streams, rivers and coastlines.'

Like lead in lead-based paints, mercury is a highly potent neurotoxin. It affects the brain and nervous system of fetuses and young children. It also may be linked to autism, Parkinson's disease, and Alzheimer's disease. Most commonly, you get mercury poison from eating fish. Although many types of fish carry a certain amount of mercury in their bloodstreams, tuna has one of the highest levels. More than 80 percent of all tuna is eaten in the form of canned tuna, and much of that is used in children's lunches. In early 2003, the Centers for Disease Control and Prevention found that 8 percent of all American women of child-bearing age (almost five million) have dangerous amounts of mercury levels, and 15 percent of the four million children born each year do as well.

An EPA study conducted before the 2000 presidential election and released in 2001 estimated that mercury emissions could be cut by as much as 90 percent if advanced technology were used.

So has the Bush administration followed this path? No. Instead it downgraded mercury as a less rigidly controlled pollutant. The EPA under the Bush White House proposed a plan to cap mercury emissions at thirty-four tons a year by 2010 and, by 2018, reduce the cap to fifteen tons. This cap, the NRDC reported, 'would allow nearly seven times more annual mercury emissions for five times longer than current law.' An EPA report that warned of mercury's danger to small children was filed in May 2002. The White House sat on it until February 2003 before it quietly released it.

How did coal interests get the White House on their side? The electric power and coal industries gave $16 million to Bush and the Republicans for the 2000 elections. And they lobbied. *The Washington Post* reported that the lobbyists' epistolary contributions helped draft the legislation that loosened the mercury regulatory standards. 'A side-by-side comparison of one of the three proposed rules and the memorandums prepared by [the energy-heavy law firm] Latham & Watkins . . . shows that at least a dozen paragraphs were lifted, sometimes verbatim, from the industry suggestions.' Jeffrey R. Holmstead, a former lawyer for Latham & Watkins, is head of the EPA's Office of Air and Radiation.

In May 2004, after an outcry over the administration's proposed mercury rules, EPA director Leavitt announced that the EPA would take the next three months to reexamine the legislation. Its final decision is due in March 2005.

FUEL EFFICIENCY STANDARDS

The United States has 5 percent of the world's population and uses between 25 percent and 30 percent of the world's oil. (The United Kingdom, by comparison, has less than 2 percent of the world's population and uses 2% of the world's oil.) We import 63 percent of that oil, at a cost of nearly $200,000 per minute. (In 1983, we imported only 28 percent.) And in the Bush administration, access to imported oil is arguably the single greatest factor in domestic and foreign policy – outside of religion. (The day I wrote this sentence, ten American soldiers died in Iraq, which has 11 percent of the world's oil reserves.) More than two-thirds of the foreign oil we use is burned as transportation fuel. Incredibly, overall fuel economy ratings in the United States are worse now than they were in 1988. By comparison, in Europe, according to *The New York Times,* gas mileage in 1998 was already close to thirty miles per gallon and now averages almost thirty-five miles per gallon. Japanese cars, by 2002, were averaging more than thirty-four miles per gallon, fast approaching Japan's 2010 goal of 35.5 miles per gallon.

Why is America so far behind? The 2.5 million SUVs sold every year is a significant factor.

Actually, that's wrong – it's essentially the *only* factor. SUVs produce almost 45 percent more air pollution than average cars. The Union of Concerned Scientists says that if SUVs and minivans were to meet the same fuel efficiency standards as cars, U.S. oil use would be cut by one million barrels per day by 2010. The federal corporate average fuel economy standards, or CAFE as they are soothingly called, set fuel economy goals for new passenger cars at 27.5 miles per gallon. But this excludes SUVs, which, together with vans and pickup trucks, comprise 50 percent of the vehicles sold today. SUVs are not even categorized as 'cars'; they're on the books as 'light trucks' and therefore have to average only 20.7 miles per gallon. Because of the complexities of the

CAFE regulations, it's technically possible for SUVs to have fuel efficiency standards as low as twelve miles per gallon. Vehicles over eighty-five hundred pounds, such as the Ford Excursion and the Hummer, are so heavy they don't even qualify as 'light trucks' and therefore are beyond the reach of any kind of fuel economy standards.

According to a report prepared by the Sierra Club, the difference in energy consumption each year between driving a regular car and a thirteen-miles-per-gallon SUV is equal to

- Leaving your refrigerator door open for six years.
- Leaving a lightbulb burning for thirty years.
- Leaving your TV on for twenty-eight years.

Not only did the White House energy bill not set fuel standards for SUVs, the Republican-led Congress changed an IRS rule increasing a tax benefit that encourages the purchase of the largest, least-efficient models. In 1986, Congress had passed a tax deduction provision for equipment purchases, including trucks weighing more than six thousand pounds. It was intended to help owners of commercial vehicles, specifically small businesses, and was capped at $25,000. In 2003, Congress quadrupled the deduction to $100,000. Never in 1986 did legislators anticipate that less than two decades later, three-ton vehicles would be needed to ferry suburban kids to soccer games or rap stars to nightclubs. If you're in the 35 percent income tax bracket and you buy a $106,000 Hummer for 'business' use, the IRS gives you a rebate of $35,000 on the purchase in the first year.

At the opposite end of the spectrum – and the tax code – are fifty-miles-per-gallon hybrids, which run on both fuel and electricity. These are the cars favored by Vermont residents and Hollywood liberals who drive them to public events when they don't want to be seen driving their SUVs. Purchasers of hybrids, which the three major auto manufacturers would rather not produce, get a $1,500 tax deduction, which shrinks by $500 a year until 2006. The NRDC estimates that if automakers greatly increased the production of hybrids and made conventional cars more efficient, overall fuel economy rates for new vehicles could rise to forty miles per gallon by 2012 and fifty-five miles per gallon by 2020. This would cut projected U.S. oil needs by 50 percent in 2020 and save consumers almost $30 billion per year by then. Even the Republican-controlled EPA estimates that a three-mile-per-gallon increase in overall fuel efficiency standards would save Americans $25 billion a year in oil costs and reduce annual CO_2 emissions by 155 million tons.

THE AIR AT GROUND ZERO

As someone who lives thirty-four blocks from where the World Trade Center towers once stood and watched them come down from the corner of Seventh Avenue and Eleventh Street, I will say this: It didn't take a scientist to know that the air downtown was foul and that it was going to have serious health effects on the tens of thousands of rescue workers and volunteers from all over the continent who spent months undoing that mountain of deformed, smoldering steel and rubble.

This is how the EPA handled the issue of air quality at Ground Zero:

- September 12. The day after the attacks, the office of EPA head Christine Todd Whitman told agency employees that 'all statements to the media should be cleared through the National Security Council, headed by [Condoleezza Rice] before they are released.'
- September 13. The agency issued a news release saying, 'EPA is greatly relieved to have learned that there appears to be no significant levels of asbestos dust in the air in New

York City.' A section in the original draft of the release had
stated that 'even at low levels, EPA considers asbestos
hazardous in this situation . . .' It was deleted by the White
House and the NSC.

- September 16. The agency issued a further notice saying,
'The new samples confirm previous reports that ambient air
quality meets [Occupational Safety and Health
Administration] standards and consequently is not a cause
for public concern.' The White House and the NSC
removed the following from the original draft of the
statement: 'Recent samples of dust gathered by OSHA on
Water Street [almost a half mile from the Trade Center]
show higher levels of asbestos than in EPA tests.'

- September 18. Whitman pronounced that the air at Ground
Zero was 'safe to breathe.'

And on it went. The White House was eager to reassure Wall
Street employees that the air around them was safe, so that the
New York Stock Exchange could be reopened quickly. The EPA
followed along by repeatedly delivering deceptively upbeat news.

In reality, the air quality was toxic and extremely dangerous. As
the 110-story buildings fell, millions of tons of pulverized material
exploded into the sky, carrying all manner of toxins. Some details:

- When they were built between 1968 and 1973, both towers
were fireproofed with material manufactured by W. R.
Grace. The fireproofing, like most installations in those
days, contained asbestos. It's not dangerous in its installed
state, but airborne asbestos is lethal, even small amounts. A
memorandum written by Cate Jenkins, while she was a
senior chemist with the EPA, states that the level of
asbestos in the apartments near Ground Zero was
'comparable to or higher' than that in the homes in Libby,
Montana, where the W. R. Grace mine had, over thirty

years, produced what is possibly the worst Superfund disaster in American history. Jenkins found that dust collected from a windowsill four blocks from Ground Zero contained seventy-nine thousand fibers per square centimeter of asbestos – twenty-two times higher than the levels found in Libby.

- Also in that enormous cloud were fumes from 150,000 gallons of fuel and 30,000 gallons of waste oil from the buildings' huge electrical transformers, containing high amounts of PCBs, one of the most toxic industrial chemicals.

- The thousands of shattered windows sent billions of microscopic glass particles into the air.

- The explosion of thousands of laptop computers and fluorescent lights released dangerous amounts of mercury, which as noted above can cause nerve damage and birth defects.

- The air was filled with tens of thousands of tons of concrete particles, as well as dioxin, another chemical that can cause neurological disorders and birth defects.

- The *St. Louis Post-Dispatch* reported that the U.S. Geological Survey had a team testing the particulate dust covering the immediate area and 'found that some of the dust was as caustic as liquid drain cleaner and alerted all government agencies involved in the emergency response.'

On December 27, 2002, the Friday between Christmas and New Year – with the site cleared, the Stock Market fully operational, and the buildings around Ground Zero filling back up with tenants – the EPA at least came clean, issuing its final report on air quality. The report said that the buildings' collapse produced the largest concentration of dioxin ever recorded.

The epilogue is both predictable and tragic. According to testimony given before a congressional hearing, as many as 50 percent of workers at the site who were screened now suffer from long-term health problems – and 40 percent of those don't have health insurance. A report prepared by the Mount Sinai School of Medicine found that 78 percent of the workers at Ground Zero were suffering from respiratory or lung ailments and 88 percent had ear, nose, or throat problems. By early 2003, twenty-four hundred members of the New York Fire Department were on disability leave. Many of the workers at the site have been unable to collect workers' compensation.

In May 2004, the New York *Daily News* reported that in 'a dramatic sign of escalating health problems stemming from 9/11, more than 1,700 cops and firefighters have filed lawsuits against the city claiming they were sickened by work at Ground Zero or the Fresh Kills landfill. To handle the unprecedented legal overload, the city's Law Department set up a special division to tackle 9/11 claims and appointed attorney Kenneth Becker as chief of the World Trade Center unit.'

Pulitzer Prize-winning reporter Laurie Garrett described John Graham, who in his capacity as a health and safety inspector for the Carpenters' Union had been at the site for 262 days and testified at the hearing, as in ill health and permanently disabled. 'He displayed a sack full of medications he now uses,' she wrote in *Newsday,* 'including an anti-asthma drug, an antibiotic, an inhaler . . . and assorted steroids.'

WATER

The Clean Water Act, passed by Congress over Nixon's veto in 1972, was established not only to regulate the nation's drinking water but also to protect its rivers and lakes for activities like fishing, swimming, and other water sports. According to the NRDC, thirty years later, 75 percent of Americans live within ten miles of a polluted river, lake, or coastal water. (The U.S. military is the biggest polluter in the world, generating an estimated 750,000 tons of toxic waste around the world every year. According to the media research group Project Censored, the Pentagon has ten thousand employees who do nothing but handle the legal technicalities of this polluting. Their budget: $2 billion.) Clean water has been under systematic, aggressive attack by the Bush administration, whose policies have sought to remove protection from twenty million acres of wetlands; permit inadequately treated sewage to be pumped into our rivers, streams, and other waters; and allow mountaintop-mining companies to dump their waste directly into waterways (more on this later).

Politicians should know that clean water is a major concern of voters. In a nationwide poll taken in 2002, 81 percent of respondents said it was an important factor in whom they vote for.

Perhaps mindful of this, on October 18, 2002, the thirtieth anniversary of the passage of the Clean Water Act, the White House named October 2002–October 2003 the Year of Clean Water with a pronouncement from the president that began, 'I George W. Bush . . . call upon all Americans . . . to join in setting good examples of environmental stewardship in our daily lives.'

This was the same George W. Bush who on January 20, 2001, his first day in office, ordered a moratorium on Clinton-era Clean Water Act regulations controlling the discharge of raw sewage from what the waste industry likes to call 'sanitary sewers.' By November 2003 – just a month after the Year of Clean Water had ended – the administration took the moratorium a step farther when the EPA announced a plan to allow sewage treatment plants to release biologically untreated waste into rivers and other waterways. But only on rainy days. The EPA is not without its own gift for euphemism: It calls the simultaneous release of treated sewage and inadequately treated sewage 'blending.'

In July 2003, smack in the middle of Bush's Year of Clean Water, the administration, through the EPA, refused to add any contaminants to the list of those regulated, including perchlorate, a rocket fuel ingredient that can cause thyroid problems and cancer. There are dangerous amounts of this chemical in twenty million Americans' drinking water. Another contaminant the administration refused to add to the regulatory list was the gasoline additive MTBE. It can affect the nervous system and cause stomach and liver illnesses and possibly even cancer. The three largest producers of MTBE were all major donors to the Bush–Cheney campaign.

Bush made countless stabs at reducing the quality of America's waters, and in a number of cases they were so outrageous that he was forced to back down following public protests.

Just before Clinton left the White House, for instance, the EPA issued a rule that the maximum arsenic level in drinking water should be lowered to ten parts per billion. The old standard, which had been established in 1942, was fifty parts per billion, a level that is estimated by the National Academy of Sciences to cause an extremely high cancer risk. Within two months of taking office, Bush sought to increase the levels of arsenic in Americans' drinking water to the old level. Following public and political protest, he quietly backed down.

On April 17, 2001, right before Bush's first Earth Day as president, the White House pledged that the 'administration will continue to take responsible steps to ensure that we preserve [wetlands] for future generations of Americans.' This should have been a balm for environmentalists. Wetlands are not only pollution filters, they also are the habitats for numerous endangered species as well as for other fish, birds, and wildlife.

By January 2002, it was revealed that the Army Corps of Engineers, which is in charge of granting permits to developers who want to build on or near wetlands, had loosened its rules to allow individual developers to destroy up to three acres of wetlands, up from the Clinton-era limit of half an acre, as well as eliminated the requirement of acre-for-acre replacement of destroyed wetlands. The plan was a violation not only of the Clean

Water Act but also of the Endangered Species Act and the National Environmental Policy Act. When the Fish and Wildlife Service predicted that the plan would cause 'tremendous destruction of aquatic and terrestrial habitat,' Interior Secretary Norton suppressed the study. She even overrode the concerns of her own biologists and scientists.

In January 2003, Bush administration officials made a brash attempt to rewrite the Clean Water Act by eliminating completely the protection of 'isolated' wetlands, ponds, bogs, and streams having a seemingly tenuous connection with other waterways, a plan that would affect upward of twenty million acres of wetlands. The White House also shifted the balance between those granting licenses and those applying for them by instructing the Corps of Engineers and the EPA to ensure that developers would no longer require permits. The rule placed the onus on government agencies – henceforth *they* would be the ones forced to apply for protection approval.

In December 2003, Bush backed down on the proposal. Why? First, more than 130,000 citizens wrote in opposing the new rule. And he came up against a special interest group he hadn't counted on: the 'hook-and-bullet' crowd – fishermen and hunters who have become an environmental force in Washington. The *Los Angeles Times* reported that 'President Bush spent more than an hour with the leaders of some 20 hunting and fishing groups.' Four days later, he dropped his proposal. 'President Bush knows full well that most of the sportsmen were part of his political base, and he doesn't want to alienate them,' Jim Martin, conservation director for Pure Fishing, the largest tackle company in the United States, told *Times* reporter Elizabeth Shogren. 'I don't think he cares what the environmental community thinks, but he cares what the sportsmen think.'

Bush had better luck with his plans for the Everglades in southern Florida. The area, which once measured 50 by 120 miles, has shrunk by half over the past century. During the

Clinton administration, Congress passed a thirty-year, $8.4 billion package to save the area. In early 2002, the Army Corps of Engineers began issuing permits for open-pit limestone mining in the Everglades, the first phase of a project that would eventually bulldoze and dynamite thirty square miles of Everglades wetlands. This move would destroy more wetlands in Florida than the EPA allowed for the whole country the year before. The Corps proposed issuing the permits before – during the Clinton years. But both the Department of the Interior and the EPA objected, saying the plan's effect on the Everglades would be 'significant' and 'irreversible.' After Bush came into office, Interior and the EPA signed off on the proposal.

By the time of Bush's 2005 budget, the White House's interest in clean water had all but evaporated. The amount allocated to water infrastructure investments was cut from $2.6 billion to $1.8 billion. The EPA's Clean Water and Drinking Water Infrastructure Gap analysis published in 2002 put the amount needed to do the job properly at $450 billion, according to Greenwatch, an environmental tracking organization.

With water safety standards declining, the administration, ever mindful of the next election, was faced with two options: make water cleaner, or just tell the public that water was cleaner. The Bush White House, being the Bush White House, chose the latter. In early 2004, the EPA's own Office of the Inspector General issued a report stating that the agency had repeatedly made false and misleading statements about the purity of the nation's drinking water. In 2002, the EPA claimed that 91 percent of Americans were drinking safe tap water. In 2003, it upped the number to 94 percent. The OIG reported that the EPA overlooked 35 percent of health standards violations nationwide. The EPA's own data show that the number of actual inspections had declined by more than half since Bush came into office. In April 2004, Brent Blackwelder, the president of Friends of the Earth, said that '60 percent of industrial facilities nationwide are now in violation of Clean Water Act discharge limits.'According to the NRDC, scientists at the EPA say the percentage of Americans drinking safe tap water can be estimated at only 81 percent.

In February 2004, Bush administration pollster Frank Luntz warned the White House in a blunt memo that ignoring the majority of Americans' strong belief 'that clean water is a RIGHT, not a privilege' would be politically dangerous. It's no surprise that two months later, on Earth Day, President Bush trumpeted a new wetlands initiative purporting to increase wetlands acreage. But as Joan Mulhern from Earthjustice points out, 'Trotting out a list of voluntary programs that already exist – and calling them a new initiative while simultaneously dismantling the nation's most important wetlands protection law – is not going to wash.'

ENDANGERED SPECIES

It was Richard Nixon who brought the 1973 Endangered Species Act into being. By 1975, the U.S. Supreme Court called it the 'most comprehensive legislation for the preservation of endangered species ever enacted by any nation.'

Not surprisingly, it has come under complete attack by the Bush White House. According to Defenders of Wildlife, the administration is the first in the act's history to declare a species in imminent danger of extinction but not list it as being endangered because the White House decided the species was 'insignificant.'

During the Clinton administration, 211 species were added to the endangered list. During the Bush administration, a mere 25 have been added – and in every single case, the listing came as a result of lawsuits by environmental groups. There is a current backlog of more than 250 endangered species waiting to be formally listed. Buckling to industry petitions, the White House has removed a record number of species from the endangered list, and the ESA is now so underfunded by the Bush administration that 200 species already on the list are on the verge of extinction because there is no money to protect them.

The U.S. Fish and Wildlife Service, which enforces the ESA, reports to Craig Manson, assistant secretary of the interior, who has been actively trying to dismember the landmark act, declaring in 2003 that 'the Endangered Species Act is broken.' Environmentalists say that the ESA has never been so threatened. 'It's the death-of-a-thousand-cuts approach,' Bart Semcer, a Sierra Club fish and wildlife policy specialist, told *The Washington Post*. 'They know that they can't win by adopting a wholesale approach to attacking the [ESA], so they're launching sneak attacks, small pieces of legislation that they're hoping the public won't notice in order to undermine the law.' Bruce Babbitt, interior secretary during the Clinton administration, says, 'There is nothing wrong with the Endangered Species Act. It works. The problem is this administration is not enforcing it and it doesn't want it to work. They want it to fail.'

Ever inventive, the administration has employed a number of tactics to undermine the ESA and reduce protections for some of America's most vulnerable wildlife. One favorite is the manipulation of science to suit their own ends. Andrew Eller Jr., a biologist employed for seventeen years by the Fish and Wildlife Service, filed a legal complaint in May 2004, charging the agency with deliberately manipulating scientific data to reduce protections for the Florida panther, of which there are only an estimated sixty to eighty left. This disregard for scientific evidence also led to one of the largest fish kills in American history in September 2002, when the Bush administration decided to favor the wishes of irrigators over endangered salmon on the Klamath River, in order to, in Karl Rove's words, 'support our base.' When the Bureau of Reclamation diverted water from the river to the irrigators, thirty-three thousand fall-run salmon and steelhead died.

The Bush administration has even taken its breezy attitude toward endangered species global. In 1973, the Convention on International Trade in Endangered Species of Wild Fauna and Flora was established to eliminate illegal trade in rare and endangered species. The treaty, now signed by more than 160 nations – including the United States – protects more than forty thousand plant and animal species worldwide, including the Asian elephant and the Bengal tiger. In October 2003, *The Washington Post* reported that the Bush administration, apparently under pressure from Safari Club International, a U.S.-based hunting advocacy group whose members are wealthy trophy hunters willing to pay tens of thousands of dollars to kill endangered elephants, antelopes, sheep, big cats, and other big game, proposed resuming trade in illegal endangered species. Three years earlier, the association, which gives heavily to the Republicans, named George W. Bush as its governor of the year.

NUCLEAR POWER

Vice President Cheney said at the time of the Energy Task Force's report that nuclear power was an integral part of the administration's plan. It may once have been considered a marvel of technology, but nuclear power has a number of factors weighing against it.

- Businesswise, it's not competitive with other forms of energy. In fact, the White House included $3.8 billion in incentives in its Energy Bill just to keep the nation's nuclear power plants afloat. (Nuclear power interests gave at least $9 million to the Bush–Cheney campaign and other Republican candidates in 2000.)
- In addition to other reactor safety issues, nuclear power plants are ripe potential targets for terrorist attack, putting

the communities near them in grave danger. (See also Chapter 1, 'The President's Wars.')

- There is no long-term plan for storing radioactive waste. (I'll come to this in a moment.)
- For something that sounds so cutting-edge, it's become an old technology. The nation's 103 nuclear power plants are licensed by the Nuclear Regulatory Commission to operate for forty years. After that they can apply for (and almost always receive) a renewal license good for another twenty years. The commission has issued renewal licenses for fourteen plants thus far. By 2015, more than half of the plants will have passed the forty-year mark.

'I believe sound science, and not politics, must prevail in the designation of any high-level nuclear waste repository. As president, I would not sign legislation that would send nuclear waste to any proposed site unless it's been deemed scientifically safe.'

– PRESIDENTIAL CANDIDATE GEORGE W. BUSH,
May 2000

That was just campaign talk. As president, Bush has acted in quite a different manner. Granted, storing seventy thousand tons of what a *Mother Jones* report on the environment calls 'some of the most deadly and long-lasting toxins ever made' is a problem for any White House. The administration decided that the ideal dumpsite was Yucca Mountain, one hundred miles northwest of Las Vegas. It sounds perfect: It's in the Nevada desert, not many people are around, and it's far away from the busy minds of environmentalists and concerned citizens.

Except that twenty-four years of government studies costing $4 billion have found problems with the site, including dormant volcanoes and a web of earthquake faults. When the GAO issued a report that criticized the Department of Energy's storage plan, Energy Secretary Abraham dismissed the agency's findings as 'fatally flawed.' He said the department was relying on engineered waste packages to store the waste.

Those engineered waste packages are also a problem. Environmental law dictates that nuclear waste must be kept in isolated containers for ten thousand years. The DOE is putting its money on canisters made of steel fused with chrome, nickel, and molybdenum, also called alloy 22. After three years of tests, the Energy Department assures us that the canisters will last twelve thousand years, according to *Mother Jones*.

Experts are not so confident. An eleven-member Nuclear Waste Technical Review Board studied the canisters and issued a report that voiced concerns that alloy 22 could corrode at high temperatures over time. Paul Craig, one of the scientists on the panel, called it 'an upscale version of stainless steel.' He went on to explain to the Associated Press, 'The report says in ordinary English that under the conditions proposed by the Department of Energy, the canisters will leak. It was signed by every single member of the board so there would be no confusion . . . The science is very clear. If we get high-temperature liquids, the metal would corrode and that would eventually lead to leakage of nuclear waste.'

The Bush administration devised a clever way of getting around naysayers. Its reclassifying what is and what is not radioactive waste, thereby exempting much of it from strict cleanup measures. At the same time, it introduced new transportation regulations that would exempt different classes of radioactive material from regulatory control while in transit. As a report by Greenwatch put it, the measure permits 'an increase in unregulated material on the nation's roads, rails, barges and aircraft [and so] is of special concern due to homeland security worries over the transportation of nuclear waste material possibly enabling a dirty bomb.'

OIL AND GAS DRILLING

Three months after taking office, Bush announced that all public lands, including wilderness areas and national monuments, would be considered for oil and gas drilling. The industry, by the way, donated $46,620,134 to Bush–Cheney, the Republican National Committee, and other Republican candidates in the 2000 and 2002 elections, according to the Center for Responsive Politics.

Three months after the president's statement, Interior Secretary Gale Norton testified before Congress that her department would not allow such drilling in national parks or wilderness areas. This seemed like an uncharacteristic statement. But a month later, hotter heads prevailed, and the president issued an executive order calling on all federal agencies to 'expedite energy-related projects' on America's public lands.

The Bureau of Land Management, which is charged with protecting 262 million acres of land assets, set its eyes on the Rocky Mountain states, where 88 percent of total BLM-managed lands are open to oil and gas drilling, and ordered that drilling permits be expedited. In order to prevent hundreds of thousands of acres from being placed under the protection of the Wilderness Act, the Bush administration is allowing the gas industry to stockpile leases and drilling permits on thirty-four million acres of public lands in the Rockies, even though energy companies are currently drilling on less than one-third of that land. Once an oil and gas company puts a road on a leased parcel, the land can no longer be protected by the Wilderness Act. In Wyoming, 94 percent of all public land is up for grabs. The administration supported plans that would cover Wyoming and Montana's twelve-million-acre Powder River Basin with seventy-seven thousand coal bed methane wells, fifty-three thousand miles of pipelines, fifty-three hundred miles of new power lines, and twenty-six thousand miles of service roads. It sounds like a lot, but not to the Bush White House. The administration would allow the amount of drilling in the region to increase by five times.

Cheney's Energy Task Force report ordered officials to look out for 'impediments' to the administration's plan and then 'modify those where opportunities exist.' The Bureau of Land Management sent a memo to its Utah field offices telling them to 'ensure that existing staff understand that when an oil and gas lease parcel or when an application for permission to drill comes in the door, that this work is their No. 1 priority.' According to *Mother Jones*, the BLM said that in the first year it intended to process forty-one hundred drilling permits, up from twenty-six hundred the year before.

This is what Bush said to a group of schoolkids who won Environmental Youth Awards in 2001: 'The whole world doesn't have to be zero sum. It doesn't have to be that we find more energy and therefore the environment suffers. We've got technologies available now to make sure that we explore and protect the environment at the same time . . . we need to be good stewards of the land.'

Offshore drilling was opened up as well off the coasts of California and Florida. California, which objected to the plan, lobbied the administration to buy back thirty-six offshore leases; Gale Norton denied the request. Florida was more successful. When the president's brother Jeb made the same request for Florida's offshore leases, the Bush administration spent $235 million buying back the leases from the energy companies. After a three-year legal battle with California in which the federal government lost two rounds in court, the administration has said it will 'try' to buy back the state's thirty-six leases.

THE ARCTIC NATIONAL WILDLIFE REFUGE

It is something of a mystery why the administration has been so fixated on the prospect of giving up the nineteen-million-acre Arctic National Wildlife Refuge with its 1.5-million-acre coastal plain to oil interests, since 95 percent of Alaska's North Slope is already open to drilling. Deputy Interior Secretary J. Steven Griles has said that opening it up is his 'greatest wish.'

Naturalists have called the ANWR, which is teeming with all manner of vegetation and wildlife, 'America's Serengeti.' Norton calls it 'a flat, white nothingness.' And she has repeatedly deceived the public and distorted the facts in her desire to let oil concerns move into this wilderness refuge.

- In the fall of 2001, Norton told the Senate Committee on Energy and Natural Resources that, according to her agency's scientific analysis, caribou would not be harmed by drilling in the ANWR. Shortly afterward, biologists from the Fish and Wildlife Service revealed that Norton had completely altered their original report, making seventeen major changes to the scientific data in order to minimize the environmental impact of the drilling. When confronted with the changes, Norton waved one of them away, claiming it was a typographical error. The other disparities were ignored.

- In April 2002, biologists at the U.S. Geological Survey, which is part of the Department of the Interior, gave Norton a report based on twelve years of research that said drilling in the ANWR would significantly harm the region's wildlife.

- Two weeks later, Norton issued a two-page report stating the exact opposite of what the Geological Survey report had stated. According to Robert F. Kennedy Jr. in *Rolling Stone*, she failed to report two studies by the Fish and Wildlife Service concluding that the drilling would harm polar-bear populations as well as violate the international treaty protecting polar-bears. One of the lawyers in her department told the Fish and Wildlife Service to tidy up the report to "reflect the Interior Department's position.'"

- Norton said that the drilling would affect only two thousand acres of the region. But as *New York Times* columnist Paul Krugman discovered, roads aren't covered in that estimate. 'And "surface acreage covered" is very narrowly defined: if a pipeline snakes across the terrain on a series of posts, only the ground on which those posts rest counts; bare ground under the pipeline isn't considered "covered."'

All this deception and environmental risk taking, and for what? Proponents of drilling in the ANWR coastal plain claim it 'may' contain between 6 and 16 billion barrels of recoverable oil. The Geological Survey estimated that, at most, the coastal plain could profitably produce 3.2 billion barrels of oil – equivalent to six months' worth of U.S. consumption. And the study said it would take fifty years to get all of the oil out of the ground. (By comparison, the NRDC estimated that making replacement tires for automobiles meet the same standards as the tires that are supplied with new cars would save 5.4 billion barrels over fifty years.)

In the end, even the Republican-led Senate felt that the administration had overreached. It blocked all the White House's proposals for drilling in the Artic National Wildlife Refuge. Bush vowed to keep trying.

MOUNTAINTOP MINING

'We were looking for friends, and we found one in George W. Bush.'
– JAMES H. 'BUCK' HARLESS, a member of the board of Massey Energy, a mountaintop-mining company

Mr. Harless has a sound instinct for friendship. Acting on behalf of coal-mining interests, the Bush administration rewrote the Clean Water Act to allow them to dump the waste from mountaintop mining into the nation's rivers and streams without worry or penalty.

By the 1980s, mining interests had pretty much given up on traditional coal mines and had come up with a new technique that involved literally blasting the top off a mountain and then digging straight down. Getting rid of the top was a problem, though. And the Clean Water Act established strict guidelines about what the mining companies had to do with it. In the Appalachia region of Kentucky, Tennessee, West Virginia, and Virginia, millions of tons of mountaintop waste have buried twelve hundred miles of streams. 'In the Carter administration, we required them to truck it down and put it in four-foot compacted lifts,' an inspector told *Vanity Fair*'s Michael Shnayerson. 'With Griles's promotion in 1983 to deputy assistant secretary of the interior for lands and minerals management, says the inspector, the rules were basically ignored. "Mining operators could push or shove fill from the top of a hollow and let it flow right down to the streambed, transported essentially by gravity."' The Bush White House has given the mining companies even more latitude. A chronology:

- Communities in coalfield regions begin going to court to have the Clean Water Act enforced.
- The mining industry (which donated $3.3 million to the 2000 Bush–Cheney campaign and other Republican candidates) appeals to the Bush administration.
- On a Friday in May 2002, the administration removes the provision in the Clean Water Act that had made it illegal for mining companies to dump mountaintop waste into the nation's streams and other waters.
- The EPA issues a press release saying the change will 'enhance environmental protections' for rivers and streams.
- The U.S. District Court for the Southern District of West Virginia rules that the administration's action was illegal. As Judge Charles H. Haden II put it, 'No effect on related environmental values is more adverse than obliteration. Under a valley fill, the water quality of the stream becomes

zero. Because there is no stream, there is no water quality.'

■ The Bush administration appeals the decision.

■ The Fourth Circuit Court of Appeals, the most conservative appeals court in the country, overturns the lower court ruling.

■ A land rush begins. Mountaintop-mining companies besiege the Army Corps of Engineers, which issues permits, with plans for twenty new mountaintop projects. In West Virginia and Kentucky, the corps reportedly has to add extra staff to handle the paperwork.

■ A September 2003 EPA report finds nearly three hundred Clean Water Act violations by the mountaintop-mining industry. How does the Bush administration react? It moves to change the law by establishing the Mountaintop Mining Self-Reporting Program, which would allow the industry to police itself and issue small fines for violations.

NATIONAL PARKS

Created by an Act of Congress in 1916, the National Park Service was established to 'promote and regulate the use of the . . . national parks, monuments, and reservations . . . to conserve the scenery and the natural and historic objects and the wildlife therein and to provide for the enjoyment of the same in such manner and by such means as will leave them unimpaired for the enjoyment of future generations.' Back then, the NPS looked after only 14 national parks and 21 national monuments. Now there are 57 national parks, 74 national monuments, and 256 other affiliated areas, covering more than 84 million acres, that receive more than 270 million visitors each year.

In the final days of the 2000 election that brought him to power, Bush declared, 'America's first environmental president, Theodore Roosevelt, talked of the value of "silent places, unworn by man." These places inspired him – and he inspired our government to protect them. I view protecting America's "silent places" as an ongoing responsibility, a shared commitment of the American people and our government.'

Six months after he was sworn into office, Bush said, 'My administration will restore and renew America's national parks . . .We are also the first administration to request full funding of the Land and Water Conservation Fund. This fund provides Florida and other states with the means to set aside new parks, vital habitats and restore threatened ecosystems.' He also pledged to fund the $4.9 billion needed to make overdue repairs on the nation's parks. In both cases he fell far short of his promises.

- In complete opposition to what he said earlier, Bush decided to limit the ability of future administrations to create new national monuments by supporting legislation that actually weakened presidential authority over the right to create them. By 2003, Norton proclaimed that the Department of the Interior would not seek any new wilderness area designations anywhere. According to Public Employees for Environmental Responsibility (PEER), the Bush administration has failed to submit to Congress previous administrations' recommendations to designate more than two million roadless acres in eight national parks as wilderness areas.
- The administration also didn't set aside the $4.9 billion as it said it would, although it did slightly increase the NPS operating budget. The White House pledged $900 million for the Conservation Fund. But even this figure is misleading. *The New York Times* said that due to accounting tricks, the amount was really only $314 million.

According to EPA studies, one snowmobile can throw off the same exhaust as one hundred cars. After ten years of looking into the subject, the National Park Service decided that snowmobiles were threatening the environment and wildlife of Yellowstone National Park in Wyoming, Montana, and Idaho, and Grand Teton National Park in Wyoming. In Yellowstone, according to the NRDC, air pollution from snowmobiles on busy days can exceed that of Los Angeles. In addition, the noise from a four-stroke snowmobile can be louder than a pneumatic drill, putting visitors and park staff at risk of hearing damage.

The Bush White House, going counter to the opinions of almost every department and agency involved in the matter, decided not to eliminate snowmobile use in the two parks – but to allow it to *increase* by 35 percent over the daily average. This was such an outrageous overreach that the National Park Service was sued by environmental groups. And in late 2003, the U.S. District Court in Washington, DC, decided against the NPS. In a harsh forty-eight-page brief, Judge Emmet Sullivan ruled the Bush administration's decision 'arbitrary and capricious.'

In early 2004, in a separate suit brought by the snowmobile industry and snowmobilers against a Clinton administration ban, the U.S. District Court for Wyoming issued a temporary restraining order against the ban. According to an editorial in *The New York Times*, 'The administration expressed satisfaction that Judge [Clarence] Brimmer [who wrote the decision] had chosen to defer to the National Park Service "experts." But this implies that the Park Service enthusiastically embraces snowmobiling. It does not. Left to its own instincts, the service would have banned snowmobiling. It signed on to the Bush plan under pressure, its science and better instincts overwhelmed by the administration's political objectives.' At the moment, both sides are appealing.

The Bush administration also increased leases for oil and gas drilling in the national park system. One of the parks, Padre Island National Seashore, is in the president's home state of Texas. It is one of only two places on earth where the Kemp's ridley sea turtle nests, the most endangered of all sea turtles. The administration pressed the NPS to allow drilling along the seashore and to open up fifteen miles of beaches and dunes to the trucks attendant to that drilling.

In early 2004, David Shaver, the chief of the park service's Geological Resources Division, sent a memo to his headquarters saying, 'Based on our review, we recommend that the book not be sold in park bookstores because the book purports to be science when it is not, and its sale in the park bookstores directly conflicts with the Service's statutory mandate to promote the use of sound science in all its programs including public educations.' What book was Shaver referring to? A slim volume that the park service, under pressure from top NPS political appointees, released for sale that suggests that the Grand Canyon was created in six days.

This Orwellian strategy of 'message control' is also evident in the official 'talking points' distributed under orders from Washington to NPS employees. Internal NPS e-mails, released in May 2004 by PEER, reveal that park superintendents were instructed to refer to budget cuts as 'service-level adjustments' when talking to the media and to use the following talking points:

- 'Despite the challenges, NPS has fared well under President Bush . . .'
- 'The Bush Administration is committed to dramatically improving air quality.'
- 'This Administration is very committed to preserving the resources of the National Park System . . .'

NATIONAL FORESTS

You may be able to repair contaminated water. You may even be able to repair contaminated air. But when you destroy a forest, it's an act that takes decades, if not centuries, to make good again. The logging industry – which donated $6,854,321 to the

Bush–Cheney campaign and the Republicans in 2000, and which gave a further $3,617,921 in the 2002 election cycle – has a vested interest in getting its hands on America's old-growth forests. And therefore so does the Bush White House. The president indicated his intent by naming Mark Rey the administration's point man on forest policy. His previous job? For almost twenty years he worked as a lobbyist for the lumber industry.

Almost a third of the United States is covered in forest – some 737 million acres. Only around 6 percent of those are protected by federal law. According to the NRDC, there are already more than 380,000 miles of roads that cut through national forests – eight times more than the entire interstate highway system. The Clinton administration, under the Roadless Area Conservation Rule, sought to protect a third of the truly wilderness national forest area from further road building. In its first month in office, the Bush administration set in motion a program to reverse that plan.

- By late 2001, the Forest Service – created in 1905 to manage national forests and grasslands – decided, under pressure from the White House, that environmental impact studies and 'compelling need' arguments on the part of loggers were no longer necessary. Henceforth, apparently, the industry would get logging and road-building permits whenever it asked for them.
- The Bush plan was tripped up by the Ninth Circuit Court of Appeals, which upheld the Clinton-era regulation.
- Not to be outdone by a federal court, in June 2003 the White House managed to slip an exemption into the Roadless Area Conservation Rule that would allow road building in Alaska's Tongass National Forest. The Tongass is not just the largest forest on the continent, it's also the biggest intact temperate rain forest on earth. According to Osha Gray Davidson in *Rolling Stone*, 'It's also one of the

only places in the country that retains every species of plant and animal found [there] in pre-Columbian times, a biological time capsule that includes grizzly bears, wolves, bald eagles, and salmon.' Bush's plan: to allow one thousand miles of new roads through the Tongass – and to get taxpayers essentially to pay for clear-cutting by giving the logging companies subsidies for 'clearing-out' the forest and by paying for the road construction and maintenance. According to the Wilderness Society, the Forest Service already loses up to $35 million per year on logging activity elsewhere in the Tongass.

- The Department of Agriculture announced its formal decision to allow road building in extreme wild forests like Tongass in December 2003. The White House did its best to put the news out quietly. It released it on the 23rd, just before the Christmas holiday.

- 'The Bush administration's doublespeak about the environment reached a new level of shamelessness with this week's announcement that it is "retaining" the rule to protect roadless areas in national forests,' said the *San Francisco Chronicle*. 'Let none be fooled: What the Bush administration did this week was carve huge exceptions and loopholes into a thoroughly vetted, well-balanced, popularly supported plan to protect the ever-shrinking swaths of untrampled national forests . . . The Bush administration's arguments for the new rules are phony and transparent.'

The White House focused much of its energy on its Healthy Forests initiative. It may have a crunchy, environmentally friendly name, but in truth it's anything but. The initiative allows big timber companies to thin out the smaller trees in national forests. But the bill presents no precise definition of a small tree. Furthermore, in return for clearing out the so-called smaller trees, timber interests would be allowed to cut down old-growth trees. Opponents of the plan say that 'thinning' is a Bush administration code word for logging. And the United States actually loses money on the deal. As Paul Krugman wrote in *The New York Times*, 'According to the General Accounting Office, the Forest Service consistently spends more money arranging timber sales than it actually gets from the sales. How much money? Funny you should ask: last year the Bush administration stopped releasing that information.'

In May 2003, Congress discarded the White House's Healthy Forests initiative, watered it down a bit, and changed the name to the Healthy Forests Restoration Act. In December 2003, the bill was passed. As the president pronounced at the time, 'We have a responsibility to be good stewards of our forests. That's a solemn responsibility. And the legislation I sign today carries forward this ethic of stewardship.' Bush added, 'The principles behind the Healthy Forest Initiative were not invented in the White House, and truthfully, not invented in the Congress. They are founded on the experience of scientists, forestry experts, and, as importantly, the firefighters who know what they're talking about.'

Except that

- 'Thinning may help reduce a fire's severity if the weather conditions are working for you,' David Calahan, a retired Oregonian firefighter, told a congressional hearing. 'But when the climate and weather turns against you, thinned areas can suffer even more than untouched areas.'
- 'Partial cutting done historically typically aggravated the fire hazard and made things worse when fire came along,' C. Phillip Weatherspoon, an emeritus research forester for the Forest Service, told the *Los Angeles Times*.
- 'The most effective place to fight fire is in a mature forest,' Dr. Patrick Withen, a veteran smoke jumper, was quoted by the Environmental Media Services (EMS) as saying. 'Yet the administration is essentially trading logging for thinning. This is just increasing the fire danger.'

■ And finally, 'It is ironic,' firefighter Timothy Ingalsbee, director of the Western Fire Ecology Center, told EMS following the congressional hearings, 'that in this time of corporate and financial scandals, President Bush wants to completely deregulate the system. They speak with the corporate elite, but never the working people. Not one of the 17,000 firefighters out on the line was ever consulted about how to protect their communities.'

The White House continues to weaken protections for old-growth forests and the wildlife that inhabits them. In March 2004, the Associated Press reported that the administration 'eased restrictions on logging old-growth forests in the Pacific Northwest, completing a rules change that will allow forest managers to begin logging without first looking for rare plants and animals.'

THE SUPERFUND

In 1980, the Carter administration established the Superfund to clean up the nation's worst toxic waste sites, forcing companies responsible for the contamination to pay for the cleanup. And it levied a 'polluter pays' fee on certain chemicals and crude oil as well as corporations that would go into a trust fund to pay for cleanups when the companies responsible for the mess went out of business or couldn't be clearly identified. (According to the General Accounting Office, one out of four people lives within five miles of a Superfund site. And children born to women living within a quarter mile of a Superfund site are more likely to have birth and heart defects.) When Tim Russert asked Dick Cheney during the 2000 election campaign if 'he would support authorizing funding for Superfund to clean up toxic waste,' the future vice president answered, 'I would.'

Nothing, unfortunately, could be farther from the truth.

Congress had eliminated the 'polluter pays' fees in 1995, which has saved the energy and chemical industries, among others, $13 billion. The Bush administration has done nothing to reimplement them. As a result, the trust fund, which once stood at $5.5 billion, is essentially bankrupt. There are at present more than twelve hundred sites in need of cleaning up, and any money owed to the trust fund is already committed to a portion of these sites. According to a February 2004 report by the GAO, 'In fiscal year 2004, the appropriation from the general fund was the only source of funds for the program,' with zero dollars coming from the Superfund trust fund. In fact, the Bush White House is the first administration since the fund was established not to demand the 'polluter pays' fees. It's no surprise that the pace of cleanups has stalled significantly. Forty sites were cleaned in 2003, whereas eighty-seven were cleaned each year, on average, between 1996 and 2000. However, the White House did ask Congress for a 10 percent increase for the program. The increase doesn't come from the polluting companies but from general revenue – in other words, taxpayers.

GLOBAL WARMING

On February 14, 2002, the day Bush announced his Clear Skies proposal, he laid out his plans for tackling the global-warming problem. 'My administration is committed to cutting our nation's greenhouse gas intensity – how much we emit per unit of economic activity – by 18% over the next ten years.' In fact, the proposal's wording and its accounting actually would allow emissions to increase by 14 percent over the next decade, according to the NRDC, exactly the rate of increase for the decade before.

The White House went on a spree, removing references to global warming from government reports, or dismissing them completely.

- On June 3, 2002, the EPA released a study linking human-made emissions to global warming. The president's offhanded response: 'I read the report put out by the bureaucracy.' A spokesman later clarified that Bush actually hadn't read the report, but a White House employee had briefed him on it. The administration told Congress that the problem needs further investigation.

- In September 2002, a section on global warming was removed from the administration's annual report to the public on the status and trends of air quality. A year later, the White House deleted critical information about global warming from a 'comprehensive' EPA draft report on the state of the environment. An internal EPA memo at the time of the removal said that the report 'no longer accurately represents scientific consensus on climate change.' In a letter to *The New York Times*, Russell Train, the EPA head during the Nixon and Ford administrations, wrote, 'I can state categorically that there never was such White House intrusion into the business of the EPA during my tenure. The EPA was established as an independent agency in the executive branch, and so it should remain. There appears today to be a steady erosion in its independent status. I can appreciate the president's interest in not having discordant voices within his administration. But the interest of the American people lies in having full disclosure of the facts, particularly when the issue is one with such potentially enormous damage to the long-term health and economic wellbeing of all of us.'

In early 2004, *Fortune* magazine and the English newspaper *The Observer* obtained a report on global warming that had been prepared by the Pentagon's Office of Net Assessment. The study was supervised by Andrew Marshall, an eighty-two-year-old Pentagon veteran who has counseled defense secretaries for the past three decades. Marshall was the man Rumsfeld had gone to when he was planning his overhaul of the U.S. military prior to the Iraq war. Inside the Pentagon, they call him 'Yoda.'

The study envisions catastrophic consequences of global warming not by 2050, or 2040, but by 2020. The Pentagon report indicated that global warming poses a greater threat to the West than does terrorism. It said that by as early as 2007, violent storms or flooding could destroy coastal barriers and render low-lying coastal areas around the world uninhabitable.

The report said that by 2020 – *sixteen years from now* – the following is more than plausible:

- Seas will submerge low-lying European cities.
- European temperatures could drop by as much as six degrees.
- Britain could have a climate the forecasters called 'Siberian.'
- There will be droughts and widescale rioting and warfare around the world.
- Famine will claim millions of lives.
- The United States and Europe will become 'virtual fortresses' in their efforts to stem the flow of the millions fleeing countries plagued by drought and famine.
- Japan, North Korea, South Korea, Iran, Egypt, and Germany will develop nuclear weapons programs to protect themselves.

Britain's chief scientist, Sir David King, wrote in the journal *Science*, 'In my view, climate change is the most severe problem we face today, more serious than the threat of terrorism . . . As the world's only remaining superpower, the United States is accustomed to leading internationally coordinated action. But the U.S. government is failing to take up the challenge of global warming.'

What did the Bush administration – the administration that removed the United States from the Kyoto Protocol – do about the Pentagon report? It never acknowledged it.

The White House had already decided that carbon dioxide (the single greatest cause of global warming) was not technically a pollutant under the Clean Air Act and therefore should not be regulated. The administration was thoroughly incorrect in this claim. According to Section 103(g) of the act, CO_2 is very much considered a pollutant necessary to regulate. How did Bush react to this? The administration removed CO_2 from regulated pollutants included in the Clean Air Act.

The White House had succeeded earlier in removing the respected American climatologist Dr. Robert Watson as chair of the Intergovernmental Panel of Climate Change, a position he had held since 1996. According to a report prepared for California Democrat Henry Waxman, 'Politics and Science in the Bush Administration,' what ticked the administration off was a study issued in 2001 by the panel that concluded that there 'is new and stronger evidence that most of the warming observed over the last 50 years is attributable to human activities,' a statement backed up by the National Academy of Sciences. After Watson was forced out – ExxonMobil had lobbied the White House for his removal – Michael Oppenheimer of Princeton University told *Science*, 'It is scandalous . . . This is an invasion of narrow political considerations into scientific process.'

By early 2004, the scientific community was in a rage over the White House's cavalier attitude of ignoring serious research in favor of the interests of the big polluting industries. The Union of Concerned Scientists, in a statement signed by more than sixty prominent members – including twenty Nobel Prize-winners – attacked the Bush administration's suppression and distortion of scientific findings. The group's chairman, Dr. Kurt Gottfried, said, 'Across a broad range of issues, the administration has undermined the quality of the scientific advisory system and the morale of the government's outstanding scientific personnel.'

'I like to tell people, Laura and I are proud to be Texas – own a Texas ranch, and for us, every day is Earth Day.'

– GEORGE W. BUSH, April 2002

6

■

EDUCATION

'Rarely is the question asked: Is our children learning?'
– GEORGE W. BUSH, January 2000

'Listen, we don't want Washington, D.C., managing public education. Trust me.'
– GEORGE W. BUSH, May 2002

FEBRUARY 27, 2001. President George W. Bush's first address to Congress. As he stressed the issue at the very heart of his claim to be a 'compassionate conservative,' which would become the cornerstone of his domestic policy in the years ahead, Bush leaned forward and declared, 'Education is *not* my top priority.'

Following a curious round of applause from the elected representatives in the chamber, Bush stopped, checked the TelePrompTer, leaned forward, and declared, 'Education *is* my top priority.' More applause.

From the evidence available, it would seem that the president was right the first time. But we're getting ahead of the story.

In January 2002, Bush signed into law his sweeping No Child Left Behind Act, which promised nothing less than a complete overhaul of the nation's public school system. With its stated goal of giving all American children a better education by holding teachers and schools to hitherto unmatched standards of proficiency, the bill sailed through both houses. The name had been chosen well and even had a familiar and worthy ring to it: Leave No Child Behind was the slogan for Marian Wright Edelman's Children's Defense Fund.

Bush's bill was the single most audacious attempt to mandate improvements in the nation's education system since the 1965 reforms put forward under President Lyndon Johnson's Great Society. With fifty-three million students being taught by three million teachers in ninety-two thousand public schools in fifteen thousand school districts, the president's seven-hundred-page plan was nothing if not ambitious.

The bill's goal seemed monumental, if relatively simple: It sought to have a 'highly-qualified' teacher in every classroom by the end of the 2005–06 school year and to have every child in America proficient in math and reading by the year 2014. And it was determined to make teachers and schools accountable not to the states and communities that employed them but to the Bush administration.

This was how No Child Left Behind was going to accomplish these goals:

- Children and schools would be given uniform annual 'proficiency' tests.
- Children would be held to standardized performance levels. Those who didn't meet these levels would receive extra help.
- Schools would be graded as well. Ones that failed the bill's 'growth targets' had pay to transport their students to

schools with higher test results. The schools also had to undergo a shape-up program to remedy their problems.

- Repeated failure could result in the school being taken over by the state or a private company and the principal and teachers being reassigned to other schools. Some of the schools could be shut down.

Like so many initiatives of the Bush administration, things haven't quite worked out the way the president sold it. To begin with, teachers are overstressed and poorly paid as it is. According to Robert Borosage in *The American Prospect*, since 1970, teachers' pay nationwide has risen at a rate of only one-third of 1 percent beyond inflation per year. The average starting pay for public school teachers in the United States was just $30,719 in 2002, according to the American Federation of Teachers. New teachers coming into the profession enter with a college loan to pay off that is 85 percent higher than it would have been a decade ago. And one out of five teachers quits his or her job in the first three years.

The average school is forty-two years old. And the chances are it's overcrowded. In major cities, Borosage says, the rising number of students 'has led to the doubling of classes, to [students studying in] half-day shifts and to the conversion of trailers, closets, libraries and gyms into classrooms.' According to Borosage, a 1995 General Accounting Office report estimated 'that it would require $112 billion simply to bring the schools up to safe standards. A more detailed estimate by the National Education Association in 2000 included funds needed to update schools for advanced technology; it estimated the cost at $322 billion.'

For educators and students, No Child Left Behind is rigid and unforgiving. The law not only encourages schools to turn out test takers rather than thinkers, it also requires every student in every ethnic and academic category to achieve a level of test-taking proficiency. And it requires almost perfect attendance on the day the tests are delivered. In *Forbes*, Dan Seligman pointed out that 'the new law provided that 95% of all students – and in some cases 95% of each ethnic group within the school – had to participate. Inevitably, some schools were flunked because they only had, say, 94.6%.'

The bill gives broad outlines for performance standards and then lets each individual state determine its levels of 'proficiency,' which it will later be measured against. Many states have gotten around that issue by lowering their academic standards going into the program. As Peter Schrag pointed out in *The American Prospect*, 'while Michigan reported that some 1,500 schools (40 percent of all the state's public ones) failed to make their adequate yearly progress goals . . . Arkansas and Wyoming, with lower proficiency standards, reported none.'

William Mathis, writing in the *Phi Delta Kappan*, the professional journal of American education, said that 'a plethora of estimates have been put forth regarding the number of schools across the U.S. that will turn out to be failing' under No Child Left Behind. 'North Carolina estimates 60%, Vermont calculated 80% . . . and Louisiana reports 85%.'

As with all Bush administration initiatives, money is an issue, and here it is an enormous one. 'The highest percentage increase in our budget should go to our children's education,' Bush said in his 2001 address to Congress. But according to the Center on Budget and Policy Priorities at the time, 'the cost of the tax cut over the next 10 years is 40 times the $1 billion . . . slated for improving the nation's education system.' Indeed, since the No Child Left Behind Act was passed, cuts to other education programs have meant that the White House has steadily lowered the budget increases slated overall for education – from an 18 percent increase in funding in 2002 to 3 percent scheduled for 2005, says the American Federation of Teachers. The 2005 budget marks the smallest increase in education funding in nine years, according to the National Education Association. In the 2005 budget, for example, Bush called for spending $36.7 billion on federal programs for public kindergartens through twelfth grade. That's just $1 billion more than was budgeted the year before.

The Bush administration plans to cut thirty-eight education programs in 2005. On the chopping block: $11 million for gifted students; $247 million for Even Start, a family literacy program; and $5 million for a dropout-prevention program, even though under No Child Left Behind schools are penalized for each student who leaves. A $149 million program called HOPE VI, designed to revitalize deteriorating housing projects, would be scrapped as well. Head Start, a forty-year-old program that helps about a million children from poorer communities prepare for kindergarten, is under threat of elimination. The White House has demanded that at least half the Head Start teachers in the country have four-year college degrees by 2008. (Their current pay averages $21,000 a year.) The extra estimated costs to hire such qualified teachers is $2 billion, which the Bush administration is reluctant to include in the budget. Head Start has few champions in the White House. When he was a congressman, Vice President Dick Cheney voted against the program's initial creation.

The *Phi Delta Kappan* estimated that meeting the goals set by No Child Left Behind would add between $84.5 billion and $148 billion per year to what nationwide education spending levels were before the law was enacted. Of the states that have studied the extra costs imposed by the law, New Hampshire, for instance, found that meeting the act's standards would cost it an additional $126.5 million but that it was receiving only $17 million from Washington. In Texas, an increase of almost $7 billion would be needed to conform to the law, while the Bush administration proposed only a $1 billion federal increase in education funding for the whole country in 2004. But 'legal scholars have opined that the federal government cannot be sued to force adequate funding of the law,' said the *Phi Delta Kappan.*

Throughout the country, educators have been doing what they can to maintain standards in the face of the onslaught of costs and conditions of the No Child Left Behind Act. Consider these drastic measures, reported by *The New York Times* in April 2003:

- In Oregon, teachers worked two weeks without pay to keep the state's school districts from shortening the school year.
- In Missouri, the governor ordered every third lightbulb removed to save money.
- In Oklahoma, teachers filled in on janitorial duty, drove school buses, and worked in cafeterias. In a few cases, students helped clean the classrooms.
- In Colorado, some schools cut back to four days a week.
- In Idaho, school auctions and bake sales were held to help pay teachers. In one town, the teachers all chipped in to keep a hearing specialist on staff at their school.
- In California, layoff notices were sent to twenty-five thousand teachers. San Francisco canceled its summer school programs for elementary school students.
- In Kansas, half the school districts cut staff. At two elementary schools, students contributed the coins in their piggy banks to keep nurses and foreign-language teachers.
- In Illinois, according to *The Wall Street Journal*, the state had to drop the $19 million it was spending on its gifted-student programs.

A year later, the story was much the same. The May/June 2004 issue of *Mother Jones* showed how desperate the situation had become. In Oregon, once known for innovative schools and the funding to match, a Republican-led legislative put together a spending package of mostly temporary tax increases that would have funneled $300 million to the state's cash-strapped schools. The measure passed.

But then Citizens for a Sound Economy came to town. Led by former House majority leader Dick Armey, the national right-wing group spent about a half a million dollars campaigning for the spending measure to be repealed. It worked. In February 2004, 59 percent of Oregonians voted to repeal the tax, meaning that Oregon will have to slash another $500 million from public spending, including $300 million from public schools. How much would the tax increase have cost the average household in Oregon? $36.

Mother Jones also found this:

- In early 2004, McDonald's sponsored McTeacher's Night in sixteen states. Teachers and principals worked the grills and fry baskets to earn their schools a cut of the night's profits. The chain says that $700,000 went to schools that night, but with more than one thousand schools participating, that meant less than $700 each.

- After Nobelsville, Indiana, lost more than $800,000 in school funding cuts in 2003, the head of the intermediate school said he'd get a Mohawk and dye it green if students could raise $30,000 in a jogathon. They ended up with more than $41,000, but the school might still have to charge kids a fee to join the math club.

- Desperate for funds, schools in Junction City, Oregon, cut classes in art, music, and gym, laid off three teachers, and ended all field trips. Then a dozen local farmers had an idea and took off all their clothes for a pinup calendar. At $17 each, the calendars earned the school system more than $225,000.

Already twenty-six thousand of the country's ninety-two thousand public schools have received failing grades, according to *The New York Times*, and experts fear that the number will grow dramatically. In Hawaii, 180 of the state's 280 public schools were found to be failing in 2003. 'How do you defend a law that is likely to result in 85% of public schools in America being labeled failing – based on a single test score?' *The Times* asked. 'And how do you defend a law that gives the federal government unprecedented control over "failing" schools – that tells local school boards when they must fire their principals and teachers – even though it pays [just 7 percent] of public education costs?'

The backlash against No Child Left Behind has taken many paths. At least twenty states are revolting against the bill, either by criticizing the law, asking for exemptions from it or, like Vermont and Connecticut, pulling out of No Child Left Behind – thereby giving up federal education money altogether. 'If Clinton had done this, Republicans would have been up in arms,' James Dillard, a Virginia state congressman (and a Republican), told *Time*. He paused for a moment, then said; 'Republicans *are* up in arms.' In Utah, where 245 of the state's 810 public schools failed to make 'adequate yearly progress,' the Bush administration sent emissaries from the Department of Education to help explain the complicated rules. *The New York Times* said that one of the officials, Ken Meyer, barnstormed the state, 'part good-will diplomat, part flak-catcher, calming emotions and clarifying misunderstandings.' In early 2004, the Republican-led Utah legislature nevertheless voted sixty-four to eight to ignore provisions in No Child Left Behind that weren't fully financed by federal money.

The transfer program is riddled with flaws. Allowing students from 'failing' schools to transfer to 'passing' schools punishes schools in poorer neighborhoods, forces students into what can be long commutes, and overburdens the teachers and facilities at the 'passing' schools. *The American Prospect* reported that of 250,000 students eligible for transfer to 'passing' schools in Chicago in 2003, only 19,000 applied, and of those, just over 1,000 were placed. In New York, eight thousand students were transferred in 2003, contributing, *The New York Times*, reported, to 'the worst overcrowding of city schools in years.' *The Times* discovered that a third of those students actually transferred from one 'failing' school to another 'failing' school.

In June 2002, the U.S. Supreme Court upheld the city of

Cleveland's school voucher program in which students can receive up to $2,250 to help pay for tuition at a private school. Bush called it a 'great victory to parents and students' and 'an important statement' to 'make sure no child is left behind.'

Bush's push for vouchers is also a clever way for the president, who claims that his favorite political philosopher is Jesus, to move students into religious schools.

- Nationwide, private, nonsectarian school tuition averages about $8,000 for elementary school and nearly $15,000 for high school, according to the Council for American Private Education.
- In the Northeast, the elite private schools cost from $15,000 a year for day students to more than $30,000 for boarding students.
- The average cost for private religious schools is less than $4,000.
- With Cleveland's voucher program giving students up to $2,250 to help pay for private school, religious schools are the only option for lower- and middle-class parents. Indeed, in Cleveland, 96 percent of the students in the voucher program wound up in religion-based schools.

The voucher program not only removes talented students from their schools, it basically undermines the whole notion of public education. In an editorial at the time of the Supreme Court decision, *The New York Times* said that 'voucher programs like Cleveland's siphon off public dollars, leaving struggling urban systems with less money for skilled teachers, textbooks and computers. They also skim off some of the best-performing students, and the most informed and involved parents, from public schools that badly need their expertise and energy.'

A further element of No Child Left Behind that has educators and parents furious is a provision buried within its seven hundred pages of rules and regulations that requires all public schools to send students' names, addresses, and phone numbers to military recruiters, who can approach them with incentives of up to $20,000 in enlistment bonuses and $50,000 in college tuition packages, reports the *News & Observer* in North Carolina. According to David Goodman in *Mother Jones*, 'School officials are given wide leeway in how to implement the law, and some are simply handing over student directories to recruiters without informing anyone.' Major Johannes Paraan, a recruiter for the U.S. Army, told the magazine, 'The only thing that will get us to stop contacting the family is if they call their congressman. Or maybe if the kid died, we'll take them off our list.'

As with so many elements in the Bush's agenda for the nation, this one goes back to his time in Texas. No Child Left Behind was based on the same formula first sketched out in Houston by Education Secretary Rod Paige. His was a success story politicians dream about. Paige's story in a nutshell:

- He's an African-American Republican from Monticello, Mississippi.
- According to a profile of him in *The Christian Science Monitor*, his father was not only a school principal but also a Boy Scout leader and a deacon of the local church; Paige's mother was a teacher and librarian.
- All five children in the family graduated from college; three went on to complete their doctorates; and four went into teaching.
- Paige was elected to the Houston school board in 1989 and was named school superintendent 1994.
- Following a flurry of awards, including one from the American Association of School Administrators naming him superintendent of the year, Bush named him secretary of education.

Once settled in Washington, Paige hit some rough patches. He told *Baptist Press* that he thought it was important for schools to teach Christian values. That got civil liberties and education groups calling for his head. Then he referred to the National Education Association, the teachers' union, as 'a terrorist organization.' That got teachers calling for his head.

Bush trumpeted Paige as a model educator and the Texas school system as a model education program for the nation. The centerpiece of the system is a statewide test called the Texas Assessment of Academic Skills. 'As a presidential candidate,' *The New York Times* said, 'Texas's former governor, George W. Bush, contended that Texas's methods of holding schools responsible for student performance had brought huge improvements in passing rates and remarkable strides in eliminating the gap between white and minority children.'

But in July 2003, the *Times* reported that discrepancies had been discovered in the Texas school system. 'A recent state audit in Houston, which examined records from 16 middle and high schools, found that more than half of the 5,500 students who left in the 2000–01 school year should have been declared dropouts but were not. That year, Houston schools reported that only 1.5 percent of its students had dropped out.' At Sharpstown High in Houston, Assistant Principal Robert Kimball wrote to Principal Carol Wichmann warning that the school was misrepresenting its dropout figures. 'We go from 1,000 Freshmen to less than 300 Seniors [in the same class four years later] with no dropouts,' Kimball wrote. 'Amazing!'

As an editorial in *The Times* noted, 'It turns out the Houston schools have not lived up to their billing. Their amazingly low high school dropout rate was literally unbelievable – the educational equivalent of Enron's accounting results.'

On the surface, No Child Left Behind was an idea both Republicans and Democrats could embrace: better education for the nation's public school students. In practice, it appears to be doing more harm than good to school systems that are far from perfect but still the envy of the world. The two liberal Democrats who appeared with Bush for the photo op organized when he signed the legislation into law in January 2002, Massachusetts Senator Ted Kennedy and Calfornia Congressman George Miller, later criticized the White House for not backing up the bill with the necessary funding. As one teacher said, it's 'like sending a child for $10 worth of groceries and giving him just $1 to buy them.'

7

*

HEALTH CARE

WE are the greatest health care consumers in history. In 2002, Americans spent $1.55 trillion on their health, according to the Department of Health and Human Services. That's $5,440 for each person in the United States, more than double the number for the next biggest per capita spender, Switzerland. Health-care spending in America rose 9.3 percent in 2002, the biggest increase in more than a decade and during a year in which inflation was only 1.6 percent.

The United States also devotes a greater percentage of its economy to health care than any other country. In 2000, health care accounted for 13.3 percent of America's gross domestic product; in 2001, it accounted for 14.1 percent; and in 2002, it rose to 14.9 percent of GDP. Health and Human Services estimates that by 2012, the United States will be devoting 17.7 percent of its GDP to health-care spending. By comparison, the Swiss spend only 10.9 percent of their GDP on health care.

We also spend more on drugs per capita than any other country. According to a *Time* magazine investigative report, annual pharmaceutical sales in America averaged $654 per person in 2001. In Britain, the figure is $197. In Italy, it's $209.

So. We spend more on health care than any other country and more on drugs, and we devote a greater percentage of our economy to health care than any other industrialized country. And this being America – we love being number one – we must have the best health care in the world. Right?

No. Not even close. According to the first-ever study of individual countries' health plans conducted by the World Health Organization and published in June 2000, out of 191 member states, France has the top slot, followed by Italy, San Marino, Andorra, Malta, and Singapore. America's not in the top ten. It's not even in the top twenty-five. The United States is way down the list, sandwiched between Costa Rica and Slovenia, in thirty-seventh place. (Iraq was number 103, between Bulgaria and Armenia.) In the Middle East, Oman is in eighth place, Saudi Arabia ranks twenty-sixth, and the United Arab Emirates is in twenty-seventh place.

When it comes to life expectancy, in comparison with other industrialized nations like Japan, France, Switzerland, Germany, Italy, Britain, and Spain, America doesn't rank first, or second, but *last*. In the United States, life expectancy is seventy-seven years. The other countries have life expectancies that vary between seventy-eight and eighty-one years.

The United States, furthermore, has the distinction of being the only industrialized country in the world that does not guarantee health coverage for all its citizens. Given the amount of money America spends on health care, the absence of universal coverage is the closest thing we have to a national disgrace. And the situation is getting worse:

- According to the Census Bureau statistics, in 1996, the year Bill Clinton was elected president, there were 38.6 million Americans without health insurance.
- In 2000, the year George W. Bush was elected, 39.8 million Americans had no health insurance.

- By the end of 2002, Bush's second year in office, the number had swollen to 43.6 million, more than 15 percent of the population.

In a December 2001 report published by the National Academy of Sciences, Dr. Arthur Kellermann wrote that eight out of ten Americans without health insurance are employed or are members of a working family. Yet in early 2004, following a three-year study by fifteen experts, the academy concluded that 'universal insurance coverage is an important and achievable goal for the country.'

Medicare and Medicaid were designed to provide health insurance for the elderly, the disabled, and the poor. The program is far from perfect. A 2004 study done by the Kaiser Family Foundation said that 'because of gaps in Medicare's coverage, the elderly spent an estimated 22% of their income, on average, for health-care services and premiums in 2002 . . . most have some form of supplemental insurance.'

Medicare took twenty years to become law. First introduced by Truman in 1945 as a coverage plan for all Americans through Social Security, it was picked up by Kennedy, who focused on coverage for the elderly. In 1965, Johnson signed Medicare and Medicaid into law. Truman, who was eighty-one at the time, received the first Medicare card. Within a year, nineteen million Americans had been enrolled. Today, more than forty million elderly and disabled Americans benefit from Medicare.

Medicaid is a corollary plan designed primarily to help low-income families pay for health care. With about forty-three million members, Medicaid accounts for 17 percent of all health care spending in the United States. Washington and the state governments finance it jointly, with the federal government picking up a little over half the $258 billion tab in 2002.

Bush's record on health care when he was governor of Texas was dismal. More than 27 percent of Texans between nineteen and sixty-five were uninsured in 1998, when the national average was 19.7 percent, wrote Adam Clymer in *The New York Times* during the 2000 campaign. More than 39 percent of poor Texas children in 1998 were uninsured, compared to about 26 percent nationwide. 'Texas has had one of the nation's worst public health records for decades,' Clymer wrote. 'The state ranks near the top in the nation in rates of AIDS, diabetes, tuberculosis and teenage pregnancy, and near the bottom in immunizations, mammograms and access to physicians.'

A Medicare prescription drug plan for the elderly achieved a grassroots momentum going into the new millennium that even this White House couldn't ignore. Drug prices were skyrocketing. Even the giant pharmaceutical and insurance companies realized this was a political movement that wasn't going to go away, that it was destined to become a very important part of their future. A Gallup poll found that 82 percent of Americans said health care was one of their top concerns.

Defeating the movement was out of the question.

Controlling and profiting from it was the way to go.

There was a lot at stake. The pharmaceutical industry is the single most profitable sector in American business. In 2002, the ten largest drug companies posted 17 percent profits on average. (The average profit for Fortune 500 companies that year was just 3.1 percent.) According to *Time,* Pfizer, which manufactures the cholesterol pill Lipitor and the antidepressant Zoloft, had a 28 percent profit margin in 2002. By comparison, Wal-Mart, considered one of the best-run companies in the world, had a profit margin of 3.3 percent. The Health Reform Program of Boston University estimates that the Medicare drug program will increase the profits of the major pharmaceutical companies by 38 percent.

According to a *Business Week* article published in April 2004, this is what the heads of five of the major drug companies made in 2003:

- Pfizer: H. A. McKinnell, $9,457,000
- Merck: R. V. Gilmartin, $2,958,000
- Johnson & Johnson: W. C. Weldon, $6,567,000
- Bristol-Myers Squibb: P. R. Dolan, $5,869,000
- Wyeth: R. Essner, $3,569,000

According to the Public Campaign Action Fund, the drug lobby spent an estimated $544 million fighting for their interests between 1997 and 2002. They hired 675 lobbyists – more than there are representatives, senators, and cabinet members combined. *Fortune* magazine reported that the industry spent $139 million leaning on politicians in the first six months of 2003 alone, just as Congress was gearing up to debate the administration's Medicare drug benefit.

The pharmaceutical industry once split its political campaign donations roughly evenly between the two parties, with Republicans getting slightly more than Democrats. More recently, sensing that a Bush administration would be friendly to its interests, the industry bet the farm on the Republicans. According to Charles Lewis, author of *The Buying of the President 2004,* 'The top five pharmaceutical contributors to the political parties in the 2000 and 2002 election cycles gave 87% of their party donations to the Republican national committees.' The party, it can safely be said, is appreciative. A letter that went out in April 1999 from Jim Nicholson, the Republican national chairman, to Charles Heimbold, CEO of Bristol-Myers, said, 'We must keep the lines of communication open if we want to continue passing legislation that will benefit your industry.' It doesn't get more appreciative than that. And Bristol-Myers responded: The company and its employees contributed $2 million to the Republican Party and its candidates during the 2000 campaign, according to the Center for Responsive Politics, which tracks campaign financing. Heimbold, by the way, subsequently left Bristol-Myers. Bush named him ambassador to Sweden.

The president and others in his party received more than $34 million in campaign contributions from the drug companies, their employees, and their interest groups from 1999 to 2003. At one Republican fund-raiser headlined by Bush in 2002, some drug giants were among donors paying $250,000 each. The event raised $30 million in a single evening, and the fact that this occurred while Congress was trying to push through the Bush-backed prescription drug benefit bill for Medicare speaks volumes about the way it was received by the big drug companies.

The Center for American Progress calculated that along with Bush, the ten senators and representatives who got the industry-backed Medicare bill passed had received a total of more than $17 million in campaign contributions from the health-care and drug industries between 1999 and 2003:

- John Breaux (D-LA)
    Received from the health industry: $118,612
    Received from the drug industry: $59,150
- Tom DeLay (R-TX)
    Health industry: $237,199
    Drug industry: $78,250
- Bill Frist (R-TN)
    Health industry: $550,264
    Drug industry: $123,957
- Dennis Hastert (R-IL)
    Health industry: $545,985
    Drug industry: $194,700
- Charles Grassley (R-IA)
    Health industry: $573,678
    Drug industry: $217,921
- Max Baucus (D-MT)
    Health industry: $646,450
    Drug industry: $145,372

- Billy Tauzin (R-LA)
    Health industry: $601,077
    Drug industry: $211,249
- Orrin Hatch (R-UT)
    Health industry: $743,940
    Drug industry: $433,324
- Bill Thomas (R-CA)
    Health industry: $1,021,920
    Drug industry: $322,514
- Nancy Johnson (R-CT)
    Health industry: $1,418,258
    Drug industry: $336,908
- George Bush
    Health industry: $7,549,695
    Drug industry: $891,208

The bill itself was pulled together almost entirely by Republicans. Negotiating sessions were closed to all Democratic members of the House and included only two Democrats from the Senate. The House received the thousand-plus page bill on Friday, November 21, 2003. Members usually get at least three days to review new legislation. The Republicans demanded a vote on the $395 billion package, the most sweeping changes to Medicare in its thirty-eight-year history, within hours. 'A thousand pages in four hours is not acceptable,' Sheila Jackson Lee, a Democratic congresswoman from Texas, told the House's Rules Committee, according to a UPI report.

When the votes were cast a few hours before dawn on Saturday, the Republicans were down two votes, and the Medicare bill was on the verge of defeat.

Voting in the House generally takes fifteen minutes. In this case, however, the Republicans kept the recording period open, dragging out the count for a modern-day record of two hours and fifty-one minutes while its leadership went to work on wayward party members who had voted against the bill. Bush, having just returned from Europe, was asleep at the time. He was awakened at 4 a.m. so that he could begin calling the holdouts. He got nos from two of his calls, according to Robert Novak in the *Chicago Sun-Times*. And then a couple of yeses. The bill passed at 6 a.m.

The day before, Novak says, Republican Nick Smith, an eleven-year veteran of the House, had been lobbied by Speaker Dennis Hastert and Health and Human Services secretary Tommy Thompson. Smith, a sixty-nine-year-old former dairy farmer, was going to retire, and he wanted his son Brad to run for his seat. Smith refused to be swayed. Later, Novak said, 'Things got personal.' Smith was told by people he refuses to identify that if he voted for the bill, 'business interests' would put up $100,000 toward his son's campaign, though he later disputed the exact figure. Still, Smith voted against the Republican initiative. The House Ethics Committee is investigating.

The day after the bill passed in the House, Senate Majority Leader Bill Frist immediately began to push it through the Senate by calling for a rare Sunday debate session and issuing a warning to Senate Democrats, saying, according to *The Washington Post,* 'Those who would support a cruel filibuster of this bill would hold our parents and our grandparents – 40 million American seniors – hostage to Washington's politics.'

Frist, a doctor, is the White House's go-to guy on health-care issues. In early 2004, *Harper's* magazine estimated the Frist household's stake in HCA – the Hospital Corporation of America, the nation's largest chain of for-profit hospitals, founded in 1968 by Frist's father and older brother – at $26 million. Lewis Lapham wrote in *Harper's* that for several decades, HCA 'required each of its hospitals to return a profit of 20 percent a year and to "upcode" their patients by exaggerating the degree and severity of their illnesses in order to receive, from Medicare, more generous reimbursements for the delivery of imaginary goods and services.' Between 2000 and 2002, HCA paid nearly $1.5 billion in fines and settlements over fraud charges.

A few points about the Republicans' overhaul of Medicare.

THE PLAN ITSELF

- It's of only marginal help to some of those already receiving Medicare. And that assistance doesn't kick in until 2006.
- *The Boston Globe* reported that the plan does little for about three million seniors near the poverty level, and that those who pay less than $835 a year for drugs will see their costs actually rise.
- For seniors, it eliminates the optional Medigap plan that covered drug costs over and above what Medicare pays for.
- Under the new plan, patients are guaranteed only drugs that can treat their general ailments and cannot choose specific medicines. Insurers can drop a drug from their coverage even after patients are already committed to their plan.
- When insurers make changes in the drugs they are willing to pay for, they need only post the new information on the Internet, hardly a primary source of information for most senior citizens.
- The bill stifles price controls on prescription drugs. Not only that, the plan actively forbids Medicare from trying to negotiate better prices for drugs from the pharmaceutical companies that make them. The inspector general for the Department of Health and Human Services produced a report in 2001 that surveyed Medicare reimbursements for twenty-four drugs. It found that they 'exceeded actual wholesale prices by $761 million a year.'
- According to a Center for Economic and Policy Research (CEPR) report, seniors with middle incomes will pay an average of $1,650 in out-of-pocket expenses for prescription drugs in 2006, up 60 percent from what they paid for them in 2000.
- Beneficiaries of the new bill pay an average premium of $35

a month, with a $250 deductible. After the deductible, the government pays 75 percent of the first $2,250 in drug costs.

- But between $2,250 and $5,100, patients are on their own – the government chips in nothing. (This coverage gap is called the 'donut hole.') There is a $3,600 out-of-pocket spending limit, after which Medicare picks up 95 percent of the tab.

- According to Lapham, the new Medicare law contains 'a $12 billion slush fund from which, over the next ten years, the secretary of health and human services may pay out bribes to HMOs otherwise reluctant to accept patients whose illnesses cannot be prepped for quick and certain gain.'

THE NEW MEMBERS, THE MONEY

- When Medicare was created in 1965, the costs were projected at an annual sum of $10 billion.

- By 2003, according to the Heritage Foundation, the cost was $244 billion a year.

- Before the new bill was signed, the administration said the extra cost was going to be $395 billion over ten years. Less than two months after Bush signed the bill into law, the White House had revised the figure upward to $534 billion.

- 'The ink isn't even dry [on the new Medicare law], there's not a single card issued yet, and the price went up by over 30%,' Rahm Emanuel, a congressman from Illinois, was quoted in *The Boston Globe*.

- Bush's Medicare chief, Thomas Scully, threatened to fire Richard Foster, the top actuary at Medicare, if he disclosed the true cost of the bill to Congress. Foster had privately warned the administration while the bill was being considered that its cost would be much higher than the

White House was leading Congress to believe. According to *The New York Times,* Tommy Thompson, secretary of health and human services, 'told lawmakers, "we knew all along" that the administration's cost estimates would be higher,' and added that people at the White House were aware of the higher preliminary estimates.

- The director of the Congressional Budget Office estimates that the drug benefit will cost between $1 trillion and $2 trillion in its second decade.
- There are forty million retired Americans now.
- The first of the baby boomers will turn sixty-five in 2011.
- By 2030, there will be seventy-six million retirees.
- According to a March 2004 trustee report, Medicare, without changes to the system, will exhaust the surplus in its trust fund by 2019, seven years earlier than what the trustees estimated last year.

WHAT SENIORS THINK OF IT

- A week after the bill passed, a poll by Hart Research found that 65 percent of the membership of the American Association of Retired People 'wanted Congress to go back to the drawing board,' according to the *Alameda Times-Star.*
- AARP members were furious at the association's leadership. 'AARP – what does it stand for?' Democratic congressman Pete Stark said in a letter to his House colleagues. 'Always Advocating for the Republican Party.'
- On December 8, the day Bush signed the bill into law, 'polls showed more Americans opposing it than supporting it,' wrote *The American Prospect.*
- And most of them still have no idea of the actual details of the plan.

THE GUIDING PHILOSOPHY BEHIND THE PLAN

- It is a step in a long-term march toward privatizing Medicare that began in the mid-1990s when, according to Trudy Lieberman writing in *The Nation* in November 2003, 'rightwing politicians and their allies at the Heritage Foundation embarked on a campaign to transform Medicare into a private insurance program and ultimately to remove the government from the business of guaranteeing healthcare for the oldest and sickest citizens.'
- By 2010, Robert Berenson of the Urban Institute estimates that much of what we think of as Medicare will be privatized.

Then there's the matter of the drug discount card, which seniors will use until 2006, when Medicare drug coverage kicks in. The elderly will be responsible for doing their own due diligence as to which of the seventy-three available discount cards is best for them.

According to the Center for American Progress, 'The Bush administration's new Medicare drug card plan is more like a shell game than a savings program.' In May and June 2004, the center reported:

- Of the seventy-three companies approved by the administration, at least twenty have been involved in charges of bilking Medicare and overcharging consumers.
- Seniors could buy a month's worth of the most popular brand-name drugs cheaper on Drugstore.com than through some of the Medicare discount cards.
- The elderly must choose a single card program, even if selecting multiple cards would save them money.
- Once that card is selected, enrollees cannot switch

programs until 2005. The drug companies, however, can change prices on a weekly basis, and the government is powerless to negotiate the lowest price possible.

'Only in this administration,' Senator Edward M. Kennedy told *The Boston Globe,* 'would the words "discount card" mean seniors get the card while corporations get the discounts.'

According to the Fort Worth *Star-Telegram,* Bush sought the help of David Halbert when the administration was drafting the drug discount card proposal, and indeed Halbert was at the president's side when he originally announced the Medicare initiative in the White House Rose Garden in July 2001.

According to the *Star-Telegram*, Halbert's company, AdvancePCS, along with four other firms control '80% of the Pharmaceutical Benefit Management market and up to 90% of the mail-order pharmacy business.' These companies will work under contract to the big health-care providers to 'negotiate with drug makers, issue discount cards and line up networks of pharmacies.' As Bloomberg News reported in 2003, the system is designed to steer 'patients away from [local] pharmacies and into mail-order businesses run by pharmacy-benefit managers such as Express Scripts Inc. and AdvancePCS.'

Halbert was brought in on the planning of the bill not because he's a widely respected authority on the subject or anything. But he did have the following going for him:

- He's been a Bush campaign contributor since 1994.
- According to the *Star-Telegram,* Halbert 'helped clean up a deal with Harken Energy that had earlier prompted an S.E.C. investigation of George W. Bush.'
- Furthermore, Bush was an early investor in Halbert's business and went on to make a $1 million profit on that investment.
- In March 2004, AdvancePCS merged with Caremark Rx to

become the number two company in the pharmaceutical benefit management industry.

- The Center for American Progress called AdvancePCS 'the Halliburton of Medicare.'

The importation of cheaper drugs from Canada is a growing annoyance to the big pharmaceutical companies, because their profit margins are so much lower when they sell drugs to Canadian rather than American drugstores. According to *Time,* in 2002, Americans spent $40.7 billion on imported prescription drugs, much of that from Canada – a nearly fivefold increase over 1995. It's not hard to see why this business is on the rise. A typical prescription for Lipitor in the United States costs between $272 and $308; in Canada, it runs $159 to $199. Pfizer, the manufacturer of Lipitor, is, says *Time,* 'aggressively seeking a pharmaceutical blacklist, warning Canadian pharmacies that if they sell drugs to Americans, Pfizer will halt supplies of all its products.'

Writing in *Fortune,* Roger Parloff had this to say: 'Manufacturers will start raising their Canadian prices – as at least four have done. Canadian price regulators will try to block those hikes – as Quebec is now trying to do. If manufacturers can't raise Canadian prices, they'll clamp down further on Canadian supply, creating shortages. If drug shortages threaten Canadians' health, Canada may cease honoring manufacturers' patents. And if Canada stops honoring U.S. patents, the U.S. might bring a complaint against Canada before the World Trade Organization. Or invade.'

Although a report by the Congressional Research Service found that drugs manufactured in Canada meet or surpass the quality-control guidelines set by the U.S. Food and Drug Administration, the FDA and the pharmaceutical industry have spread rumors that Canadian drugs aren't safe. One ear they apparently whispered in was that of the president. In early 2004, despite the findings of the Congressional Research Service report, the White

House announced a year-long study of whether drugs could be safely imported from Canada. 'But then,' Robert Pear wrote in *The New York Times*, 'it infuriated the critics by selecting Mark B. McClellan, the commissioner of food and drugs, to lead the study. Dr. McClellan has [in the past] adamantly opposed any relaxation of the rules barring drug imports. He says such imports would be unsafe, and his agency has threatened legal action against cities and states that help people import Canadian drugs.'

All this fearmongering is doubly spurious since many of the common prescription drugs sold in the United States by American pharmaceutical companies aren't even made here. Pfizer outsources the manufacture of Lipitor to Ireland. Viagra's made there too. In fact, according to *Time*, 'seventeen of the 20 largest drug companies worldwide now make drugs in Ireland, largely because of tax incentives.'

Finally, there was the matter of selling the new Medicare program to the public in an election year. The Bush White House budgeted $9.5 million in television ads, another $10 million on brochures, and a further $3.1 million in ads directed at Hispanic voters, *The American Prospect* reported in early 2004. The television ads were handled by National Media, a consulting firm that was also working on the Bush–Cheney reelection campaign. The ads were intended for use on local news programs and made to look like actual news reports praising the new Medicare law. Two of the spots ended with a woman saying, 'In Washington, I'm Karen Ryan reporting.' The packages sent out went so far as to include prepared dialogue for the news anchors to use to introduce Ryan as a 'reporter.' But Ryan is an actor and the scripts she read were written by the administration.

'If the administration wants to help the seniors of this country deal with their prescription drug costs, I might suggest using $10 million to help improve the inadequate drug benefit rather than using it to convince seniors the plan they have is "really not that bad,"' said Arkansas congressman Marion Berry.

The $9.5 million to fund the ads came from the Department of Health and Human Services – taxpayer money that should be used to implement the law, not to sell an already passed bill to the public. Democrats accused the White House of running nothing more than an election ad and argued that the funds should come from the GOP campaign war chest. In May 2004, the nonpartisan General Accounting Office ruled that the video ads were illegal, calling them a form of 'covert propaganda.'

8

▓

THE JUDICIARY

'When a President chooses a judge, he is placing in human hands the
authority and majesty of the law. He owes it to the Constitution and to
the country to choose with care. I have done so . . . All have sterling
credentials and have met high standards of legal training, temperament,
and judgment.'

— GEORGE W. BUSH, May 2002

ONCE in office, the Bush team immediately went for the court advantage. It is the single most important thing they did. And they know it.

It's one thing to effect temporary change in America – all presidents manage to do this in one form or another. It's another thing to dramatically alter the very fabric of American democracy and do it in such a way that it goes virtually unnoticed but lasts a long while. Here the Bush White House has triumphed by constructing a program to implement right-wing ideological change that stays put for a generation, or two, or more. How is it doing this?

By focusing its energies on the courts.

Give the Republicans their due: They're not stupid. By infusing the federal courts with appointees who share the president's reactionary beliefs, the White House ensures that Bush's imprint will stand for decades to come. Packing the courts with likeminded jurists is *the* fundamental chapter in the Republican playbook, and it has been for some time.

Pat Buchanan, Reagan's communications director, laid out the game plan back in 1986: Our conservative judicial appointment strategy 'could do more to advance the social agenda – school prayer, anti-pornography, anti-busing, right-to-life and quotas in employment – than anything Congress can accomplish in 20 years.'

The Clinton administration didn't seem to get this, which is strange for a White House headed by a lawyer – well, two lawyers, really. After a dozen years of Reagan and the senior Bush, all thirteen U.S. courts of appeals (circuit courts), the courts just below the Supreme Court, had Republican majorities. Clinton, during his eight years in office, never made it a priority to actively push for a liberal slate of judicial appointees. For whatever reason – it may have been laxness, an unwillingness to spend the political capital necessary to push through key nominees, or just that his administration was plum worn down by scandal and investigation – the lack of an activist program to place liberal judicial nominees on the federal courts was a major mistake.

Republicans, on the other hand, are rabid in their desire to pack the courts. So much so that according to a report in *The Boston Globe* in early 2004, 'Republican staff members of the U.S. Senate Judiciary Committee infiltrated opposition computers for a year.' How did they discover the spying? Excerpts from confidential memoranda detailing Judiciary Democrats' strategies to filibuster the Republicans' conservative nominees began showing up 'in the pages of the conservative-leaning newspapers,' says *The Globe*. A subsequent report by the Senate's sergeant-at-arms revealed that eighteen months of spying led to the pilfering of more than four thousand six hundred files – primarily from the Democratic staff. The spying has led the Justice Department to open an investigation to determine if any crimes were committed.

Supreme Court appointees are there for life; only death or retirement opens the door to opportunity. Clinton managed to put a pair of his own on the high court. (The rest of the nine-person court is made up of one Nixon appointee, one from Ford, three from the Reagan administration, and two placed by George H. W. Bush.)

The circuit courts are only slightly less important. Republicans controlled the Senate for most of Clinton's presidency, and they dogged many of his candidates with arbitrary objections and dragged out the confirmation process for as long as possible. Of the circuit court nominees he put forward between 1995 and 2000, more than a third were blocked by the Republicans. In 1996, not one of his appellate court candidates was confirmed. The result: There were eighty-one federal court vacancies by the time Bush came into office, including more than two dozen empty seats on the circuit courts.

White House Counsel Alberto Gonzales, the president's point man on judicial nominees, hit the ground running. By the end of his first year in office, Bush had successfully appointed twenty-eight judges to the federal courts. As Gonzales told the *St. Louis Post-Dispatch,* 'This may be the most important thing a president does.' Admistrative policies, executive orders, and legislative victories all matter, Gonzales said, but 'those can always be undone by the next congress.'

The thing about federal judges, especially those on the high bench, is that they seem to stick around forever. Supreme Court Chief Justice William Rehnquist, who was forty-seven when he was named to the bench, has served for more than three decades. Antonin Scalia was fifty when he joined the Court and has almost two decades under his belt. The Bush administration is being very calculating in its nominations for the feeder courts right below the Supreme Court where justices also serve for life. Most are right-wing ideologues. And 10 percent of Bush's nominees are in their thirties and early forties.

These extremist judges affect not only the judicial process, they can also play serious roles in the political arena. In February 2004, Bush named Laurence Silberman, a semiretired judge on the DC circuit, to head the committee charged with investigating U.S. intelligence failures prior to the invasion of Iraq. Silberman, a Reagan judicial appointee, is, according to Michelle Goldberg of *Salon,* a 'fierce ideologue who doesn't let his judicial responsibilities get in the way of his Republican activism.' And he's not without influence: Twenty of his former clerks went on to work for the Supreme Court, wrote Goldberg, and a number of others have jobs in the Bush administration. Silberman himself has been at the center of some of the most explosive political scandals in recent memory:

- Iran-contra. He voted to overturn Oliver North's felony conviction.
- Clarence Thomas. He championed the Republican movement to vilify Anita Hill during Thomas's confirmation hearings. David Brock wrote in his book *Blinded by the Right* that Silberman said Thomas never would have asked Hill for a date, speculating that she was a lesbian and 'had bad breath.'
- The move to have Clinton impeached. He had a hand in bringing Paula Jones forward, which led to the Monica Lewinsky investigation and the move to have Clinton impeached, and he later sat on a federal appeals court panel that rejected Clinton's efforts to keep Secret Service agents from testifying about his relationships.

And now the 'most partisan and most political federal judge in the country,' as Ralph Neas, president of People For the

American Way, has called Silberman, has been tapped by Bush to cochair the president's commission investigating U.S. intelligence in Iraq.

The Republicans were single-minded and ruthless in their quest to take over the courts.

The Bush White House is wise to the fact that while Supreme Court nominees attract the sort of attention papal appointees and reality TV show winners get, candidates for the circuit courts of appeals – the courts directly below it – generate considerably less notice. (To be honest, Americans don't follow the courts that much at all. Polls have shown that two-thirds of them can't name even one Supreme Court justice.) And while the high court typically hears fewer than one hundred cases a year, the thirteen circuit courts rule on nearly thirty thousand cases a year. Their decisions can be the last word on everything from constitutional framework issues such as civil and privacy rights cases to environmental issues and the rights of women, homosexuals, and workers.

It was the DC circuit, for instance, that decided that the White House's plan to allow power companies to modernize their plants without upgrading their pollution controls violated the 1970 Clean Air Act. The same court rejected Vice President Dick Cheney's attempt to keep secret the identity of the members of his Energy Task Force. (Cheney appealed to the Supreme Court, where he hopes to get a more favorable result: He and Justice Scalia are friends and went duck hunting together at a private camp in Louisiana, flying down on Air Force Two just three weeks after the Supreme Court agreed to hear the case. Scalia did not believe he had a conflict or that it was reasonable to question his impartiality. Several legal scholars have questioned Scalia's ability to judge the appeal with any degree of impartiality. And with good reason. When the case opened before the high court in late April, Scalia immediately defended the administration, asserting, 'I think executive privilege means that whenever the president feels that he is threatened, he can simply refuse to comply with a court order.' When the Court ruled in June, Scalia helped deliver some favorable results. The ruling ordered the Lower Court to spend more time with the case, which means the task force documents will remain sealed until the case is decided. Scalia, together with Clarence Thomas, wrote, in a separate opinion that the District Court judge "clearly exceeded" his authority in ordering the administration to release the records.)

It was the second Circuit Court that held that Bush lacked the authority to classify an American citizen who was arrested in the United States as an 'enemy combatant' and thereby deny him due process. The Ninth Circuit Court in San Francisco ruled that the indefinite imprisonment without trial of the more than six hundred non-Americans being held at Guantánamo Bay is 'at odds with' the Geneva Conventions and also violates the U.S. Constitution.

Another thing: Seven of the nine current Supreme Court justices were plucked from the benches of the circuit courts.

Reagan and the senior Bush made 125 circuit court appointments between them. Clinton, though in office for two-thirds the combined number of years of his two predecessors, made just over half their number of appointments. George W. Bush, after a mere three years in office, has made thirty, putting him on track to fill almost 25 percent more judicial seats than Clinton. Early in Bush's fourth year, nine of the thirteen courts had Republican-nominated majorities, two had Democratic-nominated majorities, and two were evenly divided. At the end of the Clinton administration, according to a report by the Alliance for Justice, 54 percent of judges on the federal courts were Democratic appointees and 46 percent Republican. At the three-year mark of the Bush administration, the numbers had more than reversed. Republicans had placed 57 percent of the judges and Democrats 43 percent.

The White House and Republican Senate have used the war on terror post–September 11 to their own ends, craftily labeling any opposition to their mandate as a lack of patriotism and general liberal wussiness.

The Bush White House's push to pack the courts has left the United States with the lowest vacancy rate on federal benches in thirteen years, according to Senator Patrick Leahy, the ranking Democrat on the Senate Judiciary Committee.

By comparison, Republican opposition to court nominees during the Clinton years was archly partisan, especially at the end of his term – in Clinton's last year in office, 89 percent of his nominees were blocked. Now, as legal scholar Cass Sunstein puts it in *The American Prospect,* 'Too often, the views of contemporary federal judges are closer to the Republican Party platform than to those of the framers [of the Constitution].'

Throughout the Bush administration, the Justice Department has been a willing accomplice to the White House's determination to make the federal courts even more conservative than they already are. Traditionally, the department has acted on behalf of Congress to advise lawmakers on constitutional boundaries in drafting laws. But the Justice Department under Bush increasingly does the *president's* bidding. Attorney General John Ashcroft is, like Bush, a man who invokes God in his day job. Ashcroft is a devout Pentecostal – they're against alcohol, dancing, and pre-marital sex; they're also into healing and speaking in tongues – who holds prayer meetings in his office or a nearby conference room every morning, and he has made the separation of church and state worryingly porous. Warning: A right-wing Supreme Court run by justices Scalia and Thomas would allow the White House unprecedented say in religious matters.

The first thing the Bush White House did was to make the Federalist Society the dominant body in reviewing judicial nominees.

An essential factor in the Republican highjacking of the nation's courts has been Bush's elevation of the Federalist Society, which the administration has used to usurp the long-standing role of the centrist, 125-year-old American Bar Association, as the vetting body for federal judgeships.

For a half century, the ABA's ratings of nominees had been instrumental in keeping incompetent or ideological jurists off the bench. The ABA is hardly a hotbed of liberal radicalism – it's an association of four hundred thousand lawyers, after all. Nevertheless, by 2001, Bush had marginalized the ABA's role in the judicial selection process.

The ominously named 'society' was started in 1982 by a cluster of conservative firebrands at the University of Chicago Law School. It has been funded and led by an assortment of right-wing groups and individuals including, says freedom of speech attorney Martin Garbus, the seriously conservative American Enterprise Institute, Charles Koch, and the Sarah Scaife Foundation, named for the mother of ideologue Richard Mellon Scaife (who, according to *The Washington Post,* has given more than $300 million over the years to various conservative groups and put aside $2.4 million during the Clinton administration just to gather information that would discredit the president). Federalists favor creationist teachings and the use of religious materials in public schools. Also this: Many of them think that Rehnquist, a Nixon appointee, is too moderate.

The Federalist Society has more than twenty-five thousand members, including John Ashcroft, Edwin Meese (attorney general under Reagan), Interior Secretary Gale Norton, and Supreme Court Justice Antonin Scalia. White House Counsel Alberto Gonzales is a member of the Federalist Society too, as are five of the eleven members lawyers of his staff. Orrin Hatch, chairman of the Senate Judiciary Committee, which holds the confirmation hearings for the nominees, is also a member. The right-wing *Washington Times* has called it the 'single most influential organization in the conservative legal world.'

The Federalist Society is counted on by Bush to vet his federal court nominees, but the group's control of the courts doesn't stop there. It is also active in filling powerful clerkship positions within the Supreme Court and the circuit courts, 'recognizing,' as Martin Garbus has said, 'the power of clerks to influence one another, justices, judges and the law itself.'

With everything in place, the Bush administration started packing the circuit courts with fellow ideologues.
The Circuit Court for the District of Columbia is a key target of the Bush administration. It's the second most important court in the land, right behind the Supreme Court, for the following reasons:

- It's located in the capital.
- It has the last word on what a host of federal agencies can and cannot regulate. Says Chris Mooney in *The American Prospect,* 'Along with its central duty of resolving disputes over the separation of powers, Congress has given the D.C. Circuit exclusive jurisdiction over challenges to numerous federal agency decisions, including Federal Communications Commission orders, national Environmental Protection Agency rulings issued under the Clean Air Act and regulations put forth under several other key environmental provisions, including the Safe Drinking Water Act.'
- It's *the* farm team for the Supreme Court. Justices Scalia, Thomas, and Ruth Bader Ginsburg were all chosen from the DC Circuit Court.

The court had an equal number of Democratic and Republican appointees until the White House got John G. Roberts, a former Rhenquist clerk and associate counsel to President Reagan, confirmed in May 2003. It now has a Republican majority.

Judge Roberts's track record is not encouraging:

- He has a dismal history where the rights of women and minorities are concerned, having taken hard-line antichoice and anti–civil rights positions.
- He's considered to be anti–workers' rights and antienvironment.
- Since being appointed to the circuit court bench, he has argued in favor of Vice President Dick Cheney's right to keep his Energy Task Force work secret from the American public and objected to a ruling upholding the constitutionality of the Endangered Species Act.

Bush's nominees to the other circuit courts are no less worrying. A primer on the courts themselves and of his more extreme appointees and nominees follows.

Note: Many of Bush's nominees have not served on courts before. And even this is part of the Republican strategy. By putting forward candidates with little in the way of a judicial record, they make it more difficult for Democrats to object to them.

Most of the judges on the First Circuit Court (which hears cases from Maine, New Hampshire, Massachusetts, and Rhode Island) were named to the bench by Republican administrations. This is the smallest of the appellate courts, with only six judgeships. Bush has had only one vacancy during his presidency. He nominated Jeffrey Howard, an antiabortionist, and the Senate confirmed him in April 2002. Since assuming his seat, Howard has ruled for the government and against plaintiffs in at least two civil-rights-related cases.

The Second Circuit Court (which hears cases from Connecticut, New York, and Vermont) is among the most balanced benches in the country in terms of women and minorities. It has a slim Democratic majority, and it is an important majority. This court has stood up to Bush's narrow view of civil liberties. It ruled that the president did not have the power to indefinitely hold American citizens in military custody on American soil without legal representation. Even Judge Barrington Parker ruled against the president on this one, and he was a Bush appointee. In January 2004, the court ruled against the Bush administration's efforts to reduce by 10 percent Clinton's energy efficiency standards for air conditioners.

Two recent Republican appointments to the Third Circuit Court (which hears cases from Delaware, New Jersey, and Pennsylvania) do not bode well for the court's historically centrist line. In July 2002, Bush filled one of the openings with a Pennsylvanian, D. Brooks Smith, a former U.S. district court judge. And in December 2003, Michael Fisher, a former Pennsylvania attorney general, was confirmed.

Judge Smith's record:

- Alliance for Justice (a non-profit Washington-based advocacy organization that also monitors judicial nominations) suggested in a report that Smith is a judge 'who will sometimes distort or ignore the law to reach his desired result, too often one favoring corporate and other powerful interests over the interest of ordinary Americans.'
- According to the Alliance for Justice, Smith initially refused to recuse himself from 'a case involving a bank at which his wife was an employee and in which he had substantial financial interests.'
- Since being appointed, he has ruled in favor of the 'streamlining' of appeals regulations for immigrants at the Board of Immigration and Appeals, thus denying immigrants, in some cases, due process by replacing the usual three-member hearing panel with a single person. The judge who dissented on the opinion wrote that Smith and the majority had thus approved a 'provision of judicial review.'

Judge Fisher's record:

- He's opposed to abortion and gun control, and has voted against increases in the minimum wage, improvements in workers' rights, and environmental protection.
- He has spoken out against gay rights.
- He's an advocate of the death penalty.

The Fourth Circuit Court (which hears cases from Maryland, Virginia, West Virginia, North Carolina, and South Carolina) has a heavy Republican majority and is considered the most right wing of the appellate courts. According to the *Cornell Law Review,* less than a quarter of the sexual harassment plaintiffs who appear before the court prevail. (By contrast, almost double that number win their cases nationwide and four times that number prevail in the more liberal Second Circuit Court.) The Fourth Circuit Court became even more reactionary with the appointment of Judge Dennis Shedd, a former district court judge who once served as Senator Strom Thurmond's chief counsel.

Judge Shedd's record:

- A report by Alliance for Justice's judicial project, Independent Judiciary said that his history as a judge 'raises serious questions about competence and commitment to the role of the federal judiciary as guarantor of equal access to justice.'
- The same report stated that he has 'often refused to let a jury hear employment discrimination and other cases, instead deciding the case himself in favor of the employer.'
- He upheld the rights of South Carolina legislators to keep their ethics violations secret from voters.
- He has dismissed female sexual harassment claims and claims by disabled workers.

- In *Condon* v. *Reno*, he struck down the Driver's Privacy Protection Act, which protected employees and patients of abortion clinics from antiabortion extremists, who use driver's license information to post their home addresses on the Internet. The Supreme Court unanimously reversed his decision. That opinion was written by Chief Justice Rehnquist.
- Since being appointed, he has ruled against workers' rights. He authored a majority opinion that reversed a National Labor Relations Board ruling against antiunion discrimination. The ruling provoked a strong dissent from Shedd's colleague on the bench, the extremely conservative J. Harvie Wilkinson, who said that the majority had 'overstepped its bounds as a reviewing court.'

The Fifth Circuit Court (which hears cases from Texas, Louisiana, and Mississippi) had a large Republican majority and a reputation for being a bastion of conservative activism. Three days before the celebration of Martin Luther King Day in 2004 (and one day after laying a wreath on the civil rights leader's grave), Bush audaciously named Charles Pickering to one of the court's openings during a congressional recess. The appointment allows Pickering to serve out the remainder of the year without being formally confirmed. (The administration had put him up for the seat twice before, in 2001 and 2003, without success.) And little wonder.

Judge Pickering's record:

- As a state senator in Mississippi, he supported a constitutional amendment overturning *Roe* v. *Wade*. He also chaired a committee that drafted a national Republican Party platform opposing abortion even in cases of rape or incest.
- He has rarely ruled for the plaintiff in cases of employment discrimination.

- His critics maintain that he has a troubling record on civil rights. This is worrying, since the Fifth Circuit has the largest percentage of minority residents of any circuit court in the country apart from the DC Circuit.
- He wrote an article suggesting ways of strengthening laws against interracial marriage, and as a federal district court judge, he managed to reduce from seven years to twenty-seven months the jail term of a man who burned a cross in the yard of an interracial couple.
- He has called the one person/one vote doctrine 'obtrusive.'
- His two previous nominations to the circuit court were opposed by scores of groups representing workers' rights, individual rights, environmental protections, and civil rights, including such organizations as the National Association for the Advancement of Colored People, the AFL-CIO, and virtually every major women's group in the country.
- President Bush has called him 'a fine jurist, a man of quality and integrity.'

Another Fifth Circuit judge Bush has appointed is Ed Prado, a former Texas district court judge who was elevated to the circuit court bench in 2003.

Judge Prado's record:

- Well, it's not his actual record that is alarming so much as the way he runs his court. An article in *Texas Lawyer* said that Prado 'uses the courtroom as a comedy club with a captive audience for his standup routine.'
- During the trial of a wealthy businessman accused of hiring a hit man to kill his wife, Prado stopped the proceedings, pulled out a boom box, and proceeded to play an unfunny parody of the Turtles' 'Happy Together':

Imagine me as God, I do
I was appointed by the president
Appointed forever,
My decisions cannot be questioned by you
I'm always right.

I'm not making this up.

- When he was growing impatient with the pace of the trial, he played the theme from the TV show *Jeopardy.* I'm not making this up, either.
- And then there was the time he put on a dress and high heels and performed Ginger Rogers's airplane wing dance from *Flying Down to Rio.* Okay, I made that one up.

The Sixth Circuit Court (which hears cases from Michigan, Ohio, Kentucky, and Tennessee) was viewed as a moderate and evenly divided court. But thanks to years of Republican-dominated Senates refusing to hold confirmation hearings on Clinton nominees, a quarter of the Sixth Circuit's seats were vacant when Bush came into office. More have opened up since then, giving Bush an opportunity to swing the court to the right. His appointments include John Rodgers, a University of Kentucky law professor who has urged the high court to overturn *Roe* v. *Wade*; Deborah Cook, who was elevated from the Ohio Supreme Court and Jeffrey Sutton, a former law clerk for Supreme Court Justice Scalia. Cook and Sutton, by the way, donated $1000 each to the Bush campaign.

Judge Rodgers is a newly minted judge and so his record thus far is slim.

Judge Cook's record:

- She has repeatedly ruled against workers, consumers, and

victims of discrimination and corporate negligence, regularly siding with governments, industry, and insurance companies.

▪ She once argued that a worker who was lied to by his employer about the presence of toxic chemicals in his workplace could not sue for injuries suffered from exposure to those chemicals.

Judge Sutton's record:

▪ He argued that a female victim of sexual assault should not be able to sue her attackers in federal court when the state university where the attack occurred did not punish the attackers.

▪ He represented tobacco companies in a 2001 lawsuit, arguing that Massachusetts laws regulating the promotion of tobacco products to children were an unconstitutional limitation on free speech.

▪ He has built a decidedly hostile reputation regarding civil rights and workers' rights.

▪ He once argued that a nurse in Alabama, who'd been told to quit or accept demotion because she had breast cancer, was not protected by the Americans With Disabilities Act. The victory had sweeping consequences for workers in the state by depriving them of basic on-the-job legal protections.

The Seventh Circuit Court (which hears cases from Illinois, Indiana, and Wisconsin) is seen as very conservative and has a Republican majority with no vacancies. (It has no Hispanics or Asian Americans on the court, and only one African American, making it one of the least ethnically diverse federal courts.)

The Eighth Circuit Court (which hears cases from Minnesota, Iowa, Missouri, Arkansas, Nebraska, North Dakota and South Dakota) is one of the most lopsided Republican-nominated courts in the country. It had one vacancy when Bush came into office; three more subsequently opened up. Bush filled the openings with Lavenski Smith, William Riley, Michael Melloy, and Steven Colloton. The four had little in the way of a public record to examine and were confirmed easily. (Smith did cause some concern with his hostility toward *Roe* v. *Wade,* however.) The first three have issued troubling opinions since their nominations:

- Smith dissented in a sexual harassment case, arguing that the plaintiff should have to accept a retrial or damages of $10,000 instead of the majority-approved award of $200,000.
- In a racial discrimination case, both Melloy and Riley joined the majority opinion that denied the plaintiff a jury trial.

The Ninth Circuit Court (which hears cases from Alaska, Arizona, California, Hawaii, Idaho, Montana, Nevada, Oregon, and Washington) is the largest such court in the country. With a heavy Democratic majority, it's considered to be liberal to centrist. As a result, its decisions are reversed by the Supreme Court more than any other appellate court in the country. Bush is working hard to shift the majority. By the end of 2003, he'd made four appointments to the court, including Attorney General John Ashcroft's former number two, Jay Bybee, who was named to the court in March 2003, and Carlos Bea, a former California superior court judge, who was elevated in September 2003.

Judge Bybee's record:

- He authored a 2002 memorandum while he was the assistant attorney general that, according to *The New York Times,* 'appeared to establish a basis for the use of torture for senior Al Qaeda operatives in custody of the CIA', on the basis that momentary or fleeting pain was not necessarily torture.

- According to the Alliance for Justice report opposing his nomination, he has 'demonstrated a breathtaking disdain for democracy and contempt for Congress. Bybee has argued that the Seventeenth Amendment – which authorized the people rather than state legislators to elect U.S. Senators – should be repealed.'
- The same report notes that 'his writings suggest that he harbors a personal animus towards gays and lesbians.' In fact, he once referred to homosexuals as 'emotionally unstable.'
- He has argued for curbing congressional power and increasing the president's.
- He has argued to strike down laws that permit victims of gender-based violence to sue their attackers and considers the Violence Against Women Act and the Americans with Disabilities Act unconstitutional.

Judge Bea's record:

- An Alliance for Justice report at the time of his nomination stated, 'Most significantly, in recent surveys, lawyers in the San Francisco area have questioned his temperament on the bench, his preparedness, and his grasp of legal issues.'
- The report also said that, among his peers in the Bay Area, he is widely seen as having an 'attitude problem' – one experienced female lawyer described Bea as 'condescending and biased against women attorneys.'
- The report also said that he has been accused of showing a tendency to favor corporations over individual plaintiffs.

The Tenth Circuit Court (which hears cases from Colorado, Kansas, New Mexico, Utah, Oklahoma, and Wyoming) was evenly divided between Republican and Democratic appointees when Bush took over. Two slots – both held by Republican appointees – opened after the election, granting Bush four vacancies. He filled all of them, giving the court a seven-to-five Republican majority. Among his appointees are Michael McConnell, a law professor at the University of Utah, named to the court in 2002, and Timothy Tymkovich, a former Colorado state solicitor general, who was elevated to the bench the next year.

Judge McConnell's record:

- According to the Alliance for Justice report at the time of his confirmation, he had 'signed a statement [in 1996] calling for a Constitutional amendment to outlaw abortion, with no exception for rape and incest.'
- He has argued against the Freedom of Access to Clinic Entrances Act, stating that the protection of women, doctors, and abortion clinic staff from potentially violent protestors is unconstitutional. He's even favorably compared antiabortion protestors to followers of Martin Luther King Jr. during the civil rights movement.
- His views that the government *should* fund religious schools would, wrote the Alliance for Justice, 'fundamentally alter the current understanding of the Constitution and tear down much of the separation of church and state.'
- He believes in weakening constitutional protections against race, gender, and sexual orientation discrimination.

Judge Tymkovich's record:

- He was cochair of the Colorado chapter of Lawyers for Bush-Cheney 2000 (Lawyers for Bush-Cheney, broken down by state chapters? This should tell you something about how organized the Republicans are.)
- He's a former member of the Independence Institute, which an Alliance for Justice report said 'advocated for laws allowing Coloradoans to carry concealed weapons, and against affirmative action in higher education.'

- The report also says that 'throughout his legal career . . . he has vigorously advocated for positions that would deny equal justice to ordinary Americans, especially women . . . gays and lesbians.'

The Eleventh District Circuit Court (which hears cases from Alabama, Florida, and Georgia) had a slim Republican majority with one vacancy, which Bush had trouble filling. Then, a scant month after installing Charles Pickering onto the Fifth Circuit Court during a congressional recess, Bush again took advantage of a recess to put Alabama Attorney General William Pryor on the Eleventh Circuit Court, sidestepping an earlier successful democratic filibuster against him. But unlike Pickering, who received his recess appointment before the current session of Congress and must give up his seat in the fall of this year, Pryor can serve until the end of the *next* session of Congress, sometime in the fall of 2005.

What's Bush's opinion of Pryor? 'His impressive record demonstrates his devotion to the rule of law and to treating all people equally under the law.' Senate majority leader Bill Frist called him 'a man of integrity,' going on to say, 'I am confident he will impartially interpret the law.'

Judge Pryor's record:

- He has described *Roe* v. *Wade* as 'the worst abomination of constitutional law in our history.' Speaking at a 1997 rally, Pryor said, 'I will never forget January 22, 1973, the day seven members of our highest court ripped the Constitution and ripped out the life of millions of unborn children.'
- Pryor considers a provision of the Voting Rights Act that requires the approval of the Justice Department when state and local authorities seek to change voting procedures that might adversely impact minorities to be 'an affront to federalism and an expensive burden that has far outlived its usefulness.'

- According to Alliance for Justice, 'under Pryor's leadership, Alabama was the only state to challenge the constitutionality of provisions of the Violence Against Women Act . . . Pryor also argued in briefs that the Supreme Court should cut back on the protections of the Age Discrimination in Employment Act, the Civil Rights Act of 1964, the Americans with Disabilities Act, the Family and Medical Leave Act, and the Clean Water Act.'

- In 2003, Pryor filed a brief with the Supreme Court in which he compared homosexual acts to 'prostitution, adultery, necrophilia, bestiality, possession of child pornography and even incest and pedophilia.'

- Commenting on the Supreme Court's ruling in *Bush* v. *Gore,* Pryor said, 'I'm probably the only one who wanted it 5–4. I wanted Governor Bush to have a full appreciation of the judiciary and judicial selection so we can have no more appointments like [Bush Sr.'s moderate Supreme Court appointee] Justice Souter.'

- He is a cofounder of the Republican attorneys general Association (RAGA), a fund-raising organization that contributes to the election campaigns of Republican attorneys general. *The Washington Post* describes RAGA as being founded 'with the explicit aim of soliciting funds from the firearms, tobacco . . . and other industries facing state lawsuits.' Pryor himself refuses to identify any donors, saying that he does not want [contributing] corporations to be punished and targeted by trial lawyers.' He once told Congress that he did not know whether any tobacco companies were RAGA members. He has also said that contributions do not influence legal decisions by RAGA members. However, *The Washington Post* reported that in 1999, Pryor called Philip Morris Inc. and Brown & Williamson to obtain $25,000 from each for 'Roundtable' memberships in RAGA. *The New York Times* reported that leaked documents revealed that RAGA targeted the insurance industry, whose donations, along with those of others, were 'funneled to the Republican National Committee, where donors were kept secret and the committee was free, in turn, to donate $100,000 to Mr. Pryor's campaign.'

■ More than 170 organizations opposed his nomination.

The Federal Circuit Court, unlike the other twelve circuit courts, has no geographical jurisdiction; rather, it hears appeals from several courts, including the U.S. Court of Federal Claims and U.S. Court of International Trade. The Court of Federal Claims has national jurisdiction on cases involving property owners and businesses that charge that the federal regulations protecting our health, environment, and safety, for example, have resulted in the taking of their property. What's particularly troubling is that this court's conservative majority, according to the Independent Judiciary, 'exhibits an anti-regulatory, pro-business bias, which could well result in decisions further dismantling important worker, consumer and environmental protections.'

The court has a solid eight-to-four Republican majority. Bush used the one vacancy available to appoint Sharon Prost, who had been counsel to Orrin Hatch, chairman of the Senate Judiciary Committee. Prost has spent relatively little time in court, and her lack of experience was evident in one of her first opinions: In a civil rights case, her ruling prompted a dissent that, according to the Independent Judiciary, said, 'Prost's opinion was without precedent and threatened basic antidiscrimination measures.'

Some candidates the Bush White House put forward were such belligerent ideologues that even Republicans began to blanch.

Nominees for the federal courts get appointed by getting a majority vote in the Senate. Once they pass that hurdle, they're judges.

For life. If one senator filibusters, the appointee needs three-fifths of the votes to get approved. (The filibuster is a grand tradition in the Senate chamber that began to be used in earnest in the late 1800s. A derivation of the Dutch word for 'pirate,' it is essentially a stalling method used to prevent legislative matters from being passed. See the filibuster scene in Frank Capra's *Mr. Smith Goes to Washington.*)

Here, the Democrats have met with some measure of success. By early 2004, six Bush nominees had been blocked by filibuster, though two of the six – Pryor and Pickering – got recess appointments. Looking at only the women that were blocked, it's not hard to see why they didn't pass muster – although they're not really all that more extreme than the successful Bush appointees.

> 'I have the job of nominating people to serve on the federal benches. I have handled my duty in the right way by picking superb men and women to serve our country as federal judges: people of integrity and honor; people of high intelligence . . . Carolyn Kuhl, Janice Brown, Priscilla Owen really represent the best of America – superb, superb women.'
>
> – GEORGE W. BUSH, November 2003

Carolyn Kuhl, a superior court judge for Los Angeles County, was nominated by the White House in June 2001 for a seat on the Ninth Circuit Court and was blocked by filibuster in the Senate at the end of 2003. Her record, according to an Alliance for Justice report:

- She has a long history of hostility toward the rights of women and minorities.
- According to NARAL (once the National Abortion and Reproductive Rights Action League, the group now calls itself NARAL Pro-Choice America), while working as a lawyer in the Reagan Justice Department, Kuhl was one of

the 'most aggressive' advocates urging the Justice Department to argue for a reversal of *Roe* v. *Wade*.

- Independent Judiciary reported that she was 'one of two Justice Department officials who persuaded the Attorney General to reverse an 11-year Internal Revenue Service policy and reinstate the tax-exempt status of Bob Jones University and other racially discriminatory schools.'

- When she was questioned by the Senate Judiciary Committee, she waffled, saying that her support of Bob Jones was a mistake, that she had been very young, and had not understood the issues fully.

- An editorial in *The New York Times* said, 'As a lawyer and as a California state court judge, [Kuhl] advocated objectionable positions on civil rights, abortion and privacy. But at her confirmation hearings, she backpedaled furiously.'

- According to Independent Judiciary, 'When senators asked Kuhl whether positions she had taken opposing a woman's right to choose, affirmative action, and punitive damages for corporate wrongdoers in both government and private practice represented her personal views, she refused to answer.'

- More than fifty organizations opposed her nomination.

Janice Rogers Brown, a California supreme court justice, was nominated to the DC Circuit Court in July 2003. *The New York Times* said Brown was among Bush's 'very worst' nominees, adding that 'she has declared war on the mainstream legal values that most Americans hold dear.' There was a filibuster, and Brown's appointment failed. 'This Bush nominee has such an atrocious civil rights record she makes Clarence Thomas look like Thurgood Marshall,' said Diane Watson, a Democratic congresswoman from California. (When Brown was nominated to the California bench in 1996, she encountered similar resistance. The state bar evaluation committee actually found her unqualified. She was appointed nevertheless.)

Some other aspects of Judge Brown's judicial record:

- She refers to the New Deal as the 'Revolution of 1937.'
- According to People For the American Way, she has argued that the United States has become a 'nation of whiners' and that policymakers are 'handing out new rights like lollipops in the dentist's office.'
- In a speech delivered before the Federalist Society the year Bush was elected president, she said, 'Where government moves in, community retreats, civil society disintegrates, and our ability to control our own destiny atrophies . . . The result is a debased, debauched culture which finds moral depravity entertaining and virtue contemptible.' That a nominee with such an extremist antigovernment position was a nominee to the DC circuit, which has primary jurisdiction for cases involving federal regulatory agencies, was, according to People For the American Way, particularly outrageous.
- When the California supreme court overturned a state law requiring minors to get parental consent for an abortion, she dissented, accusing her colleagues of wanting to be 'the final arbiters of traditional morality.'
- Brown on help for the aged: 'My grandparents' generation thought being on the government dole was disgraceful, a blight on the family's honor. Today's senior citizens blithely cannibalize their grandchildren because they have a right to get as much "free" stuff as the political system will permit them to extract.'
- More than fifty organizations, ranging from the Sierra Club to the Congressional Black Caucus to the National Council of Jewish Women, opposed her nomination.
- The *San Francisco Chronicle* quoted Eva Patterson, a

prominent civil rights lawyer: 'It's particularly painful for us to be opposing an African American's elevation. I don't want to oppose another sister. But this is a philosophical war . . . If she gets through here, she will probably be nominated to the U.S. Supreme Court. If Justice Brown is on the [Supreme] Court, there will be no more affirmative action.'

Priscilla Owen, a justice on the Texas supreme court and a former lawyer who represented oil and pipeline interests, has been nominated twice and has seen a vote on her appointment to the Fifth Circuit Court blocked a total of four times by the Senate. Some other aspects of Judge Owen's judicial record:

- Independent Judiciary says she anchors 'the far-right end of a very conservative court, [and] consistently supports big business and special interests against the claims of ordinary Americans.'

- When she first ran for the Texas supreme court (candidates for state courts are elected), she received an $8,600 donation from Enron. Two years later, she authored an opinion that saved Enron $225,000 in taxes, while resulting in lost revenue for a school district. According to the National Organization for Women, 'Since 1993, Enron contributed $134,058 – more than any other corporation – to Owen and other members of the Texas Supreme Court. A study by Texans for Public Justice found that the court ruled in Enron's favor in five out of six cases involving the company since 1993.'

- White House counsel Gonzales served on the same court as Owen from 1999 to 2000. According to People For the American Way, he agreed with more than a dozen opinions sharply criticizing opinions written or joined by Owen on the court. Nevertheless, this is the White House's assessment of Judge Owen: she is 'an accomplished jurist of exceptional integrity, character, and intellect. The superb credentials she has earned through her extensive experience as judge and private practitioner make her an extraordinarily well-qualified nominee.'

- Her nomination was opposed by more than forty organizations.

Miguel Estrada, one of the more controversial of Bush's judicial nominees, met with such resistance that after losing a series of Senate filibuster votes, he finally withdrew his name. Bush wanted him on the powerful DC Circuit Court, a move widely interpreted as the first step in moving him up to the Supreme Court.

Published evidence of Estrada's legal views was slim, and his confirmation hearing was something of a fiasco:

- He had worked in the solicitor general's office in the Justice Department, where one of his supervisors described him as 'too much of an ideologue to be an appellate judge.'
- When senators reviewing his nomination asked to see memos he wrote there, the White House stepped in and refused to release them. Estrada himself similarly refused to answer the Senate Judiciary Committee's questions.
- *The New York Times* reported that 'incredibly [Estrada] claimed to have no opinion on whether *Roe* v. *Wade* . . . was correctly decided,' adding that 'as Senator Charles Schumer has noted, no American expects to be hired for a job after refusing to answer questions at the interview.'
- When his nomination was blocked, Bush supporters claimed that the opposition was anti-Hispanic. In fact, several major Hispanic organizations along with dozens of other groups protested his nomination.

As the Federal courts increasingly become dominated by right-wing ideologues, the Bush White House has focused on five major issues.

- Eliminating the right to abortion and promoting abstinence as an effective form of birth control
- Reducing or eliminating the rights of homosexuals
- Reducing or eliminating affirmative action
- Reducing or eliminating environmental protections that have been passed over the last thirty years
- Reducing or eliminating civil liberties safeguards that have been put in place over the last thirty years

Underlying all these initiatives is the desire on the part of the Bush administration to reduce or eliminate the separation of church and state.

ABORTION

Abortions are down, by the way, having dropped almost 20 percent – from 1.6 million a year to 1.3 million – from 1990 to 2000. Still, you'd think pro-choice would be a priority issue with women. But it's not. A 2003 survey by the Center for the Advancement of Women found that only 41 percent of women polled considered abortion a top priority. That means almost 60 percent don't consider it a major issue.

Abortion clinics are down too. Threats against clinics and patients, as well as punishing government regulations, have driven many of them out of business. According to the National Abortion Federation, it is exceedingly difficult for women who live outside major cities even to access an abortion clinic – 97 percent of nonurban counties have no abortion providers whatsoever. Michelle Goldberg, writing in *Salon,* found that 'in Texas, there's no abortion clinic north of Dallas.'

The Republicans introduced a bill to suspend RU-486, the abortion pill, on the grounds that two women died after taking it, said Goldberg. (By comparison, a reported 564 American men had died from taking Viagra less than two years after its release. You certainly don't hear gray-haired Republican elders arguing for the ban of *that* drug.)

Seven of the twelve circuit courts are against abortion rights, said Martin Garbus in *The American Prospect*. When you hear justices arguing for 'states' rights,' that's right-wing code for antiabortion.

Bush, even at a time of his own contrived war, supports a Reagan-fortified policy prohibiting servicewomen from getting safe abortions at overseas military hospitals. In a decree creating National Sanctity of Human Life Day in early 2002, Bush stated, 'On September 11, we clearly saw that evil exists in this world, and that it does not value life . . . Now we are engaged in a fight against evil and tyranny to preserve and protect life.' By the way, he's not talking about Al Qaeda here.

Bush craftily downplayed abortion during his 2000 campaign. Once elected, though, it was a different matter. In his first week in office, Bush told NBC News, 'I've always said *Roe* v. *Wade* was a judicial reach.' And so he began laying the groundwork for the Supreme Court's eventual reversal of the 1973 landmark case by putting the clamps on abortion in small, less noticeable, under-the-radar ways:

- He's said he would block federal money from international family-planning organizations that promote abortion or offer counseling.
- He's made fetuses eligible for coverage under the government-subsidized Children's Health Insurance Program. Living parents might not have coverage, but their unborn children will.
- He's put advocates like Attorney General John Ashcroft in

positions where they can help push through his antiabortion platform.

- Surrounded by ten smiling white males from Congress, Bush signed the Partial Birth Abortion Ban Act of 2003, which would outlaw procedures performed during the second and third trimesters. Even pro-choice advocates get squeamish on the subject of abortions this late in the pregnancy, but these procedures are generally reserved for instances in which the mother's life is seriously in danger. It should be pointed out that according to figures published in the conservative *Washington Times,* less than half of 1 percent of the abortions performed in the country in a given year are late-term abortions. But this bill was not about that. This was about laying the groundwork for a full-scale onslaught to overturn *Roe* v. *Wade.* And sooner rather than later.

- The Republicans then drafted the Unborn Victims of Violence Act, which states that when someone kills a pregnant woman and her fetus, he has killed two people. As Pro-Choice America says, this is a 'sneak attack on a woman's right to choose . . . Despite claims that the bill protects pregnant women from acts of violence, its true intent is to undermine *Roe* v. *Wade* by granting embryos and fetuses unprecedented legal rights.' Bush signed the act into law in April 2004, his first bill signing of the year.

- Bush reimposed the Mexico City Policy, commonly called the global gag rule (which the Clinton administration had canceled by executive order in 1993) on the U.S. Agency for International Development. He did this on his first workday in office. *His first day.* (It also happened to be the twenty-eighth anniversary of *Roe.* v. *Wade.* On the thirty-first anniversary of *Roe,* Bush spoke to supporters at an anti-choice rally by phone, saying, 'We all know there is still more to do.')

- Under the gag rule, foreign nongovernment organizations are ineligible for any money from the agency if they support abortion services, lobby for abortion legislation or, according to the Center for Reproductive Rights, 'even provide accurate medical counseling or referrals regarding abortion.' Planned Parenthood, which clearly couldn't agree to the gag rule's provisions, forfeited $20 million in annual funding, a fifth of its budget. The gag rule, says Barbara Crane, executive vice president of the women's reproductive rights group Ipas, is 'interfering with [other countries'] democratic processes. Who should be making the choice, the White House or the women and governments affected?' In Kenya, for instance, where the maternal death rate is roughly thirteen per thousand live births, five vital family-planning clinics were forced to close because of the gag rule. (Bush believes the myth that sex education and information about contraception send teens 'a contradictory message. It tends to undermine the message of abstinence.' He has also said, 'The best sex education takes place at home.' For more – or, rather, less – on this, keep your eyes on the president's twin daughters in the coming years.)

- Arguing that abstinence is the best approach to sex education and proposing doubling the $135 million in federal funding to abstinence-only programs has had a devastating effect on HIV/ AIDS programs. As Joanne Csete, director of HIV/AIDS programs at Human Rights Watch, told *The Washington Post*, 'Whenever AIDS educators are repressed and harassed and kept from doing their jobs, the epidemic is the big winner.'

- Bush's proposed budget for 2005, according to *Salon*'s Michelle Goldberg, 'provides less than one-sixth of the increase needed to close the budget shortfall in the AIDS Drug Assistance Program, which helps low-income HIV patients access medical care and lifesaving drugs.'

- On the other hand, Bush wants that $135 million he allocated in 2004 for abstinence-only programs to be doubled to $270 million in 2005. As Goldberg says, 'Much of that money would be given in grants to Christian organizations such as Youth for Christ and to anti-abortion groups operating so-called crisis pregnancy centers, outfits that masquerade as women's health clinics but deliver a strongly anti-abortion message and often medically inaccurate information.'

- Goldberg quotes James Wagoner, president of Advocates for Youth, a nonprofit organization devoted to sex education: 'To promote abstinence-only in the era of AIDS is to promote ignorance. It's inexplicable.'

- The Centers for Disease Control's Web site used to include comprehensive information on the use and effectiveness of condoms, including studies that demonstrated that condom education did not promote sexual activity. In late 2002, according to Scientific Integrity in Policymaking, the Bush White House pressured the CDC to replace that information with passages that stressed condom failure rates and promoted abstinence.

- The State Department's Agency for International Development's Web site, which once called condom distribution a 'cornerstone of USAID's HIV prevention strategy,' has, under the Bush administration, all but removed condom education from its site.

- In his 2003 State of the Union message, Bush promised $15 billion to fight tuberculosis, malaria and, most important, AIDS in developing countries, mainly in Africa, where about one of every twelve people from fifteen to forty-nine living south of the Sahara is infected with HIV. (He repeated this pledge at the following G-8 Summit and on a tour of Africa months later.) The Bush initiative sounded admirable and bipartisan, except for one thing: Because of the gag rule, many organizations that work to promote HIV prevention through the use of condoms were conveniently no longer eligible for funding due to their related family-planning work involving abortion. A third of the money must be directed to programs promoting abstinence – this in countries where virtually all women have had sexual intercourse by the age of twenty-five.

- The Bush administration will use any kind of science to bolster its challenge to abortion. Until 2002, the National Cancer Institute had information on its Web site that some studies had found no link between abortion and breast cancer. This information was based on numerous studies, the most sweeping of which had been published in The *New England Journal of Medicine* in 1997. In the fall of 2002, the Bush administration forced the NCI to remove the accurate information from its Web site and replace it with a fact sheet stating that there *was* a link between abortion and breast cancer, a move *The New York Times* labeled 'an egregious distortion of the evidence.'
- As far as America's reputation around the world is concerned, the situation is downright mortifying. In December 2002, at the UN's Asian and Pacific Population Conference, the U.S. delegation attempted to eliminate from the conference's population and poverty plan any language referring to condom use as a means of preventing HIV infection. The United States was voted down thirty-two to one.

GAY RIGHTS

As Bush himself has said somewhat cryptically, 'I support equal rights, but not special rights for people.'

The Bush White House purposely uses the somewhat fringe

issue of gay marriage as a means of getting voters hopped up on the rights of homosexuals. If he is successful in amending the Constitution to ban gay marriages, he will be the first president to change the document – which has been amended over the years to give greater rights to women and African Americans – in ways that would *limit* the rights of a segment of the population. Even though most Americans are opposed to gay marriages, there is the argument that homosexuals have every right to the same blissful agonies of matrimony that heterosexuals enjoy. So if you want to get married to your same-sex partner, there are options (as of May 2004, anyway): Massachusetts, Oregon, or Canada. And all are nice places for honeymoons too.

Bush's intolerance for homosexuals and pro-choicers is thorough, to say the least. *The Washington Post* reported that a federal auditor looking over the books of a Washington, DC, AIDS group advised one of its employees on the 'sin of homosexuality' and transcribed helpful passages from the Bible on her business card. An eight-minute video shown at the Lincoln Memorial's visitors' center used to feature footage of events and demonstrations that had taken place there. Under pressure from right-wing groups, the National Park Service, which operates the memorial, has promised to remove clips of gay rights rallies and replace them with footage of conservative events.

Most recently, the Republican-appointed head of the Office of Special Counsel removed information about sexual orientation discrimination from its Web site, from a brochure titled 'Your Rights as a Federal Employee,' and from a slide show that is used to train new federal employees. *The Washington Post* reported that the head of the agency had the material removed because of what he perceived as 'uncertainty over whether a provision of civil service law applies to federal workers who claim unfair treatment because they are gay, bisexual, or heterosexual.'

AFFIRMATIVE ACTION

The president was certainly a beneficiary of a helping hand, and on more than one occasion. Coming out of Andover, he had a combined SAT score of 1,206 – 566 verbal and 640 math – nearly 200 points lower than the average score of his Yale classmates in 1964. Despite the fact that he was neither a scholar, an athlete, nor a war hero (as his father was), Bush was from a wealthy family and both his father and grandfather had gone to the school. Whew – cliffhanger here – George got into Yale. And he went on to earn an illustrious C average. According to Peter Dreier in *The American Prospect*, 'It probably didn't hurt that three of the seven members of Yale's admissions committee who reviewed Bush's application had been in Skull and Bones, the exclusive college club that also included [his] grandfather and father . . . and who would later "tap" [him] for membership during his junior year.'

When Bush was in the National Guard after college, he scored just 25 percent on the pilot aptitude test. Even so, he was immediately made an airman. And when he applied to the Harvard Business School, with that C average from Yale, he was accepted as well.

And yet, with all these helping hands in his own past, Bush is against affirmative action and has actively filed a Supreme Court brief opposing it. As he said in a speech in early January 2003, about the University of Michigan's consideration of race as one factor in admissions, 'I strongly support diversity of all kinds . . . in higher education. But the method used by the University of Michigan to achieve this important goal is fundamentally flawed.'

Condoleezza Rice, the first African American to head the National Security Council, and a graduate of the University of Denver and Notre Dame, was a beneficiary of affirmative action, as was Justice Clarence Thomas, who attended Holy Cross and Yale Law School. In classic cases of raising the drawbridge once you're on the other side, Thomas opposes affirmative action, and

Rice is, at best, less than enthusiastic about it, stances which, given their circumstances, are simply beyond comprehension.

Coming up is the full-on push to dominate the big leagues.
When it comes to abortion, gay rights, and affirmative action, the Supreme Court is still the Circus Maximus of major constitutional issues. By its very construct and appearance – legal mandarins in long black robes – it's a proper, sober assembly. The Court is already conservative leaning – seven out of its nine members were appointed by Republican presidents, after all – and as the Bush administration continues, it could become perilously ever more so. The Court, led by Chief Justice William Rehnquist, has become a law unto itself and has a reputation for striking down laws passed by Congress – more than thirty, in whole or in part, since Rehnquist took over in 1987. It rules on the most important issues of the day as well as the marginal. In 1887, it took the U.S. Supreme Court to rule once and for all that the tomato was a vegetable. Today's conservative court would become drastically more so if it were eventually dominated by Scalia and Thomas, as many legal scholars fear it might under four more years of Bush. It would become radically conservative on cases having to do with the environment, the disabled, affirmative action, women's rights, and the elderly – the last four especially curious for a group made up of an African American, two women, and eight senior citizens.

The right wing of the Court is led by Rehnquist. Nominated to the bench by Nixon and sworn in 1972, he was named chief justice fourteen years later under Reagan. Although firmly conservative (for instance, he voted against the McCain–Feingold bill in 2003 overhauling the campaign finance laws), he nevertheless is capable of guiding his colleagues toward moderate stands, as he was on issues involving free speech.

The other members of the court's right-wing flank are

- Antonin Scalia, appointed to the Court by Reagan in 1986; he is Rehnquist's mini-me, a conservative activist.
- Clarence Thomas, a George H. W. Bush appointee, who joined the court in 1991. Only the second African American to serve on the Court (the first being the liberal jurist and civil rights activist Thurgood Marshall), Thomas's votes invariably concur with those of Rehnquist and Scalia. (Like a schoolgirl in the sixties naming her Beatle of preference, during the 2000 election, George W. Bush announced that Scalia and Thomas were his favorite judges.)

The more centrist wing is made up of Sandra Day O'Connor, a Reagan nominee who was named to the bench in 1981. Unanimously endorsed by the Senate at her confirmation, O'Connor sometimes votes in line with Rehnquist but has nevertheless been known to toe a more liberal line as well, providing the swing vote on issues such as affirmative action and laws affecting homosexuals. As Jonathon Turley pointed out in *Legal Times* in August 2003, nearly 20 percent of the Supreme Court's cases for that term were settled by five-to-four votes. In twelve of those fourteen cases, O'Connor was a swing vote. *The Washington Post*'s David Broder says that by dint of her swing vote on the Court, she might well be the 'most influential single public official in the country.'

The other members of the court's centrist faction are

- Anthony Kennedy, a Reagan appointee who joined the court in 1988. Kennedy, like O'Connor, was a Senate shoo-in. Although a conservative, he has been instrumental in steering the Court toward the center on hot-button issues such as abortion rights and equal treatment for homosexuals. There is speculation that he would like to be chief justice once Rehnquist steps down. Deomocrats would consider this a far better option than the likes of Scalia or Thomas, but Bush's conservative base would likely bristle at his centrist ways.

- David H. Souter, appointed by the senior Bush in 1990, has proved to be something of a wild card, an influential moderate who defends, much to the dismay of Rehnquist's majority, the power given to Congress to protect fundamental freedoms such as the right to privacy and equality for minorities. He is also a strong defender of the separation of church and state.

The more liberal wing of the court is represented by Ruth Bader Ginsburg, a Clinton nominee who was named to the bench in 1993, and two swing members, John Paul Stevens, a holdover from the Ford administration who joined the Court in 1975, and Stephen G. Breyer, a Clinton appointment who arrived in 1994.

- Ginsburg is only the second woman to serve on the Court (O'Connor being the first) and, perhaps predictably, has proved herself partisan in the area of women's rights.
- Stevens is another wild card and is, according to Jason Manning, the national editor for Online NewsHour, the Web site for PBS's *NewsHour with Jim Lehrer,* 'more practical than ideological, [and] is known for taking independent stances, showing deference to the legislative branch and paying special attention to the individuality of each case brought before the court.'
- Breyer is known to toe the more liberal line alongside Ginsburg, Stevens, and Souter in affirmative action cases and on issues involving homosexuals' rights. He is also comfortable with the centrist faction of the Court, agreeing with O'Connor and Kennedy roughly three-quarters of the time.

Looking back, there was that turning point in history.
It could fairly be argued that the most momentous Supreme

Court decision of the last half century was its decision over the 2000 election, on which Rehnquist formed the majority opinion. Al Gore had won the popular vote, and with a dead heat in the electoral college, it all came down to Florida. With Bush ahead by just 537 popular votes, and all sorts of claims of voting irregularities, a flurry of lawsuits demanded recounts in districts where it appeared that chicanery was afoot. The Florida Supreme Court ruled to allow some of the recounts to proceed. But after an emergency appeal by lawyers for the Bush team, the U.S. Supreme Court overruled the decision. (With the election over, Clarence Thomas's wife raised money for Bush's inauguration and became a member of his transition team, according to Charles Lewis in *The Buying of the President 2004*. Both of Justice Scalia's sons worked for firms – one in Miami, the other in Washington – that represented Bush in the 2000 Florida recount fight. Bush's lawyer in the appeal, Theodore Olson, a member of the Federalist Society, was subsequently appointed solicitor general.)

And so George W. Bush, who was unable to realize his ambition of overseeing professional baseball, became the country's forty-third president.

As Charles Lewis observed in *The Buying of the President 2004*, never in our lifetime has the high court decided who would occupy the White House. Justice Stevens was one of the most vocal dissenters at the time of the ruling, arguing, 'Preventing the recount from being completed will inevitably cast a cloud on the legitimacy of the election.' He went on to say, 'Although we may never know with complete certainty the identity of the winner of this year's presidential election, the identity of the loser is perfectly clear. It is the nation's confidence in the judge as an impartial guardian of the rule of law.' History, as it becomes written over the years, will almost certainly agree with him on this matter.

The final tally in Florida was hair-raisingly close: 2,912,790 for Bush and 2,912,253 for Gore, a difference of 537 votes. (The

Florida Supreme Court had ruled that about 62,000 votes needed to be recounted.) Ponder that the next time you think your vote doesn't matter much.

And now get ready for the hard right turn.

The simple fact is that the Supreme Court over the past two decades has moved incrementally to the right. What would have been considered the *far* far right in the 1970s is now the right; far right is now the center; the center is now called liberal; and the traditional liberals have all but disappeared.

During the Reagan administration, the right wing of the Republican Party had its sights on taking the Court back to the days before Chief Justice Earl Warren, who oversaw the high bench through the 1950s and 1960s and produced landmark decisions on civil rights, the right to counsel, freedom of speech, and individual liberties.

More recently, there is the sense that the far right wing wants to take the high bench back even farther – more than seventy years to the Roosevelt Supreme Court.

Writing in *The American Prospect*, Robert Kuttner asked, 'How would such a Supreme Court change American democracy? We already know from *Bush* v. *Gore* that even the current high court is a partisan rubber stamp for contested elections. A Scalia–Thomas court would narrow rights and liberties, including . . . the right to vote, disability rights, and sexual privacy and reproductive choice.'

And they may well get their wish. The last Supreme Court opening was a decade ago, one of the longest periods without a change to the high court in the nation's history. None of the justices have expressed a desire to step down. But Rehnquist and the other conservatives will almost certainly not leave their replacements to chance. If any of them do retire, you can bet they'll do it during a Republican administration. One, let alone two fresh ideologues on the Supreme Court would enable a bench lead by

Scalia and Thomas to have a clear ultraconservative run well into the chilly, unforgivable, distant future. As Chief Justice Charles Evans Hughes, a Hoover appointee who served on the Court during the 1930s, said, 90 percent of 'judicial decisions are based on bias, prejudices and personal and political motivations, and the other 10% based on law.' All those five-to-four moderate decisions of the Rehnquist court – decisions friendly to free speech, human rights, civil rights, privacy, and civil liberties – would be a thing of the long distant past.

9

▪

THE STATE OF THE UNION

'[The president] shall from time to time give to the Congress Information of the State of the Union, and recommend to their Consideration such Measures as he shall judge necessary and expedient.'

– U.S. CONSTITUTION, Article II, Section 3

THE State of the Union address is equal parts annual report, sales pitch, wish list, and shell game. It's been a factor in American politics for 214 years, and the 'from time to time' phrase has evolved into an annual event.

Throughout most of the nineteenth century, the address was a report on the nation's condition, often read by one of the president's representatives. In 1913, Woodrow Wilson became the first president since John Adams to add a more exciting live performance element to the speech, by giving the address himself. Presidents have been delivering differing amounts of baloney to their fellow citizens pretty much every year since.

In 1923, Calvin Coolidge became the first president to have his address broadcast on radio, and in 1947, Harry S. Truman became the first president to have his speech broadcast on television. With these new mediums, the State of the Union became an essential public relations tool for sitting administrations. It allowed them not only to parade their perceived accomplishments, but it also offered a platform from which they could give the country a head's-up to what they had in store for the year ahead.

This is not to say that the State of the Union speech is without merit. In James Monroe's 1823 address, he outlined what became the Monroe Doctrine, warning European powers to stay out of North American affairs. Abraham Lincoln's 1862 speech warned of civil war and the emancipation of American slaves. And Franklin Delano Roosevelt's 'Four Freedoms' speech in 1941 prepared Congress and the radio audience for U.S. entry into the Second World War. 'In the future days, which we seek to make secure,' Roosevelt thundered, 'we look forward to a world founded upon four essential human freedoms . . . freedom of speech . . . freedom of every person to worship . . . freedom from want . . . and freedom from fear.'

Given now that all the big broadcast networks as well as the cable news networks carry the State of the Union address, it's something of a ratings hit. The numbers of viewers can reflect either a president's popularity at a particular moment, or the country's interest in what he has to say. Or both. Or neither. Look at Bush's numbers:

- His 2002 post–September 11 'axis of evil' speech drew fifty-two million viewers.
- His 2003 address given before the invasion of Iraq pulled sixty-two million viewers.
- His 2004 delivery drew forty-three million viewers. A drop to be sure but still roughly what the Academy Awards did that year and almost double the audience that watched an average episode of *Friends*. Even with Bush's ratings slipping, you can be sure there will be a time in the not too

distant future when the networks talk a president into drawing breath long enough for them to squeeze in a few commercial breaks.

In recent years, the State of the Union address has become a series of talking points for the president's budget, laced with dozens of hollow, do-good 'initiatives' that he knows the country can't afford but will make the audience feel all warm and fuzzy. With Bush in office, it has also become perhaps the greatest annual outpouring of Orwellian doublespeak in American politics.

Like most recent presidents, Bush assembles his annual address with the help of others. White House speechwriter Michael Gerson is the president's point man, and he works alongside Bush's Svengali – attack dog Karl Rove. Once the basic architecture of the address is sketched out, former White House aide Karen Hughes, Chief of Staff Andy Card, and National Security Adviser Condoleezza Rice get to put their two cents in. Bush, perhaps characteristically, keeps his addresses short. His 2004 speech was a little over half the length of the epic eighty-nine-minute one Clinton delivered in 2000, his last year in office. In 2000, Clinton outlined 104 initiatives. In 2004, Bush managed a more modest 31. Judging his 2002, 2003, and 2004 addresses solely by the number of times he mentioned certain words, you get an idea of where the president's priorities lay.

THE STATE OF THE UNION, JANUARY 29, 2002

- terror[ism] and terrorist[s]: mentioned 34 times
- freedom: 14
- weapons: 12
- regime[s] (as in change): 11
- jobs: 11
- tax[es]: 7

- evil: 5
- weapons of mass destruction: 3
- unemployment: 2
- Iraq[i]: 2
- deficit: 1
- environment: 1
- health care: 1
- Al Qaeda: 1
- pollution: 0
- Saddam Hussein: 0
- Saudi Arabia: 0
- Osama bin Laden: 0

THE STATE OF THE UNION, JANUARY 28, 2003

- weapons: 27
- Iraq[i]: 22
- Saddam Hussein: 19
- terror[ism] and terrorist[s]: 19
- tax[es]: 11
- Al Qaeda: 8
- regime[s]: 8
- health care: 7
- evil: 4
- weapons of mass destruction: 4
- environment: 4
- job[s]: 3
- pollution: 2
- unemployment: 1
- deficit: 1
- Saudi Arabia: 0
- Osama bin Laden: 0

THE STATE OF THE UNION, JANUARY 20, 2004

- Iraq[i]: 24
- terror[ism] or terrorist[s]: 20
- tax[es]: 20
- health care: 9
- regime[s]: 8
- jobs: 6 (he never once used the word 'unemployment')
- Saddam Hussein: 5
- weapons of mass destruction: 3
- Al Qaeda: 3
- steroids in professional sports: 2
- weapons of mass murder: 1
- deficit: 1
- environment: 0
- pollution: 0
- Saudi Arabia: 0
- Osama bin Laden: 0

From here, we'll go through George W. Bush's 2004 State of the Union address and see how what he says measures up to the facts. Excerpts from the speech are in bold italics, followed by comments and amplification.

'For diplomacy to be effective, words must be credible, and no one can now doubt the word of America.'
You've got to give it to the Bush administration, it's focused. When it wants to go to war – as it did with Iraq – it goes to war come hell or high water, the justification for doing so be damned.

'We're seeking all the facts — already the Kay Report iden-
tified dozens of weapons of mass destruction–related
program activities and significant amounts of equipment
that Iraq concealed from the United Nations. Had we failed
to act, the dictator's weapons of mass destruction programs
would continue to this day. Had we failed to act, Security
Council resolutions on Iraq would have been revealed as
empty threats, weakening the United Nations and encour-
aging defiance by dictators around the world.'

David Kay, the former chief United Nations weapons inspector
who headed the administration's hunt for Saddam Hussein's
weapons of mass destruction before the war, told the House and
Senate intelligence committees in the fall of 2003 that he and his
Iraq Survey Group discovered 'dozens of WMD-related program
activities . . . that Iraq concealed from the United Nations during
the inspections that began in late 2002.'

But Kay also said, 'We have not yet found stocks of weapons . . .
We have not yet been able to corroborate the existence of a mobile
[biological weapons] production effort . . . Multiple sources [say]
that Iraq did not have a large, ongoing, centrally controlled [chem-
ical weapons] program after 1991 . . . [and] to date we have not
uncovered evidence that Iraq undertook significant post-1998
steps to actually build nuclear weapons or produce fissile material . . . [and] no detainee has admitted any actual knowledge of
plans for unconventional warheads for any current or planned
ballistic missile.'

'Weapons of mass destruction–related program activities' is a very
long way from Bush's unfounded claim in the previous year's address
that Iraq absolutely possessed 'weapons of mass destruction.'

As Stephen Zunes wrote in *Foreign Policy in Focus,* 'With strict
sanctions remaining in place against the importation of military
equipment, dual use technologies, and raw materials to Iraq that
could be used for WMD development (which, unlike the economic sanctions, were strongly supported worldwide) it is hard to

imagine how Saddam Hussein could have ever restarted his WMD programs.'

Kay and Zunes aren't the only ones who felt that Saddam's chemical, biological, and WMD capabilities had foundered. Weapons inspectors Scott Ritter and Hans Blix concurred.

'*Inside the United States, where the war began, we must continue to give homeland security and law enforcement personnel every tool they need to defend us. And one of those essential tools is the Patriot Act, which allows Federal law enforcement to better share information, to track terrorists, to disrupt their cells, and to seize their assets. For years, we have used similar provisions to catch embezzlers and drug traffickers. If these methods are good for hunting criminals, they are even more important for hunting terrorists.*'

The administration has claimed huge increases in the prosecution of individuals it says have been found guilty of terrorism-related crimes. The successes are being promoted not only to justify the intrusion on civil liberties under the USA Patriot Act but also to argue for a further expansion of their powers in the Patriot Act II.

On September 10, 2003, Bush told cadets at the FBI Academy in Quantico, Virginia, that since September 11, 2001, U.S. prosecutors had charged 260 people for their involvement in terrorist activities and had convicted 140 of those. This sounds like certain progress in the war on terror. But it's mostly smoke and mirrors. According to a study by Syracuse University's Transactional Records Access Clearinghouse, the average sentence for those 'terrorists' Bush mentioned amounted to just fourteen days. And in some of the cases, convicted offenders were sentenced to community service. The Syracuse report using Justice Department documents included the following information about those arrests:

- The Justice Department said that in the two years prior to September 11, it won convictions in 24 cases relating to international terrorism and 184 cases in the two years following September 11.
- Of those cases, the number of offenders who received jail sentences of five or more years dropped from six prior to the attacks to three in the two years following them.
- Similarly, the Justice Department boasted of 96 convictions in cases involving domestic terrorism during the two years prior to September 11 and 341 in the two years following.
- Of those cases, the number of offenders who received jail sentences of five or more years also dropped from twenty-four prior to the attacks to sixteen in the two years following them.

According to Michael Riley in *The Denver Post*, 'Federal authorities in New Jersey initially included attempts by 65 Middle Eastern men to cheat on an English-language entrance exam among their "terrorism-related" cases, briefly boosting terrorism prosecutions in that state from two to 67. The categorization was changed after it was reported in the media.'

'Some critics have said our duties in Iraq must be internationalized. This particular criticism is hard to explain to our partners in Britain, Australia, Japan, South Korea, the Philippines, Thailand, Italy, Spain, Poland, Denmark, Hungary, Bulgaria, Ukraine, Romania, the Netherlands, Norway, El Salvador, and the 17 other countries that have committed troops to Iraq. As we debate at home, we must never ignore the vital contributions of our international partners, or dismiss their sacrifices. From the beginning, America has sought international support for operations in

Afghanistan and Iraq, and we have gained much support.'
No offense to the nations listed above, but this group is a far cry
from the Allied Forces of the Second World War. Nor is it even the
coalition that backed the first Gulf War in 1991. In that conflict,
other nations committed 200,000 troops and the United States
540,000. For the war in Iraq, the coalition force numbered about
20,000 troops, with almost half of them from the United
Kingdom. (The countries not part of the coalition include Canada,
France, Germany, and Russia as well as India, Pakistan, and
Turkey.)

Then there are the '17 other countries' that joined the coalition.
Among them are Azerbaijan, Kazakhstan, Estonia, and Honduras.
As for the bigger names Bush mentioned:

- The United Kingdom sent nine thousand troops. Polls have
  shown that when the war began, more than 50 percent of
  Britons were against the war. Prime Minister Tony Blair's
  credibility as well as his political reputation and aspirations
  have been severely diminished by his support of Bush's
  unilateral invasion. By late spring 2004, 60 percent of the
  British population was antiwar.
- Australia sent fewer than one thousand troops. So strong
  was the opposition to the war in Australia that critics of
  Prime Minister John Howard said he was in Bush's pocket.
  About 70 percent of Australians opposed the war, and a
  parliamentary inquiry into Australia's handling of prewar
  intelligence, released in March 2004, determined that the
  Howard government had exaggerated the threat posed by
  Saddam's weapons of mass destruction.
- Japan sent under one thousand. Two-thirds of its citizens
  were against the war.
- South Korea sent about seven hundred troops.
- Italy sent about twenty-five hundred troops. Almost 70
  percent of Italians were against the war.

- Spain sent thirteen hundred troops despite the fact that 85 percent of the nation was against the war. Three days after the March 11, 2004, terrorist train bomb attacks in Madrid that killed 191 people and wounded more than 1,400, voters threw out Bush ally Prime Minister José Maria Aznar in favor of antiwar candidate José Luis Rodriguez Zapatero, who intended to shift his country's allegiance to Paris and Berlin and away from Washington.
- Poland sent about twenty-four hundred troops. More than half the country was opposed to the war.
- Hungary sent about three hundred troops. More than 80 percent of the country's citizens were against the war.

Not only were many of our allies persuaded to join the coalition with promises of being able to bid on prime contracts in the reconstruction effort, the war also forced leaders into positions completely counter to the wishes of the voters who elected them, thereby putting their own leadership in jeopardy. What happened in Spain may be just the beginning.

And where are the Muslim countries this time around? In 1991, Kuwait committed 11,000 troops, Syria 17,000, and Oman 25,500 in the effort to oust Saddam from Kuwait. Egypt and Saudi Arabia also pitched in thousands of troops. The number of troops from Muslim nations this time around: fewer than 200, compliments of Azerbaijan and Kazakhstan.

'We're tracking Al Qaeda around the world, and nearly two-thirds of their known leaders have now been captured or killed.'

The bulk of the Al Qaeda leadership responsible for the September 11 attacks may have been rounded up, but it is just the tip of the iceberg. U.S. troops invading and then occupying a Middle Eastern country is catnip for fundamentalist recruiters.

Islamic fanatics, mostly in their thirties, and presumably those in their twenties are moving to the front of the war against America. Some of the next generation:

- Abu Mousab al-Zarqawi, thirty-seven, who is believed to have directed twenty-five suicide bombings and, according to *Time* magazine in April 2004, is 'now the most wanted terrorist kingpin in Iraq.'
- Abu Walid, thirty, a Saudi, is believed to be the new leader of the rebel movement in Chechnya and was probably the mastermind behind the Moscow subway suicide bomb in early 2004 that killed thirty-nine people.

Faye Bowers, writing in *The Christian Science Monitor,* says, 'The new fighters are probably not as dynamic and swashbuckling as their former counterparts, jihadists who came of age during the early 1980s fighting the Soviets alongside bin Laden in Afghanistan . . . The younger acolytes, though, are believed to be at least as religiously zealous, better educated, more computer savvy, and better organization builders.' As Bruce Hoffman, a terror expert at the Washington-based RAND Corporation, told her, 'despite the loss of Afghanistan, the call of jihad remains a compelling voice to this new generation of recruits populating the ranks.'

'Of the top 55 officials of the former regime, we have captured or killed 45. Our forces are on the offensive, leading over 1,600 patrols a day [in Iraq], and conducting an average of 180 raids a week.'
Speaking at the Ronald Reagan Presidential Library in Simi Valley, California, a few months before the 2004 State of the Union address, Rumsfeld said that news reports exaggerated the lawlessness in Iraq. He said that of the then seventeen hundred

daily patrols, one-tenth of 1 percent were being attacked. By Rumsfeld's math, that's 1.7 attacks per day. Less than two weeks later at a press conference in Baghdad, Lieutenant Ricardo Sanchez said that since early October, the number of attacks on soldiers had fluctuated between twenty and thirty-five per day, up from about fifteen per day over the summer.

As the casualty count for American and coalition forces continues to rise, so does the number of Iraqi civilians killed. By summer 2004, the number dead had reached upward of ten thousand, according to iraq-bodycount.net.

'We also hear doubts that democracy is a realistic goal for the greater Middle East, where freedom is rare. Yet it is mistaken, and condescending, to assume that whole cultures and great religions are incompatible with liberty and self-government. I believe that God has planted in every heart the desire to live in freedom. And even when that desire is crushed by tyranny for decades, it will rise again. As long as the Middle East remains a place of tyranny, and despair, and anger, it will continue to produce men and movements that threaten the safety of America and our friends.'

With the nonexistence of WMDs or biological weapons facilities, two of the cornerstones of the Bush administration's justification for the war in Iraq, the White House switched gears and announced that the invasion was a humanitarian effort. If so, what about Saudi Arabia, a monarchy with a long history of human rights abuses?

But the Bush family's ties to the Saudis put the country off-limits following September 11, despite the fact that fifteen of the nineteen hijackers that day were from Saudi Arabia. As is Osama bin Laden. Yet not once in his three post–September 11 State of the Union addresses did Bush mention Saudi Arabia. He mentioned terrorism or terrorists seventy-three times, but not Saudi Arabia.

Saudi Arabia is ruled by an absolute monarchy that strictly enforces Sharia (Islamic law). Its economic imbalances and religious claustrophobia have spawned a generation of disenfranchised middle-class youth – a model breeding ground for Al Qaeda.

And the Saudis love to execute people. In this respect, and in others, they have much in common with the president's home state:

	TEXAS	SAUDI ARABIA
POPULATION	22 MILLION	24 MILLION
OIL	YES	YES
DESERT	YES	YES
INCOME DISCREPANCY	YES	YES
RELIGIOUS FUNDAMENTALISTS	YES	YES
EXECUTIONS 1980–2002	899	1,409

'To cut through the barriers of hateful propaganda, the Voice of America and other broadcast services are expanding their programming in Arabic and Persian – and soon, a new television service will begin providing reliable news and information across the region.'

The new television service the president referred to is Al Hurra, which is Arabic for 'The Free One.' Bush said it would provide 'reliable news and information across the region.' Iraqis were justifiably suspicious. Rumsfeld essentially gave the game away less than a month after the president's speech. Asked to comment on the Arab language Al Jazeera news service, he called it 'inexcusably biased' and said there was nothing the United States could do 'except try to counteract it.' Norm Pattiz, a board member of the Broadcasting Board of Governors, the U.S.-government overseer for the new network, says it will offer a 'new perspective' – code for broadcasting to Arabs what the administration wants them to hear.

'Sir, America stands with you and the Iraqi people as you build a free and peaceful nation.'

Presidents regularly have special guests in attendance at their State of the Union addresses. They are usually dignitaries, young children, or Americans who have pulled themselves up by their bootstraps – anyone who might make the commander in chief look caring and progressive. Among the guests at Bush's 2004 address was Ahmad Chalabi, the pseudohead of Iraq's pseudo-government in exile, the Iraqi National Congress, and at the time one of the members of the U.S-backed Iraqi Governing Council. It was Chalabi who had so successfully wound up the neocon tri-umvirate of Paul Wolfowitz, Richard Perle, and Douglas Feith with his Scheherazade-like tales of Baghdad's nuclear stockpiles and biological warfare factories – stories they had filled the pres-ident's ears with in order to get him to go to war.

Sitting in front of Chalabi and beside First Lady Laura Bush was Adnan Pachachi, the gentleman the president referred to in the quote above. He had already distanced himself from the White House. Back in July 2003, Pachachi told *Scotland on Sunday* that he thought 'the Iraqi people might take up arms against America were it not for the fact that they were "tired" of war.' He was especially critical of the killing of Saddam's sons, Uday and Qusay, at the hands of American soldiers in Mosul. 'The previous regime was based on a family organization sur-rounding Saddam,' he said. 'So killing the two sons means that the neck has been cut. But we would have preferred it if they had been captured. Killing is not our preferred option.'

Note: Title 18, Section 1001 of the United States Criminal Code, otherwise known as the Fraud and False Statements statute, provides a penalty of up to five years in prison, a fine, or both, to 'whoever, in any matter within the jurisdiction of the executive, legislative, or judicial branch of the Government of the United States, knowingly and willfully (1) falsifies, conceals, or covers up by any trick, scheme or device a material fact; (2) makes any materially false, fictitious, or fraudulent statement or representation; or (3) makes or uses any false writing or document knowing the same to contain any materially false, fictitious, or fraudulent statement or entry . . .'

10

※

OUR REPUTATION

'Nobody needs to tell me what I believe. But I do need somebody to tell me where Kosovo is.'

– GEORGE W. BUSH, September 1999

IN early 2001, just months after Bush was sworn in as president, *The Washington Post* reported that the White House had approached officials at the State Department for advice on how it could retract Clinton's signature from the Kyoto Protocol, the 1997 treaty ratified or accepted by 122 countries that set out to reduce global warming.

Among other initiatives, the agreement would require thirty-eight industrialized nations to cut greenhouse gas emissions an average of 5.2 percent of their 1990 levels by 2012. The United States was to cut its level by 7 percent. Inasmuch as America is responsible for a quarter of the earth's airborne pollutants, its cooperation was critical, and indeed the United Nations said that without U.S. cooperation, the world could see a 17 percent increase in greenhouse gases by 2010.

The Bush administration made it clear that it refused to live with any kind of restrictions on its energy use. Paula Dobriansky, undersecretary of state for global affairs, wrote in *The Financial Times* that the protocol was 'an unrealistic and ever-tightening regulatory straitjacket, curtailing energy consumption.'

Republicans stated during Bush's presidential campaign that if the United States didn't withdraw from Kyoto, Americans might have to 'walk to work.' In March 2001, when the White House officially pulled the United States out of the agreement, it was the first in a series of defiant snubs to allies, trading partners, and neighbors that began the slow and then dramatic decline of America's reputation around the world.

As could be expected, the withdrawal from the Kyoto Protocol drew a swift and negative response from the international community. 'China can't accept any attempt to violate the principles of the convention and eliminate the protocol,' *The New York Times* quoted Sun Yuxi, a spokesman for the Chinese Foreign Ministry. 'It is totally groundless to refuse the ratification of the Kyoto Protocol on the excuse that developing countries such as China have not shouldered their responsibility.'

> 'The US, with 5% of the world's population, emits almost a quarter of the world's carbon dioxide, the main climate changing gas. It promised to cut emissions by 7% over 1990 levels by 2012 at the latest, but its emissions in fact rose by more than 10% between 1990 and 2000. Bush's campaign for the US presidency was backed by major US oil giants, including Exxon, which also led the campaign in the US against the Kyoto treaty.'
>
> – CHARLES SECRETT in Britain's *The Guardian*

> 'The story behind the singular determination of Bush to fly in the face of world opinion, the sentiments of most Americans and even many in his own government reveals adherence to ideological rigour and a payment of debts to the business interests that helped him to the White House – above all, oil and coal. Oil runs through every sinew and vein of the

Bush administration; rarely, if ever, has a Western government been so intimately entwined with a single industry.'

– ED VULLIAMY in Britain's *The Observer*

The Kyoto withdrawal was just the beginning, though. Within months, the Bush White House pulled out of two more international treaties, further turning its back on the world.

The Biological Weapons Convention, signed by 143 nations including the United States, forbade the development, production, and stockpiling of biological weapons. The BWC lacks mechanisms for enforcement, however, and since 1995 the signatories have been trying to create some sort of enforcement provision. As the *Chicago Tribune* reported in July 2001, 'The Bush administration has decided to reject a draft agreement endorsed by many of its allies to enforce the 26-year-old [convention], citing concerns the proposal would subject American industry secrets to international scrutiny while doing little to stop the spread of biological weapons.'

Bush also refused to sign a UN pact restricting the illegal flow of small arms until provisions regulating the sale of military weapons to civilians and rebel groups were eliminated.

'The administration has, from day one, engaged in a wholesale assault on international treaties,' Ivo Daalder, a National Security Council official under Clinton, told *USA Today*. The message from UN Secretary-General Kofi Annan's office was no less stinging. The Bush White House is 'practically standing alone in opposition to agreements that were broadly reached by just about everyone else.'

Three months after September 11, in a Rose Garden press appearance, Bush formally announced that the United States would withdraw from the vital 1972 Anti-Ballistic Missile Treaty with Russia (originally signed during the Nixon administration). Exactly six months later, when the decision became official, the United States became the first nation ever to withdraw from a major arms-control pact.

'Russia still possesses approximately 6000 deployed strategic nuclear weapons, many of which are on hair-trigger alert; an even larger number of tactical nuclear weapons; and the huge inventory of weapon-grade fissile materials and chemical-weapon stocks. This arsenal constitutes the largest single threat to the U.S. and the most potent proliferation risk in the world. It can be handled only through negotiation and cooperation between the U.S. and Russia, especially mutual nuclear weapons reductions. This task will be near impossible if President Bush acts unilaterally on the ABM Treaty, which Russia, U.S. allies and the Nuclear Non-Proliferation Treaty community (including the U.S. through 2000) regard as a cornerstone of strategic stability.

'The more the United States disassociates itself from the ABM Treaty, the less likely it is that Russia will cooperate in nuclear reductions or keep their nuclear infrastructure open to intrusive inspections.'

– JOHN B. RHINELANDER, a nonproliferation expert who helped negotiate the ABM Treaty, writing for the Coalition to Reduce Nuclear Dangers

'As with Russia, China has opposed U.S. abandonment of the bilateral treaty that Leonid Brezhnev and Richard Nixon signed in May 1972 and that has been the cornerstone of the disarmament architecture built over three decades . . . some Russian commentators have expressed their fears of a new arms race.'

– MADRID'S *El País*

'History will one day judge the U.S. decision to withdraw from the Anti-Ballistic Missile Treaty in the same way it views the U.S. failure in 1919 to join the League of Nations – as an abdication of responsibility, a betrayal of humankind's best hopes, an act of folly. By announcing the decision now, in the midst of a war on terrorism that commands worldwide support, the Bush administration has also displayed a cynicism that will adversely affect the mood of cooperation that has characterized international relations since . . . Sept. 11.'

– SINGAPORE'S The Straits Times

'Lacking the political instinct of his predecessors, Bush is the bull who cannot find his way out of the China shop.'

– MANILA BULLETIN

Bush's decision to impose tariffs on steel imports was an almost comic exercise in arrogance and ultimate futility. The tariff hoo-ha caused the United States to run afoul of the World Trade Organization, it damaged America's relations with its trade partners, and it was a telling case study into the ways the Bush White House goes about its business.

STAGE I

- In May 2001, Stand Up for Steel – a coalition of industry and labor – retains the powerful lobbyist Ed Gillespie, who had worked on the president's inaugural celebrations and would later become Republican Party chairman.

STAGE II

- In March 2002, Bush, ever mindful of the 2004 election, announces steel tariffs designed to make him more popular in steel-heavy swing states like West Virginia, Ohio, and Pennsylvania. In complete opposition to the president's free-trade rhetoric, the tariffs range from 8 percent to 30 percent on a variety of imported steel products from countries like Russia, South Korea, Japan, Brazil, and the European Union, who warn that they will challenge the trade restrictions before the World Trade Organization.

'By imposing tariffs on many steel imports, the Bush administration is straining relations with key allies at a time when the US needs all the friends it can get to help fight the war on terrorism.'
– PETER GRIER in *The Christian Science Monitor*

- A chain reaction of sorts begins. The European Union

calculates that not only will more than half of the four million tons of steel it exports to the United States each year be hit with duties, but as much as sixteen million tons of cheap steel from places like South Korea might wind up in Europe. Even Bush loyalist Tony Blair calls the White House's decision 'unwarranted, unacceptable and wrong.' Moscow decides to retaliate against the steel tariffs by banning U.S. poultry imports. Japan announces that it will impose tariffs in the 30 percent range on U.S. iron and steel and tack a 5 percent duty onto American-made clothing, leather, and household goods. The European Union threatens to put tariffs on a variety of items from the United States. It backs down when Bush eases up tariffs on seven hundred thousand tons of European steel.

- Bush rebuffs criticism by blithely saying that he was just enforcing the law. What law he is talking about is never quite made clear. And as Paul Krugman writes in *The New York Times*, 'Nothing in U.S. law obliged him to impose tariffs – and it's pretty clear that the tariffs violate our international trade treaties.'

STAGE III

- In November 2003, the World Trade Organization decides that the U.S. tariffs are indeed a violation of international trade treaties and therefore are illegal. The decision opens the way for the European Union to impose more than $2 billion in tariffs on U.S. goods – the largest penalty ever permitted by one WTO member against another.
- The decision includes a detail that might have caught the president's eye: Among the list of goods to be sanctioned are citrus products from Florida, a state governed by Jeb Bush, the president's brother.

STAGE IV

- A month later, Bush quietly issues a written statement that he is lifting the tariff on imported steel. 'I took action to give the industry a chance to adjust to the surge in foreign imports and to give relief to the workers and communities that depend on steel for their jobs and livelihoods,' he says. 'These safeguard measures have now achieved their purpose, and as a result of changed economic circumstances it is time to lift them.'

- A White House fact sheet adds, 'Since [the tariffs went into effect], steel prices have stabilized, imports are at their lowest level in years, and U.S. steel exports are at record levels.'

- According to the International Iron and Steel Institute in September 2002, monthly steel production in the United States was 8,088 metric tons.

- In September 2003, following Bush's reputation-damaging sanctions, monthly steel production in the United States had dropped to 6,846 metric tons, 15.4 percent less than it had been a year earlier.

In the election that brought Bush into the White House, big agriculture was nothing if not supportive – 74 percent of its campaign contributions went to the Republican Party. The Bush administration has particularly close ties to agribusiness. Take one company, Monsanto, a leader in genetically modified foods:

- Attorney General John Ashcroft received more than $50,000 in campaign contributions from Monsanto and a spin-off company when he was a U.S. senator.

- Ashcroft's former second in command, Larry Thompson, worked in the legal department at Monsanto with future Supreme Court justice Clarence Thomas when they were both young attorneys.

- April 2002. In a lawsuit against Monsanto and two other companies, the three businesses were found liable for contaminating the city of Anniston, Alabama, with PCBs. An unusual settlement was reached, by which 'the federal government assumed jurisdiction over the cleanup,' reported the Associated Press, 'in what critics called a watered-down deal that could save the companies hundreds of millions of dollars in cleanup fees.'

The coziness between the Bush White House and big agriculture is most evident in the 2002 farm subsidy bill, a program created by President Roosevelt in the 1930s to help poor working farmers during the Depression. Since then, the money has grown dramatically – the bill President Bush pushed through will send $180 billion in payments to farm interests over the next decade, a 70 percent increase over the last subsidy program. (The Heritage Foundation estimates that the actual figure will be $462 billion over the next ten years.) And while family farms have been on the decline since the 1930s, overtaken by giant agricultural combines, the subsidies increasingly go to those who need it least: Nearly 75 percent of the funds allocated for farmers go to the wealthiest 10 percent of them, many of whom aren't what most Americans think of as real farmers.

The Washington Times's George Archibald reported in 2002 that among the leading 'corporate farm-aid recipients were billionaire David Rockefeller of Chase Manhattan Bank ($352,187); [Ted] Turner, top Time-Warner entertainment executive ($176,077); NBA player Scottie Pippen ($131,575); and Fortune 500 firms – Westvaco Corp. ($268,740), Chevron ($260,223), John Hancock Mutual Life Insurance Co. ($211,368), DuPont ($188,732) and Caterpillar ($171,698).'

The farm subsidies, which resulted in an international outcry because they make it difficult for poorer countries to compete, not only run counter to U.S. proposals to eliminate trade barriers but also actively undermine accords established by the World Trade Organization. And in a perfect example of the old saying that when America sneezes, the rest of the world catches a cold, the farm subsidies have consequences that reach far beyond U.S. shores. Bill Reinsch, president of the National Foreign Trade Council, said, 'Logically, it will have an adverse impact on most of the rest of the world.'

Jo Marie Griesgraber, the former policy director for Oxfam America, told *The Washington Post* that the bill means the United States '"stands in violation of its commitments' to the world's developing nations. "What it does is promote products so that we can sell them below market prices overseas, and put poorer producers out of work – people for whom this is a life and death matter."'

After reneging on agreements with the Kyoto Protocol, the Biological Weapons Convention, the ABM treaty, and the World Trade Organization, the Bush White House withdrew the United States from the International Criminal Court, which dates back to the 1969 Vienna Convention on the Law of Treaties. The new court, the world's first permanent war crimes tribunal, was negotiated in Rome in 1998. The United States became a signatory on Clinton's last day in office.

The Bush administration, defiant in its disregard for international law, vehemently opposed the creation of the ICC, stating, 'We do not want to have anything to do with it.' Secretary of State Colin Powell, who announced the decision, said the court undermined American judicial sovereignty and that the United States would not be accountable to a higher authority that might attempt 'to second-guess the United States after we have tried somebody.' Powell added, 'We are the leader in the world with respect to bringing people to justice.'

'It's outrageous. The U.S. should be championing justice. It shouldn't be running it down,' Alex Arriaga, director of government relations for Amnesty International U.S.A., told *The New York Times*. 'The U.S. have really isolated themselves and are putting themselves into bed with the likes of China, the Yemen and other undemocratic countries,' added Judge Richard Goldstone, the first chief prosecutor at The Hague war crimes tribunal on the former Yugoslavia, to the BBC.

'The administration is putting itself on the wrong side of history,' Kenneth Roth, executive director of Human Rights Watch, said. ' "Unsigning" the treaty will not stop the court. It will only throw the United States into opposition against the most important new institution for enforcing human rights in fifty years. The timing . . . couldn't be worse for Washington. It puts the Bush administration in the awkward position of seeking law-enforcement cooperation in tracking down terrorist suspects while opposing an historic new law-enforcement institution for comparably serious crimes.'

Faced with equally blistering criticism from America's European allies, Bush was unfazed. 'The International Criminal Court is troubling to the United States,' he said. 'As the United States works to bring peace around the world, our diplomats and our soldiers could be drug into this court, and that's very troubling – very troubling to me.' (In fact, not one UN peacekeeping official has ever been tried for war crimes under the existing tribunals.)

The moment after those jets piled into the World Trade Center towers, the United States had the sympathy of most of the world. But rather than using that goodwill to unite its allies in a global battle against terrorism, the Bush administration squandered it with an unattractive swagger and a cavalier disrespect for the wishes and nuances of the international community. Even before the invasion of Iraq, Bush's unilateral actions had sent America's reputation into a tailspin. Most traditional allies were quick to point out that they knew the difference between Americans – the people, their spirit, their way of life – and official America, the one operating on Pennsylvania Avenue.

> 'One year on, the United States is more isolated and more regarded as a pariah than at any time since Vietnam, possibly ever. The bookends of that year are headlines in the French newspaper *Le Monde*. On 12 September 2001 it declared: "Now We Are All Americans" But last month, in *Le Monde Diplomatique*: "Washington Dismantles the International Architecture"; a reflection on a year of treaties broken or ignored, and a brazen assertion of the arrogance of power.
>
> 'But no matter: America presses on, riding the slipstream of 11 September, leaving many bitter that an opportunity for real change has been lost.'
>
> – ED VULLIAMY in *The Observer*

In 2002, ABC News produced several round-ups of foreign opinion toward the United States. Some of the comments:

- Dominique Moisi, deputy director of the French Institute for International Relations: 'The emotions of Sept. 11 have faded. If you read the French press today, you have the feeling that the threat is America.'
- The Belgian newspaper *De Standaard*: 'Americans may not yet be fully aware of this, but the fact is that anti-American sentiments are resurfacing in Europe. It was striking how short the period of widespread solidarity and sympathy with the United States was in the wake of September 11.'
- Rosa Montero, columnist for Madrid's *El País*, on the treatment of Afghan detainees in Guantánamo, Cuba: 'One of the most harmful aspects of American society is its Calvinist notion of vengeance . . . the primitive "eye for an eye" of frontier law, the moral intolerance.'

- Natasha Walter, columnist for Britain's *The Independent*: 'Everybody from left to right was talking about it in shocked tones. I thought [the treatment of the prisoners] was a turning point.' (And this, remember, was before the revelations about the torture and humiliation of prisoners at Abu Ghraib.)
- Peter Kloeppel, of Germany's RTL television network: 'The people in Germany, we accept that you are, in a way, stronger. But what we don't accept is that you just come to conclusions and make decisions without ever putting into consideration what it might mean for other nations.'
- Christian Malar, senior foreign analyst for France 3 TV: Americans 'are too much interested in their own personal business . . . not caring enough about the interest or sharing interest with their own friendly countries and their own allies.'
- Hidetoshi Fujisawa of the Japanese television NHK network: 'Japanese people think the American people are a friendly people. But these days, some are thinking of them as a little bit self-centered and not knowing much about what is happening outside of the United States.'

This last point is a major concern of our international neighbors. And it would appear that American xenophobia and sheer lack of curiosity about what the outside world thinks and does is getting worse. A 2002 National Geographic–Roper survey found that 85 percent of American young adults couldn't find Afghanistan, Iraq, or Israel on a map; nearly 30 percent couldn't find the Pacific Ocean; and 56 percent didn't know where India was.

Regrettable attempts at humor by the president and members of his administration have done little to ease relations with anybody. Cocky, unilateral boasts and challenges made by the president and his cabinet haven't helped, either. Some examples:

- May 2002. Following a tense meeting with French president Jacques Chirac at the Élysée Palace in Paris, Bush and Chirac held a joint press conference. When NBC White House correspondent David Gregory asked Chirac a question in French, Bush said with a smirk, 'Very good. The guy memorizes four words, and he plays like he's intercontinental.' When Gregory kindly offered to continue in French, Bush snapped back, 'I'm impressed.' And then, in a remark that Chirac is sure not to forget, Mr. Bush added, '*Que bueno.* Now I'm literate in two languages.'

- January 2003. 'You know, how much time do we need to see clearly that [Saddam Hussein's] not disarming? As I said, this looks like a rerun of a bad movie and I'm not interested in watching it.' According to *The New York Times,* the president's spokesman, Ari Fleischer, said that 'Mr. Bush would continue working to "put spine into the United Nations and the rest of the international community" in enforcing the resolutions. Should the United Nations fail to back up its original resolutions demanding Iraq's disarmament, Mr. Fleischer said, the organization would risk becoming irrelevant in the same way the League of Nations did between the two world wars.'

- January 2003. In response to a question about European opposition to the war with Iraq, Donald Rumsfeld said, 'You're thinking of Europe as Germany and France. I don't. I think that's old Europe.'

- February 2003. Colin Powell tells ABC's *This Week* that sending in UN forces was pointless. 'What are these blue-helmeted U.N. forces going to do? Shoot their way into Iraqi compounds?' He went on to say there was no point in UN inspectors playing 'detectives or Inspector Clouseau running all around Iraq looking for this material.'

- February 2003. Bush's message to the United Nations: 'Show backbone . . . [or] fade into history as an ineffective, irrelevant debating society.'

- February 2003. Dick Cheney to French ambassador to the United States Jean-David Levitte: 'Is France an ally or an adversary of the United States?'
- March 2003. Bush: 'When it comes to our security, we really don't need anybody's permission.'

All this bluster and arrogance, not to mention the flawed justifications for invading Iraq and the nightmare of occupation, have produced around the world hitherto unimagined levels of hatred for America and its president. A Eurobarometer survey conducted in late 2002 found that in the United Kingdom – our closest ally – 55 percent of those surveyed thought the United States was a threat to global peace. The survey found that residents of Greece, Finland, Sweden, and Spain considered the United States a greater threat to world peace than even North Korea.

In comparing a 1983 *Newsweek* poll that surveyed foreign attitudes toward America and a 2002 Pew Global Attitudes Project survey of thirty-eight thousand people in forty-four countries, the Pew Research Center's Andrew Kohut commented that 'the United States has been down this road before, struggling with a battered image and drawing little in the way of support even from close allies. But for a variety of reasons, this time it is different: the anti-Americanism runs broader and deeper than ever before. And it's getting worse.' When Pew returned to the subject in the spring of 2003, interviewing sixteen thousand people in twenty countries, 'it was clear,' said Kohut, 'that favorable opinions of the U.S. had plummeted.' Some of the Pew findings:

- Germany: In 2002, 61 percent had a favorable opinion of the United States. In 2003, the number had dropped to 45 percent. (When the State Department conducted a similar study in 1999, the approval rate among Germans was 78 percent.)

- France: In 2002, 63 percent had a favorable opinion of the United States. In 2003, the number had dropped to 43 percent.
- Russia: In 2002, 61 percent had a favorable opinion of the United States. In 2003, the number had dropped to 36 percent.
- Brazil: In 2002, 52 percent had a favorable opinion of the United States. In 2003, the number had dropped to 34 percent.
- Indonesia: In 2002, 61% had a favorable opinion of the United States. In 2003, the number had dropped to just 15 percent.
- Turkey: 71 percent of respondents believe the United States is a threat to their country. In Lebanon, 58 percent do.

In ratings of countries that are considered a threat to world peace, the United States ranked fourth, behind Israel, Iran, and North Korea. Considered less dangerous were Iraq and Afghanistan, and, well down the list, China and Russia.

The Pew survey was careful to pinpoint the reasons for the anti-Americanism, says Kohut. 'Is it President Bush or America generally? Not surprisingly, solid majorities in most countries blamed the president, not America.' At the same time, Kohut said, 'Global publics believe the United States does too little to solve world problems and backs policies that increase the yawning gap between rich and poor.'

Just when it seemed our reputation couldn't get any worse, photographs of American troops 'abusing' – administrationspeak for torturing – Iraqi prisoners at Abu Ghraib prison surfaced. Thus the distinction that the world had previously drawn between Americans and the Bush administration was blurred. The photographs implicated 'real' Americans – from places like Fort Ashby, West Virginia – in America's perceived hegemony. The photos from Abu Ghraib may well become the iconic images of this conflict in the years to come.

> 'If I were an American, I would be red-faced. If I were an American citizen, I would write my very own individual letter of apology to the world, to the people of Iraq and to the detainees at Abu Ghraib.'
>
> – CERES P. DOYO in the *Philippine Daily Inquirer*

Many of the photos showed detainees being forced to pose in sexually humiliating positions, only reinforcing the notion in Muslim countries that America is a perverse, sex-obsessed nation. 'From the harsh torments inflicted on incoming students in many American suburban high schools,' wrote Susan Sontag in the *New York Times Magazine*, 'to the hazing rituals of physical brutality and sexual humiliation in college fraternities and on sports teams, America has become a country in which the fantasies and the practice of violence are seen as good entertainment, fun.'

It was soon revealed that the abuses at Abu Ghraib weren't the pranks of a few rogue young MPs, as Rumsfeld would have it. They'd been egged on by military intelligence officers and private contractors, who were in charge of interrogations at the prison. Seymour Hersh wrote in *The New Yorker* that there may have been a serious objective to taking the photographs: 'It was thought that some prisoners would do anything – including spying on their associates – to avoid dissemination of the shameful photos to family and friends.' But the damage to America's reputation is just the same. 'Shock and awe were what our military promised the Iraqis,' wrote Sontag. 'And shock and the awful are what these photographs announce to the world that the Americans have delivered: a pattern of criminal behavior in open contempt of international humanitarian conventions.'

'Is abuse now par for the course in America's secretive military prison system? What really goes on at Guantánamo Bay in Cuba, where claims of abuse by recently released British detainees were scornfully dismissed in Washington? And what about the other prisons that the Pentagon rarely mentions – in Iraq, Afghanistan and (it is believed) elsewhere?'

– TONY ALLEN-MILLS in London's *Sunday Times*

'Chinese human rights experts . . . unanimously condemned the abuse of Iraqi prisoners by US soldiers, saying that the issue exposed the United States' double standard in human rights and unmasked its true features as a hypocrite rather than a "world human rights guard."'

– CHINA'S XINHUA GENERAL NEWS SERVICE

'"[The photo of a smiling Private Lynndie England pointing at the genitals of a naked Iraqi] will become the recruiting poster of radicals trying to attack the West," said Akbar Ahmed, a professor of Islamic studies at American University in Washington and a columnist for Religion News Service. "If Osama bin Laden had come to Madison Avenue and asked for an advertising image to help him recruit, this would be it."'

– MARK O'KEEFE in Saskatchewan's *The Leader-Post*

'It is a shame that a spineless leadership allowed our government to be sucked into an illegitimate enterprise. The Abu Ghraib debacle provides the Philippine government with the perfect opportunity to withdraw our support for the Occupation and withdraw our troops from Iraq.'

– WALDO BELLO in the Philippines' *Business World*

11

THE PRESIDENT BY
THE NUMBERS

GEORGE BUSH: SCOURGE OF TERRORISTS EVERYWHERE

- 1: Number of Bush administration public statements on national security and defense issued between January 20, 2001, and September 10, 2001, that mentioned Al Qaeda.
- 104: Number of Bush administration public statements on national security and defense in the same period that mentioned Iraq or Saddam Hussein.
- 101: Number of Bush administration public statements on national security and defense in the same period that mentioned missile defense.
- 65: Number of Bush administration public statements on national security and defense in the same period that mentioned weapons of mass destruction.
- 0: Number of times Bush mentioned Osama bin Laden in his three State of the Union addresses.
- 73: Number of times Bush mentioned terrorism or terrorists in his three State of the Union addresses.

- 83: Number of times Bush mentioned Saddam, Iraq, or regime (as in change) in his three State of the Union addresses.

- $1 million: Estimated value of a painting the Bush Presidential Library in College Station, Texas, received from Prince Bandar, Saudi Arabia's ambassador to the United States, and Bush family friend.

- 1,700%: Percent increase between 2001 and 2002 of Saudi Arabian spending on public relations in the United States.

- 79%: Percent of the September 11 hijackers who came from Saudi Arabia.

- 0: Number of times Bush mentioned Saudi Arabia in his three State of the Union addresses.

- 3: Number of the September 11 hijackers whose entry visas came through a special United States–Saudi Arabia 'Visa Express' program.

- 140: Number of Saudis, including members of the bin Laden family, evacuated from the United States almost immediately after September 11.

- 14: Number of Immigration and Naturalization Service agents assigned to track down 1,200 known illegal immigrants in the United States from countries where Al Qaeda is active.

- $0: Amount approved by Bush to hire more of these special agents.

- $10 million: Amount Bush cut from the INS's existing terrorism budget.

- $690 million: Amount the Pentagon spent bringing oil into Iraq in just 2003.

- 4: Number of treasury agents investigating Osama bin Laden's and Saddam Hussein's money.

- 21: Number of treasury agents investigating Cuban embargo violations.

- 7: Number of Arabic linguists fired by the U.S. Army between mid-August and mid-October 2002 for being gay.
- $3 million: Amount the White House was willing to grant the 9/11 Commission to investigate the September 11 attacks.
- $5 million: Amount a 1996 federal commission was given to study legalized gambling.
- $50 million: Amount granted the commission that looked into the *Columbia* shuttle crash.
- 69: Number of documents, many of which included references to Al Qaeda and Osama bin Laden, the White House attempted to withhold from the 9/11 Commission.

GEORGE BUSH: MILITARY MAN

- 1972: Year Bush walked away from his pilot duties in the Texas National Guard, nearly two years before his six-year obligation was up.
- $3,500: Reward a group of veterans offered in 2000 for anyone who could confirm Bush's Alabama guard service.
- 600–700: Number of guardsmen who were in Bush's unit during that period.
- 0: Number of guardsmen from that period who came forward with information about Bush's guard service.
- 0: Number of minutes President George W. Bush, Vice President Dick Cheney, Secretary of State Donald Rumsfeld, Assistant Secretary of State Paul Wolfowitz, former chairman of the Defense Policy Board Richard Perle, and White House Chief of Staff Karl Rove – the major proponents of the war in Iraq – served in combat (combined).
- 0: Number of principal civilian or Pentagon staff members who planned the war who have immediate family members serving in uniform in Iraq.

- 535: Number of members of the U.S. Senate and House of Representatives.
- 8: Number of members of the U.S. Senate and House of Representatives who have a child serving in the military (less than half of them in Iraq).
- 10: Number of days that the Pentagon spent investigating a soldier who had called the president 'a joke' in a letter to the editor of a newspaper.
- 46%: Increase in sales between 2001 and 2002 of G.I. Joe figures.

GEORGE BUSH: AMBITIOUS WARRIOR

- 2: Number of nations George W. Bush has attacked and taken over since coming into office.
- 130: Approximate number of countries (out of a total of 191 recognized by the United Nations) with a U.S. military presence.
- 43%: Percent of the entire world's military spending the United States spends on defense. (That was in 2002, the year *before* the invasion of Iraq.)
- $401.3 billion: Proposed military budget for 2004.
- 2,300: Approximate number of accounting systems in use at the Defense Department.
- 44.1%: Percent increase in defense spending in the second quarter of 2003, after two quarters of 1.4% growth.
- 0.001%: Percent which the Defense Department proposed cutting its budget in 2003 by closing its 10-year-old Peacekeeping Institute.
- 9: Number of the government-appointed Defense Policy Board members out of 30 who sit on the corporate board of, or advise, companies that won more than $76 billion in defense contracts in 2001 and 2002.

GEORGE BUSH: SAVIOR OF IRAQ

- 1983: Year in which Donald Rumsfeld, Reagan's special envoy to the Middle East, gave Saddam Hussein a pair of golden spurs as a gift.
- 2.5: Number of hours after Rumsfeld learned that Osama bin Laden was a suspect in the September 11 attacks that he brought up reasons to 'hit' Iraq.
- 237: Minimum number of misleading statements on Iraq made by top Bush administration officials between 2002 and January 2004, according to California representative Henry Waxman.
- 237: Number of these that cherry-picked, misstated, or ignored intelligence on Iraq.
- 10 million: Estimated number of people worldwide who took to the streets on February 21, 2003, in opposition to the invasion of Iraq, the largest simultaneous protest in world history.
- 470,000: Number of U.S. service members in the Gulf War.
- 148: Number of combat deaths in the Gulf War.
- 124,000: Number of U.S. service members in the Iraq war.
- 713: Number of U.S. service members killed in Iraq since the onset of hostilities, as of May 1, 2004, the anniversary of the day Bush landed on the USS *Lincoln* and declared, 'Mission accomplished.'
- 4,924: Number of American troops killed or wounded in Iraq by May 1, 2004.
- 10,000: Estimate of the number of Iraqi civilians killed in Iraq to date.
- 3,466: The Pentagon's official tally of U.S. combat injuries by April 2004.
- April 2006: The date that the U.S. death toll in Iraq, if it continues at the same rate as it did in April 2004, will pass the U.S. death toll from September 11.

- 53%: Estimated percent of recruits who have deserted from the U.S.-trained Iraqi army, mostly over complaints about the low pay.

- $2 billion: Estimated monthly cost of the U.S. military presence in Iraq projected by the White House in April 2003.
- $4 billion: Actual monthly cost of the U.S. military presence in Iraq according to Secretary of Defense Donald Rumsfeld in 2004.
- $400,000: Estimated cost for every American who trains Iraqi police recruits, including salary and living expenses.
- $15 million: Amount of a contract awarded to a U.S. firm to build a cement factory in Iraq.
- $80,000: Amount an Iraqi firm spent (using Saddam's confiscated funds) to build the same factory, after delays prevented the American firm from doing it.
- $400 million: Amount requested by the Bush administration to build two 4,000-bed prisons in Iraq.
- $112 million: Estimated cost to build those two prisons in the United States.
- $500: Reward the U.S. military offered for each weapon turned in by Iraqi citizens.
- $5,000: Amount one weapon can fetch on the black market.

- 2000: Year Cheney said that his policy as CEO of Halliburton was that 'we wouldn't do anything in Iraq.'
- $73 million: Price of oil field supplies sold to Iraq by two Halliburton subsidiaries during Cheney's tenure there.
- $1.7 billion: Estimated value of Iraq reconstruction contracts awarded by the U.S. Army Corps of Engineers to Halliburton.
- $4.7 billion: Total value of Halliburton contracts in Iraq and Afghanistan.
- $680 million: Estimated value of Iraq reconstruction contracts awarded to Bechtel.

- $2.8 billion: Total value of Bechtel Corp. contracts in Iraq.
- $120 billion: Amount the war and its aftermath are projected to cost for fiscal year 2004.
- 20%: Percent of the billions of taxpayer dollars going toward the rebuilding of Iraq that is reportedly lost to theft, kickbacks, and corruption.
- 17: Average number of Iraqi civilians killed by gunfire in Baghdad each day in August 2003.
- 92%: Percent of Iraq's urban areas with access to potable water in late 2002.
- 60%: Percent of Iraq's urban areas with access to potable water in late 2003.
- 55%: Percent of the Iraqi workforce unemployed before the war.
- 80%: Percent of the Iraqi workforce unemployed a year after the war.
- 1%: Approximate percent of American personnel employed by private contractors during the Gulf War.
- 15,000–20,000: Number of outsourced private military contractor employees in Iraq.
- $32 million: Amount 10 leading private military firms spent on Washington lobbyists in 2001.
- 0: Number of American combat deaths in Germany following the Nazi surrender in May 1945.
- 37: Death toll of U.S soldiers in Iraq in May 2003, the month combat operations 'officially' ended.
- 79: Death toll of U.S. soldiers in Iraq in May 2004.
- 0: Number of coffins of dead soldiers returning home that the Bush administration has permitted to be photographed.
- 0: Number of memorial services for the returned dead that Bush has attended since the beginning of the war.

GEORGE BUSH: SAVIOR OF AFGHANISTAN

- $672 million: Amount budgeted for the rebuilding of Afghanistan through 2004.
- 9%: Percent of eligible Afghan voters that the United Nations has registered as of March 2004.
- 1.7 million: Number of Afghans directly involved in the production of opium (6% of the population).
- $184: Average yearly wages for an Afghan family not involved in the opium trade.
- $3,900: Average yearly wages for an Afghan family involved in the opium trade.
- 50%: Percent of Afghanistan's gross domestic product that comes from the opium trade.
- 75%: Percent of the world's opium that now comes from Afghanistan.

GEORGE BUSH: A MAN WILLING TO TAKE A STAND

- 35: Number of countries to which the United States suspended military assistance after they failed to sign agreements giving Americans immunity from prosecution before the International Criminal Court.

GEORGE BUSH: A SOLDIER'S BEST FRIEND

- 40,000: Number of soldiers in Iraq seven months after the start of the war still without Interceptor vests. Made of Kevlar, they are designed to stop a round from an AK-47, the most common automatic rifle in the world.
- $60 million: Estimated cost to outfit those 40,000 soldiers with Interceptor vests.

- $300 million: Approximate cost of a single F-22 air superiority fighter.
- 62%: Percent of gas masks army investigators discovered didn't work properly in the fall of 2002.
- 90%: Percent of chem/bio detectors, which give early warning of a biological weapons attack, that were found to be defective.
- 87%: Percent of Humvees in Iraq not equipped with armor capable of stopping AK-47 rounds and protecting against roadside bombs and land mines, at the end of 2003.
- 36%: Percent increase since 1999 in the number of U.S. Army deserters.
- 7: Number of months that veterans in some parts of the country have to wait for an appointment at a VA hospital.
- $250: First-ever enrollment fee Bush wanted to charge returning troops to enroll in the VA medical plan
- $1,000: Average amount each of the 20,000 private contractors earns per day working in Iraq.
- $100: Average amount a marine earns per day working in Iraq.

GEORGE BUSH: MAKING THE COUNTRY SAFER

- $3.29: Average amount allocated per person nationwide in the first round of homeland security grants.
- $94.40: Amount allocated per person for homeland security in American Samoa.
- $36: Amount allocated per person for homeland security in Wyoming, the vice president's home state.
- $17: Amount allocated per person in New York State.
- $5.87: Amount allocated per person in New York City.
- $77.92: Amount allocated per person in New Haven,

Connecticut, home of Yale University, Bush's alma mater.

- 76%: Percent of 215 cities surveyed by the U.S. Conference of Mayors in early 2004 that had yet to receive a dime in federal homeland security assistance for their first-response units.

- $100,000: Approximate amount the Transportation Security Administration spent in late 2003 to host a party to salute lobbyists, contractors, workers, and other federal agencies.

- 5: Number of major U.S. airports at the beginning of 2004 that the Transportation Security Administration admitted were not fully screening baggage electronically.

- 22,600: Number of airplanes carrying unscreened cargo that fly into New York's airports each month.

- 5%: Estimated percent of U.S. air cargo that is screened, including cargo transported on passenger planes.

- 6,000: Number of federal airport screeners laid off in 2003 because of budget reductions brought on by Bush's tax cuts.

- 95%: Percent of foreign goods that arrive in the United States by sea.

- 2%: Percent of those goods subjected to thorough inspection.

- $5.5 billion: Estimated cost to fully secure U.S. ports over the next decade.

- $0: Amount Bush allocated for port security in 2003.

- $46 million: Amount the Bush administration has budgeted for port security in 2005.

- 15,000: Number of major chemical facilities in the United States.

- 100: Number of U.S. chemical plants where a terrorist act could endanger the lives of more than 1 million people.

- 0: Number of new drugs or vaccines against 'priority pathogens' listed by the Centers for Disease Control that have been developed and introduced since September 11.

- $379.7 million – Amount Energy Secretary Spencer

Abraham estimated in 2002 it would cost to adequately secure the nation's nuclear facilities.

- $26.4 million: Amount Bush approved for the task.
- 20 to 1: Ratio of missile defense spending to spending aimed at securing unprotected stockpiles of warheads and bomb-grade material in the former Soviet Union.
- 4: Number of times terrorists with ties to Al Qaeda are known to have carried out reconnaissance missions of these stockpiles in 2001 and 2002.
- 171: Number of positions in the Department of Homeland Security that are unfilled out of 500 career jobs.
- 90%: Percent of port security positions at the department that are vacant.
- 51: Number of confirmed cases in 2003 of illicit trafficking in the radiological materials usable in dirty bombs, according to the United Nations.
- 8: Number of cases in 1996.

GEORGE BUSH: GIVING A HAND UP TO THE ADVANTAGED

- #1: The Bush cabinet is the wealthiest cabinet in U.S. history.
- $10.9 million: Average wealth of the members of Bush's original 16-person cabinet.
- 75%: Percent of Americans unaffected by Bush's sweeping 2003 cuts in capital gains and dividends taxes.
- $42,000: Average savings members of Bush's cabinet received in 2003 as a result of cuts in capital gains and dividends taxes.
- 10: Number of fellow members from the Yale secret society Skull and Bones Bush has named to important positions (including Associate Attorney General Robert McCallum Jr. and SEC chief Bill Donaldson).

- 79: Number of Bush's initial 189 appointees who also served in his father's administration.

GEORGE BUSH: A MAN WITH A LOT OF FRIENDS

- $113 million: Amount of total hard money the Bush–Cheney 2000 campaign received, a record.
- $11.5 million: Amount of hard money raised through the Pioneer program, the controversial fund-raising process created for the Bush–Cheney 2000 campaign. (Participants pledged to raise at least $100,000 by bundling together checks of up to $1,000 from friends and family. Pioneers were assigned numbers, which were included on all checks, enabling the campaign to keep track of who raised how much.)
- $30.2 million: Amount raised through the Pioneer program in 2003.
- $24.1 million: Amount raised through the new Ranger program in 2003. (Participants pledge to raise at least $200,000.)
- 37: Number of Pioneers on Bush's postelection team, which helped place political appointees in key regulatory positions affecting industry.
- 64: Number of Rangers and Pioneers who are lobbyists.
- 12: Total number of Pioneers identified by the Bush 2000 campaign.
- 511: Total number of Bush–Cheney 2000 Pioneers later revealed through court documents.
- 104: Number of Bush–Cheney 2000 Pioneers subsequently named to government posts.
- 23: Number of Bush–Cheney 2000 Pioneers subsequently given ambassadorships.
- 3: Number of Bush–Cheney 2000 Pioneers subsequently

appointed to the cabinet. (Donald L. Evans, Commerce Department; Tom Ridge, Department of Homeland Security; Elaine L. Chao, Labor Department).

- 12: Number of Rangers and Pioneers living in Florida.
- $175 million: Approximate amount of the Bush–Cheney 2004 campaign's preconvention budget.
- $5.3 million: Amount Bush raised on one day in September 2003 toward his reelection campaign, breaking the one-day record he himself had set.
- 270: Number of people the Bushes have invited to stay over at the White House since taking office.

GEORGE BUSH: HATES TO TRAVEL UNLESS THERE'S A REAL PURPOSE

- 65: Number of fund-raisers attended by Bush or Cheney in 2002.
- 100: Number of fund-raisers attended by Bush or Cheney in 2003.
- 0: Number of trips to Afghanistan by Bush or Cheney before waging war against that country.
- 0: Number of trips to Iraq by Bush or Cheney before waging war against that country.
- $56,800: Cost, per hour, to operate Air Force One.
- 68,000: Number of miles – all within the continental United States, and one trip to Mexico – Bush has logged on Air Force One through May 2004.
- 117: Number of trips Bush made between January 2003 and May 2004.
- 20: Number of trips to 5 key states (Pennsylvania, 5; Missouri, 4; Florida, 4; Ohio, 4; Wisconsin 3)
- 1%: Percent of the $203 million Bush has raised for reelection that has gone toward his travel costs in 2004.

GEORGE BUSH: MONEY MANAGER

- #1: Record for most U.S. bankruptcies filed in a single year (1.661 million in 2003).
- 4.7 million: Number of bankruptcies declared during Bush's first three years in office.
- 440,257: Number of bankruptcies filed during the second quarter of 2003, more than in any other quarter in U.S. history.
- 4,277: Average number of people who file for bankruptcy each day.
- #1: Record for biggest 2-year point drop in the history of the stock market during the first half of a presidential term.
- $200 billion: Approximate aggregate amount of state budget gaps in Bush's first 3 years in office, the highest figure since World War II.
- #1: Record, in 2003, for most residential real-estate foreclosures in a one-quarter period.
- #1: 2002 was the worst year for major markets since the recession of the 1970s.
- 15%: Percent the Dow, S&P 500, and Nasdaq collectively fell in 2002.
- $7 trillion: Amount of money investors lost in 2001 and 2002.
- $17 billion: Amount of government money the Treasury Department was unable to account for in 2001.
- #1: The $489 billion U.S. trade deficit in 2003 was the worst in history for a single year.
- #1: The $48.3 billion U.S. trade deficit in April 2004 was the worst in history for a single month.
- 44%: Percent the dollar declined in value against the euro between 2002 and 2004.

- $242 billion: White House projected U.S. budget surplus for 2003, issued in February 2001.
- $375 billion: Actual U.S. budget deficit for 2003.

- #1: 2003 budget deficit was, at that point, the largest in U.S. history.
- #1: $521 billion forecast 2004 budget deficit from the Office of Management and Budget will likely overtake 2003 to become the largest deficit in U.S. history.
- $275 billion: Amount of 2004 U.S. budget deficit caused by the Bush tax cuts.

- $5.6 trillion: Projected national surplus forecast by the end of the decade when Bush took office in 2001.
- $7.22 trillion: U.S. national debt by mid-2004.
- $9.7 trillion: Estimated national debt by 2014.
- $1.73 billion: Average amount the national debt increases every day.
- $24,419: Amount of each U.S. citizen's share of the national debt by the end of 2003.

GEORGE BUSH: FRIEND OF THE FARMER

- 74%: Percent of agribusiness campaign contributions that went to the Republican Party in the 2000 election.
- 75%: Percent of federal farm subsidy funds that went to the wealthiest 10% of American farmers.

GEORGE BUSH: TAX CUTTER

- 87%: Percent of American families in April 2004 that say they have felt no tax relief whatsoever from Bush's tax cuts.
- 53%: Percent of American families that received a tax cut of $100 or less in 2003.
- 39%: Percent of the tax cuts that will go to the top 1% of American families when fully phased in.

- 49%: Percent of Americans in April 2004 that found that their taxes had actually *gone up* since Bush took office.
- 88%: Percent of American families that will save less than $100 on their 2006 federal taxes as a result of 2003 cut in capital gains and dividends taxes.
- $30 billion: Amount the tax cuts will bestow on the nation's 257,000 millionaires in 2004 alone.
- 61%: Percent of Americans who say they would prefer a balanced budget to tax cuts.
- $30,858: Amount Bush saved in taxes in 2003.
- $42,409: Median U.S. household income in 2002.
- 2%: Percent of estates in the United States large enough to qualify for the estate tax.
- $6–$12 million: Amount Bush's heirs stand to gain if the White House succeeds in repealing the estate tax.
- $10–$45 million: Amount Cheney's heirs stand to gain if the White House succeeds in repealing the estate tax.
- #1: In 2004, federal revenues (from taxes) as a percent of gross domestic product hit 15.8%, their lowest level since 1950 – a time before Medicare and Medicaid.

GEORGE BUSH: EMPLOYMENT CZAR

- 5.95 million: Number of unemployed when Bush took office.
- 9.3 million: Number of unemployed in April 2004.
- 2.3 million: Number of Americans who lost their jobs during first three years of the Bush administration.
- 22 million: Number of jobs gained during Clinton's eight years in office.
- 3.9%: Unemployment rate when Bush took office.
- 5.7%: Unemployment rate in April 2004.
- 7.4%: Unemployment rate in early 2004 if the 'missing labor

force' (unemployed people who have given up looking for work) had been included.

- 2.8 million: Number of manufacturing jobs lost during the Bush administration through May 2004.
- 4.8 million: Number of people working part-time because they cannot find full-time work.
- 19.2: Average number of weeks an unemployed person was out of work in 2003, the longest period at any time in the past 20 years.
- #1: The Bush administration is well on its way to being the first since Herbert Hoover's to preside over an overall loss of jobs during its first term in office.
- #1: The Bush administration would be the first in history to win a second term having lost net jobs in its first term.
- 5.5 million: Number of new jobs the administration claimed the tax cuts would create between July 2003 and December 2004.
- 130,000: Number of new jobs the Bush administration predicted would be added in December 2003 as a result of his tax cut plans.
- 1,000: Number of new jobs created in December 2003.
- 21,000: Number of jobs created in February 2004.
- 0: Number of those 21,000 jobs that were outside the government.

GEORGE BUSH: FRIEND OF THE POOR

- 17%: The 'relative' poverty rate in the United States in 2003. ('Relative' poverty is defined as a household making less than 50% of the national median income.)
- 18.8%: The 'relative' poverty rate in Russia in 2003.
- 34.6 million: Number of Americans living below the poverty line (1 in 8 of the population).

- 6.8 million: Number of people in the workforce but still classified as poor.
- 35 million: Number of Americans the government defines as 'food insecure,' or in other words, hungry.
- 9.4 million: Number of people the Department of Agriculture defines as suffering from an 'uneasy or painful sensation caused by lack of food.'
- 250,000: Estimated number of American families that could be forced off the federal rent-subsidy program in 2005, which prevents low-income families from losing their homes, as a result of Bush's changes to Section 8 housing vouchers.
- 600,000: Estimated number of American families that could be forced off the program by 2009.
- $300 million: Amount cut from the federal program that provides subsidies to poor families so they can heat their homes.
- 40%: Percent of wealth in the United States held by the richest 1% of the population.
- 18%: Percent of wealth in Britain held by the richest 1% of the population.
- 17.1 million: Americans receiving food stamps when Bush came into office.
- 23.5 million: Americans receiving food stamps in January 2004.

GEORGE BUSH: AND ONE SPECIAL FRIEND

- $60 billion: Loss to Enron stockholders, following the largest bankruptcy in U.S. history.
- 90%: Percent loss in retirement assets of Enron employees who were prohibited from selling their stock.
- $13,500: Proposed maximum individual compensation for 4,500 former Enron employees.

- $205 million: Amount Enron CEO Kenneth Lay earned from stock option profits over a 4-year period.
- $101 million: Amount Lay made from selling his Enron shares just before the company went bankrupt.
- $50,000: Estimated cost of a single trip on a corporate jet.
- $59,339: Amount the Bush campaign reimbursed Enron for 14 trips on its corporate jet during the 2000 campaign, including 2 to Florida after the election.
- #1: Enron is the largest overall contributor to George Bush's political career.
- 30 months: Length of time as of spring 2004 between Enron's collapse and Lay (whom the president called 'Kenny Boy') still not being charged with a crime.

GEORGE BUSH: LAWMAN

- #1: As governor of Texas, Bush approved the execution of more prisoners (152) than any governor in modern U.S. history.
- 15: Average number of minutes Bush spent reviewing each capital punishment case while governor of Texas.
- #1: First president to approve the execution of a federal prisoner in the last 40 years.
- 8: Number of days after that first execution that a second federal prisoner was executed.
- 46%: Percent of Republican federal judges when Bush came to office.
- 57%: Percent of Republican federal judges after 3 years of the Bush administration.
- 33%: Percent of the $15 billion Bush pledged to fight AIDS in Africa that must go to abstinence-only programs.
- 1: Number of days in office before Bush reintroduced the global gag rule, which made foreign nongovernment

organizations ineligible for federal money if they support abortion services or lobby for abortion legislation.

GEORGE BUSH: CIVIL LIBERTARIAN

- #1: Bush became the first American president to ignore the Geneva Conventions by refusing to allow inspectors access to U.S.-held prisoners of war.
- 45: Number of days after September 11 that the USA Patriot Act was signed into law.
- 5: Number of the amendments in the Bill of Rights that are violated by the Patriot Act.
- 15: Number of additional crimes punishable by death under Bush's proposed Patriot Act II.
- 15: Number of days the government would be able to wiretap a suspect without a judge's approval under the proposed Patriot Act II.
- 10%: Approximate percent of the Patriot Act that is set to expire December 31, 2005.
- 325: Number of American cities, towns, and counties that have passed resolutions opposing the Patriot Act as of June 2004.
- 4: Number of states that have passed resolutions opposing the Patriot Act.
- 75%: Percent of 'international terrorism' convictions in 2002 that the General Accounting Office discovered were mislabeled.
- 680: Number of suspected Al Qaeda members the United States admits are detained at Guantánamo Bay, Cuba.
- 42: Number of nationalities of those detainees.
- 22: Number of hours prisoners were handcuffed, shackled, and made to wear surgical masks, earmuffs, and blindfolds during their fiight to Guantánamo.

- 32: Number of confirmed suicide attempts by Guantánamo Bay prisoners.
- 24: Number of prisoners in mid-2003 being monitored by psychiatrists in Guantánamo's new mental ward.
- 30%: Percent increase in new members of the American Civil Liberties Union in the first 2 years of the Bush administration (the organization's highest membership level ever).

GEORGE BUSH: A STUDENT'S BEST FRIEND

- 38: Number of education programs Bush proposed to cut in his 2005 budget.
- One third of 1%: Percent the average American teacher's salary has risen since 1970, taking inflation into account.
- 100%: Percent of U.S. high schools receiving federal aid whose students Pentagon recruiters now have access to under the No Child Left Behind act.
- 559: Page of the No Child Left Behind act on which the Pentagon's access to students' addresses and phone numbers is noted.
- $762,083: Average amount of aid each school district stands to lose if its schools do not supply the information to the Pentagon.

GEORGE BUSH: A HEALTH-CONSCIOUS PRESIDENT

- 43.6 million: Number of Americans without health insurance by the end of 2002 (more than 15% of the population).
- 2.4 million: Number of Americans who lost their health insurance in Bush's first year in office.

- 800,000: Number of those who lost their health insurance in 2001 who had incomes of more than $75,000 a year.
- 3%: Percent increase in the U.S. infant mortality rate in 2002.
- 1958: The last year there was an increase in the U.S. infant mortality rate.

- $1.55 trillion: Amount Americans spent on health care in 2002.
- $74 million: Amount of hard and soft money political contributions from the drug industry Bush and Republicans have received since 2000.
- $25.9 million: Political contributions from the insurance industry to Republicans in 2002, the year before the new Medicare bill was signed.
- $17 million: Amount 10 senators and representatives who got the Medicare bill passed received in campaign contributions from health-care interests between 1999 and 2003.
- $26 million: Estimated value of Senate majority leader Bill Frist's stake in HCA, his family's hospital chain. (Frist was a chief proponent of the bill.)
- 675: Number of Washington lobbyists who work only for the drug industry.
- $395 billion: Amount the White House claimed the Medicare bill would cost when Congress passed it.
- $534 billion: The actual cost of the bill.
- 6 months: Amount of time the Bush administration withheld from Congress chief Medicare actuary Richard S. Foster's estimate that prescription drug legislation would cost 25% to 50% more than the White House said it would.
- $272–$308: Cost of a prescription for Lipitor in the United States.
- $159–$199: Cost of the same prescription for Lipitor in Canada.

- 3.1%: Average profit margin of Fortune 500 companies.
- 3.3%: Average profit margin of Wal-Mart, considered one of the world's best-run companies.
- 17%: Average profit margin of the top 10 U.S. pharmaceutical companies.
- 38%: Estimated percent of increased profits to the major pharmaceutical companies as a result of the new Medicare bill.
- 3: Number of months after Bush signed the Medicare bill in 2003 that health maintenance organizations began to receive more money from the government.
- 25: Number of months after Bush signed the Medicare bill that elderly Americans will begin to receive their drug benefits.
- 2.4 million: Number of elderly Americans dropped by an HMO in the first three years of the Bush administration.
- #37: Rank of the U.S. health-care system compared with those of other countries around the world, according to a survey by the World Health Organization (France is #1, Saudi Arabia is #26, Iraq is #103, Costa Rica is #36, Slovenia is #38).

GEORGE BUSH: ENVIRONMENTALIST

- $44 million: Amount the Bush–Cheney 2000 campaign and the Republican National Committee received in contributions from the fossil fuel, chemical, timber, and mining industries.
- 31: Number of Bush administration appointees who are alumni of the energy industry (includes 4 cabinet secretaries, the 6 most powerful White House officials and more than 20 other high-level appointees).
- 200: Number of regulation rollbacks downgrading or

weakening environmental laws in Bush's first three years in office.

- 50: Approximate number of policy changes and regulation rollbacks injurious to the environment that have been announced by the Bush administration on Fridays after 5:00 p.m., a time that makes it all but impossible for news organizations to relay the information to the widest possible audience.

- 50%: Percent decline in Environmental Protection Agency enforcement actions against polluters under Bush's watch.

- 34%: Percent decline in criminal penalties for environmental crimes since Bush took office.

- 50%: Percent decline in civil penalties for environmental crimes since Bush took office.

- $6.1 million: Amount the EPA historically valued each human life when conducting economic analyses of proposed regulations.

- $3.7 million: Amount the EPA valued each human life when conducting analyses of proposed regulations during the Bush administration.

- 0: Number of times Bush mentioned global warming, clean air, clean water, pollution, or environment in his 2004 State of the Union speech. His father was the last president to go through an entire State of the Union address without mentioning the environment.

- 1: Number of paragraphs devoted to global warming in the EPA's 600-page 'Draft Report on the Environment' presented in 2003.

- 68: Number of days after taking office that Bush decided not to ratify the Kyoto Protocol, the international treaty to reduce greenhouse gases by roughly 5.2% below 1990 levels, by 2012. The United States was to cut its level by 7%.

- #1: Rank of United States worldwide in terms of greenhouse gas emissions.
- 25%: Percent of overall worldwide carbon dioxide emissions the United States is responsible for.
- 53: Number of days after taking office that Bush reneged on his campaign promise to regulate carbon dioxide emissions from power plants.
- 14%: Percent carbon dioxide emissions will increase over the next 10 years under Bush's own global-warming plan (an increase of 30% above their 1990 levels).
- 408: Number of species that could be extinct by 2050 if the global-warming trend continues.
- 5: Number of years the Bush administration said in 2003 that global warming must be further studied before substantive action could be taken.

- 62: Number of members of Cheney's 63-person Energy Task Force with ties to corporate energy interests.
- 0: Number of environmentalists asked to attend Cheney's Energy Task Force meetings.
- 6: Number of months before September 11 that Cheney's Energy Task Force investigated Iraq's oil reserves.

- 2%: Percent of the world's population that is British.
- 2%: Percent of the world's oil used by Britain.
- 5%: Percent of the world's population that is American.
- 25%: Percent of the world's oil used by Americans.
- 63%: Percent of oil it used that the United States imported in 2003, a record high.

- 8 million: Number of barrels of oil a day SUVs and other light trucks use.
- 50%: Percent of the passenger vehicle market SUVs and light trucks comprise.

- 2.5 million: Number of SUVs sold each year.
- 1 million: Number of barrels of oil per day the United States could save if SUVs had to meet the same fuel efficiency standards as cars.
- $100,000: Amount of the $106,185 price of an 11-mile-per-gallon Hummer H1, used for 'business', that owners can deduct under the Bush tax plan.
- $1,500: Amount of the $21,000 price of a 55-mile-per-gallon fuel-efficient hybrid that owners can deduct under the Bush tax plan in 2004, down from a $2,000 deduction in 2003.

- 48: Tons of mercury that coal-powered plants emit each year.
- 5.5: Tons of mercury that coal-powered plants were going to be limited to in 2008 by the Clean Air Act.
- 34: Tons of mercury that coal-powered plants will be allowed to emit in 2010 by Bush's Clear Skies initiative.
- 42 million: Tons of air pollutants permitted to be released by 2020 under Bush's Clear Skies initiative.
- 24,000: Estimated number of premature deaths that will occur under Bush's Clear Skies initiative.
- 300: Number of Clean Water Act violations by the mountaintop-mining industry in 2003.
- 750,000: Tons of toxic waste the U.S. military, the world's biggest polluter, generates around the world each year.
- 20 million: Number of acres of wetlands, lakes, and streams opened to development under Bush's proposal to end federal oversight of 'isolated' waters (an area equivalent to Maine).
- 473,000: Number of miles of streams, rivers, and coastlines that mercury pollution has contaminated.
- 80%: Percent of tuna eaten in the form of canned tuna, a favorite of school children. Tuna carries some of the highest mercury levels of any food.

- 8%: Percent of all American women of childbearing age whose mercury levels are dangerously high.
- 15%: Percent of the 4 million children born each year whose mercury levels are dangerously high.
- 88%: Percent of total public land in the Rocky Mountain states on which the administration want oil- and gas-drilling permits speeded up.
- 220 million: Number of acres of public land the administration announced in April 2003 it would open to logging, road building, and mining (an area equal to just less than the size of California and Texas combined).

- 25%: Percent of people in the United States who live within 5 miles of a Superfund toxic waste site.
- 1,200: Number of Superfund sites that need cleaning.
- $3.8 billion: Amount in the Superfund trust fund for toxic site cleanups in 1995, the year 'polluter pays' fees expired.
- $0 million: Amount of uncommitted dollars in the Superfund trust fund for toxic site cleanups in 2003.

- 270: Estimated number of court decisions citing federal negligence in endangered-species protection that remained unheeded during the first year of the Bush administration.
- 100%: Percent of those decisions that Bush then decided to allow the government to ignore indefinitely.
- 68.4: Average number of species added to the Endangered and Threatened Species list each year between 1991 and 2000.
- 0: Number of endangered species voluntarily added by the Bush administration since taking office.

- 40%: Percent of screened workers at Ground Zero who now suffer from long-term health problems, almost half of whom don't have health insurance.

- 78%: Percent of workers at Ground Zero who now suffer from lung ailments.
- 88%: Percent of workers at Ground Zero who now suffer from ear, nose, or throat problems.
- 22%: Asbestos levels at Ground Zero were 22 times higher than the levels in Libby, Montana, where the W. R. Grace mine produced one of the worst Superfund disasters in U.S. history.

GEORGE BUSH: IMAGE BOOSTER FOR THE UNITED STATES

- 2,500: Number of public-diplomacy officers employed by the State Department to further U.S. image abroad in 1991.
- 1,200: Number of public-diplomacy officers employed by the State Department to further U.S. image abroad in 2004.
- #4: Rank of the United States among countries considered to be the greatest threats to world peace according to a 2003 Pew Global Attitudes study (Israel, Iran, and North Korea were considered more dangerous; Iraq was considered less dangerous).
- 85%: Percent of Indonesians who had an unfavorable image of the United States in 2003.
- $66 billion: Amount the United States spent on international aid and diplomacy in 1949.
- $23.8 billion: Amount the United States spent on international aid and diplomacy in 2002.

GEORGE BUSH: NO FOOL WHEN IT COMES TO THE PRESS

- 11: Number of press conferences during his first 3 years in office in which Bush referred to questions as being 'trick' questions.

GEORGE BUSH: SHY RETIRING TYPE, NOT ONE TO TOOT HIS OWN HORN

- 12: Number of solo or joint press conferences Bush held in the first 3 years of his administration, the lowest number for any president since the advent of television.
- 72: Number of solo or joint press conferences both his father and Clinton had held by the same point in their first terms.

- 1: Number of executive orders signed by Bush permitting him singlehandedly to suppress the release of his presidential papers and those of his 3 predecessors.
- #1: In 2002, the administration classified more documents as official secrets than had been done in any year in U.S. history.
- 8 million: Number of documents classified in 1999, the last year of the Clinton administration.
- 23 million: Number of documents classified in 2002, the second year of the Bush administration.
- $5.7 billion: Cost of making those 23 million documents official secrets.
- 150: Number of pages of Reagan–Bush White House archives to be kept from the public indefinitely by order of George W. Bush.
- 0: Number of names released by the administration of people arrested after September 11.

GEORGE BUSH: SECOND-PARTY ENDORSEMENTS

- 90%: Percent of Americans who approved of the way Bush was handling his job as president on September 26, 2001.
- 67%: Percent of Americans who approved of the way Bush was handling his job as president on September 26, 2002.

- 54%: Percent of Americans who approved of the way Bush was handling his job as president on September 30, 2003.
- 50%: Percent of Americans who approved of the way Bush was handling his job as president on October 15, 2003.
- 49%: Percent of Americans who approved of the way Bush was handling his job as president in May 2004.

GEORGE BUSH: MORE LIKE THE FRENCH THAN HE WOULD CARE TO ADMIT

- 28: Number of vacation days Bush took in August 2003, the second-longest vacation of any president in U.S. history. (Record holder: Richard M. Nixon.)
- 28: Number of vacation days Bush took in August 2001, the same month he received an August 6 Presidential Daily Briefing headed 'Osama bin Laden Determined to Strike U.S. Targets.'
- 13: Number of vacation days the average American receives each year.
- 500: Number of days Bush has spent all or part of his time away from the White House at his ranch in Crawford, Texas, his parents' retreat in Kennebunkport, Maine, or Camp David as of April 1, 2004.
- 40%: Percent of Bush's presidency he has spent at these three vacation retreats.

GEORGE BUSH: FACTORS IN HIS FAVOR

- 3: Number of companies that control the U.S. voting-technology market.
- 52%: Percent of votes cast during the 2002 midterm elections that were recorded by Election Systems &

Software, the largest voting-technology firm, a big Republican donor.

- 29%: Percent of votes that will be cast via computer voting machines that don't produce a paper record.
- 11/17/01: Date *The Economist* printed a correction for having said George Bush was properly elected in 2000.
- $113 million: Amount raised by the Bush–Cheney 2000 campaign, the most in American electoral history.
- $185 million: Amount raised by the Bush–Cheney 2004 reelection campaign, through the end of March 2004.
- $200 million: Amount the Bush–Cheney 2004 campaign expects to raise by November 2004.
- 268: Number of Bush–Cheney fund-raisers who had earned Pioneer status (by raising $100,000 each) as of March 2004.
- 187: Number of Bush–Cheney fund-raisers who had earned Ranger status (by raising $200,000 each) as of March 2004.
- $64.2 million – Amount Pioneers and Rangers had raised for Bush–Cheney as of March 2004.

- 85%: Percent of Americans who can't name the Chief Justice of the United States.
- 69%: Percent of Americans who believed the White House's claims in September 2003 that Saddam Hussein was personally involved in the September 11 attacks.
- 34%: Percent of Americans who believed in June 2003 that we'd found Saddam's WMDs.
- 22%: Percent of Americans who believed in May 2003 that Saddam had used his WMDs on U.S. forces.
- 85%: Percent of American young adults who cannot find Afghanistan, Iraq, or Israel on a map.
- 30%: Percent of American young adults who cannot find the Pacific Ocean on a map.
- 75%: Percent of American young adults who don't know the population of the United States.

- 53%: Percent of Canadian young adults who don't know the population of the United States.
- 11%: Percent of American young adults who cannot find the United States on a map.
- 30%: Percent of Americans who believe that 'politics and government are too complicated to understand.'

GEORGE BUSH: ANOTHER FACTOR IN HIS FAVOR

- 70 million: Estimated number of Americans who describe themselves as Evangelicals who accept Jesus Christ as their personal savior and who interpret the Bible as the direct word of God.
- 23 million: Number of Evangelicals who voted for Bush in 2000.
- 50 million: Number of voters in total who voted for Bush in 2000.
- 46%: Percent of voters who describe themselves as born-again Christians.
- 92%–96%: Bush's job approval rating among Christian conservatives in 2003.
- 5: Number of states that do not use the word 'evolution' in public school science courses.

Of the 404 numbers listed above, 368 came from multiple reliable sources. Thirty-six were single-sourced from the following: American Civil Liberties Union, Associated Press, Center for American Progress, Center for Biological Diversity, Center for Responsive Politics, Center on Budget and Policy Priorities, Children's Defense Fund, Council on American-Islamic Relations, *The Economist*, *The Guardian*, Hasbro, *Harper's*, *The Independent*, Information Security Oversight Office, Federal Election Commission, iraqbodycount.net, The International

Institute for Strategic Studies, *LA Weekly*, *Mother Jones*, National Geographic–Roper Survey, *New Republic*, *Newsweek*, Natural Resources Defense Council, Office of Management and Budget (Washington), Pew Global Attitudes Project Survey, Physicians for a National Health Program (Chicago), Project on Managing the Atom, Harvard University, Ronald Reagan Presidential Library (Simi Valley, CA.), Royal Embassy of Saudi Arabia, *Salon*, Service members Legal Defense Network (Washington), Sierra Club, *Time*, Tom Matzzie on Tompaine.com, *The Week*, *The New York Times*, Tax Foundation (Washington), U.S. Army War College, U.S. Fish and Wildlife Department, *Washington Post*, World Health Organization.

12

■

AND FINALLY . . .

BY early April 2004, the president had made his thirty-third trip to his ranch in Crawford, Texas, since taking office. *The Washington Post* and CBS News estimated that by that time he had spent all or part of 233 days there, and another 78 visits to Camp David and his family's summer house in Kennebunkport, Maine. That's almost 500 days spent at one of the three retreats during just a little over three years in office. It could reasonably be argued that it's not what Bush did on days away from the office that are the problem so much as what he did during his days at the office.

In his book on the Bush Family, *American Dynasty*, Kevin Phillips found little in the way of a history of public service in the lives of the forty-first and forty-third presidents. Indeed, much of the Bush family's interest in political life has its roots in a clamoring for raw, unfettered power. Vice President Dick Cheney, similarly, seems to have an appetite for politics only when he is the politician involved. Pete Slover of *The Dallas Morning News* discovered that in the sixteen elections that took place since Cheney registered in Texas, he didn't vote in fourteen of them – including the March 2000 presidential primary in which George Bush was a candidate.

An administration that came into power with the slimmest margin since 1876, when Rutherford B. Hayes won the presidency by one electoral vote, should never have assumed that it had a mandate for sweeping, permanent changes affecting the nation's environment, its poor, and its civil liberties. Nor should it have assumed it was justified in steamrolling over the wishes of our allies and the rest of the world community when it decided to go into Iraq. Bush promised to be a uniting president, not a dividing one. The truth is, he has polarized the country in ways not seen since Vietnam or before: rich against poor, right against left, South against North, the middle against the coasts. 'We have not seen this split since the Civil War,' pollster John Zogby was quoted in the New York *Daily News*. 'We're at stalemate.'

The Bush administration's methods of governing have been kept largely secret from both the public and Congress, its tactics being obstruction, deception, and intimidation. It is this last trait-cum-philosophy that is most telling. During his father's administration, George W. Bush was tagged as the 'loyalty thermometer' because of his untitled role as plugger of leaks and controller of criticism. As president, he created a White House that lashed out early and often at dissenters and whistle-blowers. A few examples:

- When the Bush administration was trying to sell Congress on its $395 billion Medicare overhaul, Richard Foster, the government's top Medicare actuary, calculated that the program would in fact cost between $500 and $600 billion over ten years. The Bush administration, however, told Foster that if he informed Congress of the actual costs, he would lose his job.
- When Ron Suskind's book *The Price of Loyalty*, on former treasury secretary Paul O'Neill, came out in early 2004 and was highly critical of the administration's Iraq policy, the White House attempted to smear O'Neill as a disgruntled

former cabinet member and launched a probe into whether
the documents cited in the book had been properly cleared.
The investigation showed that they had been cleared.

■ When Larry Lindsey, the White House economic adviser,
told *The Wall Street Journal* prior to the invasion of Iraq that
the war could cost upward of $200 billion, he was fired. In
June 2004, the *Chicago Tribune* wrote, 'With the cost of the
operation hitting $119 billion and slated to reach at least
$170 billion by the end of 2005, a growing number of
experts believe Lindsey's estimate might have been low . . .
The Bush team originally predicted the war would cost
closer to $60 billion . . . Steven Kosiak, [a director] for the
Center for Strategic and Budgetary Assessments, said if a
large military presence is required for a long time, the cost
could run as high as $300 billion over the next decade.'

■ When retired marine general Anthony Zinni, Bush's
mediator for the Middle East, told a foreign policy forum six
months before the war that Iraq should not be a pressing
issue and that if an invasion occured, the aftermath could
prove long and difficult, he was not reappointed.

■ When ground troops in Iraq questioned the White House's
mission there, as well as living conditions and indefinite
tours of duty, General John Abizaid reminded soldiers of
their code of conduct, which is not to 'say anything
disparaging about the secretary of defense, or the president
of the United States . . . Whatever action may be taken,
whether it's a verbal reprimand or something more stringent,
is up to the commanders on the scene.'

■ When ABC News correspondent Jeffrey Kofman reported
on plummeting morale among the troops on the ground
during the war, someone in the White House
communications office attempted to discredit him by
tipping off Internet columnist Matt Drudge with the
horrifying news that Kofman was gay. And a Canadian!

- When army chief of staff General Eric Shinseki told Congress a month before the invasion began that the occupation might require 'several hundred thousand troops,' he was disparaged by Defense Secretary Rumsfeld and Deputy Defense Secretary Wolfowitz, who called his estimate 'wildly off the mark.'

- When the White House's prewar claims that Saddam Hussein had been trying to buy nuclear weapons turned out to be false, the administration pointed the finger at the CIA. As *The Washington Post* reported, 'President Bush and his national security adviser . . . placed full responsibility on the Central Intelligence Agency for the inclusion in [the 2003] State of the Union address of questionable allegations that Iraq's Saddam Hussein was trying to buy nuclear materials in Africa.'

- When Cheney was looking for ways to link Iraq to WMDs in the run-up to the war, the CIA asked former ambassador to Africa Joseph C. Wilson IV to go to Niger to investigate reports that Saddam had tried to buy weapons-grade 'yellowcake' uranium there. Wilson returned and told both the CIA and the State Department that the rumors were 'highly doubtful.' When the president stated the opposite in his 2003 State of the Union speech – claiming that Saddam had tried to buy uranium from Niger – Wilson demanded that National Security Adviser Rice correct the record. When his pleas went unheeded, Wilson allowed his findings to be published in *The New York Times* and *The Washington Post* in July 2003. A month later, Rice told Tim Russert on *Meet the Press*, 'Maybe someone knew down in the bowels of the agency, but no one in our circles knew that there were doubts and suspicions that this might be a forgery.' In retaliation against Wilson's revelations, members of the administration attempted to discredit him by telling at least six journalists that he had been chosen to go to Niger only because his wife was a CIA officer. The White House staff members also leaked the name of Wilson's wife, Valerie Plame, an undercover agent – a federal offense punishable by up to ten years in prison. When *Hardball*'s Chris Matthews quizzed Republican National Committee chairman Ed Gillespie whether the leak was 'worse than Watergate,' Gillespie replied, 'Yeah, I suppose in terms of the real-world implications of it.' (By June 2004, Bush and Cheney had been interviewed, separately, by federal prosecutors in conjunction with the grand jury investigation into the Plame incident.)

■ When retired Lieutenant General Jay Garner, the U.S. envoy to Iraq, after the war called for an Iraqi government to be formed quickly and rejected the Bush administration's program of imposing privatization on the country, he was removed from his post after a month on the job.

The Plame leak and the threats against Richard Foster are at the center of two inquiries. A number of other investigations into the Bush administration could, in time, prove damaging. It's not unusual for administrations nearing the end of their first term to become bogged down in scandal and investigation. That the Republicans controlled both the House and the Senate during the second half of the term limited both the scope and the timing of the investigations surrounding the Bush White House.

One would think that an investigation looking into the intelligence and judgment failures leading up to the attacks of September 11 – the most devastating assault on U.S. soil in more than half a century – would be at the very top of any administration's agenda. Not here. The 9/11 Commission's goal was to determine how the worst attack on American soil in half a century could have been avoided and to recommend systems the United States needs to put in place to protect its citizens against further catastrophic incidents. The Bush White House characteristically did everything in its power to derail an open inquiry. Then, when faced with its inevitability, it sought to limit its scope, its access, and its funding. Had its attitude and actions taken place in a court of law, they could only be described as obstruction or perjury. A brief rundown on the administration's search for the truth surrounding September 11:

- January 2002. Both the president and the vice president approach Senate majority leader Tom Daschle to shut down any form of inquiry, whether a congressional probe or an independent bipartisan commission. This, despite calls for one from victims of the atrocity and from a bipartisan assortment of House and Senate members. Daschle tells Tim Russert on *Meet the Press* that Cheney phoned him on January 24, requesting that no September 11 investigation be started. Cheney's argument was that the inquiry would divert attention from the war on terror. Four days later, Bush relays the same message to Daschle during a breakfast meeting at the White House.
- May 2002. In the face of growing support for an inquiry, the administration attempts to limit the probe to a joint investigation by the House and Senate intelligence committees.
- September 2002. Even as the White House is forced to begin consideration of the formation of an independent commission, it works behind the scenes to limit its scope.
- November 2002. Bush signs legislation creating the 9/11 commission and appoints former secretary of state Henry Kissinger as chairman. *The New York Times*, in an editorial, suggests the White House chose Kissinger 'to contain an investigation it long opposed.'
- December 2002. Kissinger steps down rather than release the names of clients his consulting firm represents. Former senator George Mitchell, the vice chairman, resigns as well.

- December 2002. Former New Jersey Republican governor Tom Kean is picked to replace Kissinger as chairman, and Lee H. Hamiliton, a former Indiana Democratic congressman, is named vice chairman.
- January 2003. The 9/11 commission holds its first official meeting.
- January 2003. The Bush administration allots a budget of $3 million for the inquiry. Jon Corzine, the Democratic senator from New Jersey, tells NPRs *Morning Edition,* 'That's not enough for a full-blown investigation.' Indeed, a 1996 federal commission looking into casino gambling was given a $5 million budget, $50 million was spent on the inquiry into the *Columbia* shuttle explosion, and $50 million was spent investigating the Clintons' failed Whitewater deal.
- March 2003. Chairman Thomas Kean tells the administration that the commission needs an additional $11 million to investigate the attacks and complete its report. He is, according to *Time* magazine, 'brushed off' by the White House. Finally, the White House grudgingly agrees to an additional $9 million. (Congress eventually goes further by appropriating an additional $12 million for the commission.)
- July 2003. Bush suppresses twenty-eight pages of a congressional report on the attacks of September 11. According to *The New York Times,* 'People who saw the section have said that it focuses on the role foreign governments played in the hijackings, but centers almost entirely on Saudi Arabia.'
- January 2004. The commission, whose report is due May 27, 2004, asks for two more months for its inquiry. The commission cites noncooperation and the withholding of documents by the White House as prime reasons for the necessity of an extension, according to the *Chicago Tribune.* Bush and House Speaker Dennis Hastert turn down the

commission's request for more time. A White House spokeswoman says, 'The administration has given them an unprecedented amount of cooperation . . . and we expect they will be able to meet [the May 27] deadline.'

- February 2004. Following pressure from within Washington as well as public outcry, Bush finally agrees to an extension until July.

- February 2004. After almost a year of wrangling, the commission threatens to subpoena the White House for access to the Presidential Daily Briefs. The administration concedes but restricts the access to four of the 9/11 panel members. The commission requests 360 PDBs going back to 1998. The White House says it will allow the panel members access to only 24 PDBs. As Michael Isikoff in *Newsweek* noted, 'One panel member was allowed to read all 360 – but couldn't share the contents with colleagues.' This is particularly galling because, as *Newsweek* also reported, the White House had shared some of them with Bob Woodward for his book *Bush at War*.

- February 2004. Former senator Bob Kerrey, a member of the commission, tells the *Daily News,* 'Resigning is on my list of possibilities,' alluding to the White House's refusal to allow panel members appropriate access to intelligence reports and officials.

- February 2004. Bush and Cheney place strict limits on their interviews with the commission. They say they will testify together and will submit to only an hour of questioning. The commission rejects the one-hour demand.

- March 2004. The White House backs down on the one-hour limit. Spokesman Scott McClellan says, 'The president's going to answer all of the questions that they want to raise. Nobody's watching the clock.' The administration insists, though, that the questioning take place in the Oval Office.

- March 2004. White House Counsel Alberto Gonzales attempts to besmirch the reputation of former counterterrorism czar Richard A. Clarke prior to Clarke's addressing the panel. Gonzales had improperly called Republican commission members Fred Fielding and James R. Thompson. When Clarke testified, both Fielding and Thompson presented evidence intended to bring his credibility and reputation into question.
- March 2004. Condoleezza Rice tries to justify her refusal for months to testify publicly before the commission (she had earlier met with the panel in private): 'Nothing would be better, from my point of view, than to be able to testify. I would really like to do that. But there is an important principle here . . . it is a longstanding principle that sitting national security advisers do not testify before Congress.' (In fact, on three prior occasions National Security advisers have testified before Congress.) Later in the month, the White House agrees to allow her to appear, but on the condition that it be in private and not under oath. Days later, the White House caves to pressure and says Rice will testify in public, and under oath.
- April 2004. *The New York Times* discovers that although Bill Clinton had given the okay to the National Archives to release his papers to the commission, the Bush administration had obstructed, releasing just 25 percent of the eleven thousand documents requested.
- April 2004. The commission says that sixty-nine documents from the Clinton administration involving Al Qaeda, Osama bin Laden, and other subjects that it had requested had been withheld by the White House. Under pressure, Bush turns over just twelve of the documents.
- April 2004. The White House refuses to release a comprehensive national security address Rice was to have given on September 11, 2001. According to *The Washington*

Post, the speech 'was designed to promote missile defense as the cornerstone of a new national security strategy, and contained no mention of al Qaeda, Osama bin Laden, or Islamic extremist groups.'

▪ April 2004. Rice goes before the commission for questioning. For almost three hours, under oath and on live television, Rice is grilled. She tells the commissioners that 'there was no silver bullet that could have prevented the 9-11 attacks' and that an August 6 PDB '. . . did not, in fact, warn of any coming attacks inside the United States.' But as Rice noted earlier in her testimony, 'I believe the title [of the PDB] was, "Bin Laden Determined to Attack Inside the United States."' She also dismissed the document as being 'historical information.' Days later the White House reluctantly released the PDB to the public.

▪ April 2004. Bush and Cheney meet with the commission for three hours and ten minutes. They are not under oath, a tape recorder is not allowed, and the questioning takes place in the Oval Office. *The Buffalo News* wrote, 'Commissioners were summoned to a closed-door meeting on presidential turf, with Bush and Cheney fielding questions as a team. Panel members were searched going in, and their notebooks were taken for security review as they left. There was no doubt who was in control.' When the president and vice president emerge from their 'discussion' Bush comments, 'They had a lot of good questions . . . I'm glad I did it. I'm glad I took the time . . . I enjoyed it . . . probably best that I not go into the details of the conversation.'

One would think that following the horrors committed in the United States' name at Abu Ghraib prison – a devastating blow not only to America's image but also to its self-image – an administration would want a full investigation of the matter, if only to ensure that the abuses didn't happen again. Or that it would be shamed into conducting a full investigation to make sure they didn't happen again. Not here.

In June 2004, *The Wall Street Journal* reported that since early 2003, the Bush administration had not only not been policing prison abuse, it had been actively picking through international treaties regarding the treatment of prisoners, looking for loopholes. In a draft memo to the president labeled 'secret' and not to be declassified until 2013, administration lawyers advised the White House to disregard the Geneva Conventions as well as the army's own manual for conducting interrogation. The memo said the president could 'approve almost any physical or psychological actions during interrogation, up to and including torture.' According to *The Journal*, the report stated that 'the president has virtually unlimited power to wage war as he sees fit, and neither Congress, the courts nor international law can interfere. It concluded that neither the president nor anyone following his instructions was bound by the federal Torture Statute, which makes it a crime for Americans working for the government overseas to commit or attempt torture, defined as any act intended to "inflict severe physical or mental pain or suffering."'

The report was drawn up as a result of complaints from officers at Guantánamo Bay, who were saying that their normal routine of dealing with prisoners was not yielding the desired results. The administration has maintained that foreigners held at Guantánamo don't have constitutional rights – the lawyers who drafted the classified report for the president contended that the federal Torture Statute did not apply to the prisoners at Guantánamo because the statute applies only to American behavior in foreign lands, and Guantánamo is officially part of the United States. The chief architect of the report was Pentagon general counsel William Haynes, Bush's nominee for the Fourth Circuit Court of Appeals.

The Convention Against Torture was proposed by the United

Nations in 1984 and ratified by the United States a decade later. It firmly states that 'no exceptional circumstances whatsoever, whether a state of war or a threat of war, internal political instability or any other public emergency, may be invoked as a justification of torture.' It further declares that orders from a superior 'may not be invoked as a justification of torture.'

While the administration spent a great deal of time parsing definitions of the word 'torture,' it certainly wasn't a word they wanted out there, especially after the photographs from Abu Ghraib had been splashed all over the world. It's a terrible word, with terrible consequences. Adam Hochschild, whose book *King Leopold's Ghost* documented the torture and human rights abuses that took place in the Belgian Congo, criticized administration officials, including Rumsfeld, for manipulating the meaning of the word. Writing in *The New York Times* in May 2004, he said, 'As Orwell pointed out most effectively, governments control language as well as people . . . But torture is torture. It permanently scars the victim even when there are no visible marks on the body, and it leaves other scars on the lives of those who perform it and on the life of the nation that allowed and encouraged it. Those scars will be with us for a long time.'

Indeed, as Jamal al-Harith, a British citizen who had been held at Guantánamo, told *The Guardian*, 'The whole point of Guantanamo was to get to you psychologically. The beatings were not nearly as bad as the psychological torture – bruises heal after a week, but the other stuff stays with you.' Another freed British prisoner, Tarek Dergoul, said that the camp had a torture squad called the Extreme Reaction Force, whose members 'recorded on digital video camera everything that happened,' reported *The Observer*.

In Brooklyn, within eyesight of the attack on the World Trade Center towers, is another holding center for post–September 11 detainees. Of the more than twelve hundred foreign nationals rounded up and held there in the months after the attacks, not a single person was charged with a terror-related crime, wrote *Newsweek*. When the inspector general of the Justice Department launched an investigation into complaints of prisoner treatment at the Brooklyn facility, he discovered a pattern of abuse similar to that at Abu Ghraib. He also discovered more than three hundred hours of videotape containing scenes similar to those from Abu Ghraib. The Justice Department refused to release the tapes.

Despite *The Journal*'s discovery of the March 2003 draft memo, Attorney General John Ashcroft refused a Senate Judiciary Committee demand in June 2004 to turn over an official copy of the finished report. After reminding Ashcroft of the humiliating images from Abu Ghraib, Democratic senator Joseph Biden of Delaware glared at Ashcroft and hissed, 'There's a reason why we sign these treaties – to protect my son in the military. That's why we have these treaties, so when Americans are captured they are not tortured. That's the reason in case anybody forgets it.' Another committee member, Republican senator Larry Craig of Idaho, told Ashcroft that he was concerned with the president's growing powers. 'I hope that in the end, Saddam Hussein will not have taken away from us something that our Constitution, in large part, granted us, and that we have it taken away in the name of safety and security.'

And as George Bush said in October 2003, 'We welcome Muslims in our country.'

It is more than possible that the Bush White House will be looked at years from now as one of the most secretive, deceptive, vindictive, unaccountable, reckless, and downright venal administrations in American history. It is also more than possible that the invasion of Iraq will be looked on as the defining event of the age, an unnecessary conflict that set in train a future devastating to the United States and to the rest of the world. This war without reason, this war without end, could in time become our great undoing.

Comparisons with Vietnam are, in their own way, incorrect. That was a political war: democracy vs. communism. The war in the Iraq is a political war, but it is also a religious war. Communism has all but disappeared from the political landscape. Islam has been around for more than a millennium and will be around for millennia to come. Furthermore, the people in the Middle East think in terms of centuries – they're still exercised by the Spanish having run the Moors out of Spain in the fifteenth century. America, by contrast, has become a nation of serial obsessives, interested in a subject, a trial, a scandal, or a war for only as long as a television season.

The goodwill that poured in from around the world after September 11 has dissolved in the president's hands. America has gone from being loved to being hated. Electing George Bush the first time around may be seen by the rest of the world as an aberration, a mistake. His reelection would send a message of hostile intent to the rest of the world.

As Robert B. Reich, secretary of labor under Clinton, pointed out in *The American Prospect,* a second term would see possible advances on Iran and North Korea, and a cabinet with Rice running State, Rumsfeld running National Security, and Wolfowitz running Defense. A second term would see more tax cuts for the wealthy. As Reich says, 'Economic policy . . . will be tilted even more brazenly toward the rich. Republican strategist Grover Norquist smugly predicts larger tax benefits for high earners . . . The goal will be to eliminate all taxes on capital gains, dividends, and other forms of unearned income and move toward a "flat tax." ' A second term would see further encroachment on civil liberties as the administration pushes for passage of Patriot Act II. A second term would see right-wing ideologues further transform the nation's health, education, and environmental departments. A second term would see one, and possibly two, new right-wing justices on the Supreme Court. A second term would see the Bush administration back Antonin Scalia for chief justice.

Already, the administration has put in place policies that will have long-term impact on the environment, the economy, the judiciary, health care, education, and civil liberties, not to mention our reputation and self-image. America's reputation for strength and justness, which has taken more than two centuries to establish, has been rent asunder by a single administration. America itself has been rent asunder, more divided along party lines than at any time in recent memory. It is safe to say that history will not be kind to the Bush administration. Long after it is out of office, after the investigations have run their course, after we examine the wreckage to our land and to our fragile but enduring democracy, only then will we fully comprehend all that the Bush presidency has done. And only then will we fully realize what we've lost.

'I'm the Commander – see, I don't need to explain – I don't need to explain why I say things. That's the interesting thing about being President. Maybe somebody needs to explain to me why they say something, but I don't feel like I owe anybody an explanation.'

– GEORGE W. BUSH, August 2002